BIRDINGTRAILS™
TEXAS

Prairies and Pineywoods • Panhandle

216 Birding Trails for the Avid Birder

FROM THE COVER - THE PAINTED BUNTING

With bright blue, green, and red plumage, the breeding male painted bunting is one of the continent's most gaudily colorful birds. The species breeds in two different populations, one in the south-central United States which includes Texas, and one along the seaboard of the southeastern states. This photo was taken at the South Llano State Park, near Junction, Texas.

Upcoming titles from Sandhill Crane Press™

Birding Trails™

Birding Trails™ Texas: Gulf Coast & West Texas

Birding Trails™ Montana

Birding Trails™ Northern California

Birding Trails™ Oregon

Birding Trails™ Washington

BIRDINGTRAILS™
TEXAS

Prairies and Pineywoods • Panhandle

216 Birding Trails for the Avid Birder

By Jim Foster

Birding Trails Series™

Sandhill
Crane
Press™

PRAIRIES AND PINEYWOODS EAST

Birding Trails" Series

Published by Sandhill Crane Press ",
An imprint of Wilderness Adventures Press, Inc."
45 Buckskin Road
Belgrade, MT 59714
866-400-2012
Website: www.wildadvpress.com
email: books@wildadvpress.com

First Edition 2011

Printed in China

ISBN 978 -1-932098-90-7 (8-09206-98907-8)

Table of Contents

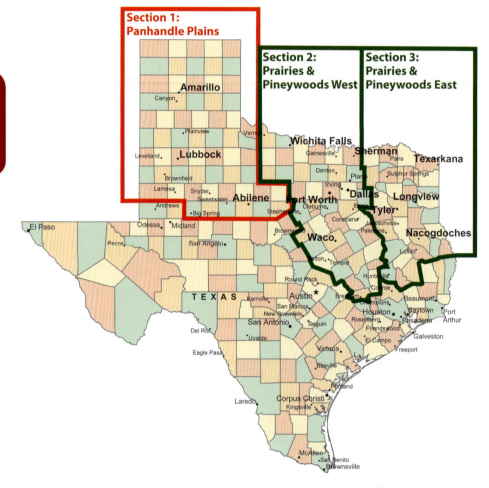

Section 1:
Panhandle Plains

Section 2:
Prairies &
Pineywoods West

Section 3:
Prairies &
Pineywoods East

BIRDING TRAILS: TEXAS
PRAIRIES AND PINEYWOODS - PANHANDLE

Introduction

As a young man, and in my early years with a camera, it would appear my interest in regard to image subjects always leaned toward animals, with wildlife being of most interest. Sometimes the frustration of not having the right equipment or a longer lens led to a long line of frustrations and then inner pleasure when the image was on film. Capturing what I could and sharing that with others became the goal — along with producing an income, of course.

Remembering well my first outing for "just" wildlife images. It was more years than I wish to remember near the town of Lubbock, Texas. It seemed there was a large park with a black-tailed prairie dog community or, as some call it, a prairie dog town.

I learned quickly that readiness was the key to catching a good shot. In other words, the idea here was to be ready to photograph these little critters at the time they popped up and just before they went back down into their holes.

This was a task I found consumed a lot of film, and not that easy to accomplish within the confines of a rather small film and processing budget. Getting close I learned meant spending a good bit of time moving into position and then sitting still long enough for them to start coming out of the holes and beginning to move around.

It was during one of these "sitting" spells I noticed a pair of yellow eyes watching me from one of the prairie dog holes. The eyes seemed to shine and a quick thought flashed through my mind that some evil underground demon was guarding the town and would punish any invader — so, closer movement at this point might not be a good idea. I snapped a couple of frames — photography was only on film at that time you know. As I watched and snapped, the eyes became a bird and the bird hopped out on the rim of the abandoned prairie dog hole still watching me closely, maybe with just a little concern. This was not the aforementioned demon.

What had just been found and photographed was a burrowing owl. The little bird of prey stayed there for quite some time until a passing truck on the road sent him back underground. It was shortly after the slides came back from the processor that I invested in a bird book to help identify the species of animal and bird I was photographing. The well-worn and earmarked copy of Sibley's Field Guide is still one of my guarded possessions.

In spite of the brief time spent photographing the little bird, I was now solidly hooked. Although not admitting it at the time, this one experience had started my birding life, and the adventure of a lifetime. At this time my birding life list was my image catalog. This was only a small flicker of a future flame that would become my passion for photographing birds of all kinds and shapes on several continents.

Being a native Texan — a rare bird indeed these days — my birding and photography of the same began. Although not known at the time, the state of Texas is a birder's Mecca, and as time went on I would spend days and weeks discovering all the state has to offer.

Some of my birding adventures are now only pleasant memories, to be relived only through my images. Getting around the country has changed and travel is somewhat more difficult, but still possible, while other adventures may never be repeated. One example of this is photographing from a canoe at the Heard Museum in McKinney, Texas. Spending time exploring the property with two birders, and shooting as many photographs as I could, made me aware just how short my time there was going to be. A parting image of an eastern bluebird is one of my favorites.

No other state in the United States has more species within its boundaries. There are currently over 620 species documented in Texas - almost 75 percent of all bird species recorded in the continental United States. One of the reasons Texas is so "birdy" is due to its variety of habitats. Mountains, deserts, beaches, grasslands, swamps, riparian woodlands, and coniferous forest can all be found and each holds its own variety of birds and other wildlife.

Texas is the only state in the U.S where golden-cheeked and Colima warblers can be found. Many endangered and threatened birds are either residents in, or winter visitors to, the state.

As I mentioned above, several of my photo outings have incorporated the use of some type of watercraft.

Leaning on the generosity of friends I made my way very close to nesting islands and sand bars where hundreds or maybe thousands of water birds and gulls lived and raised their respective families. Their shallow draft boats and outboards took me to these islands. Then it was pure manpower with a long pole or paddle that moved us quietly into camera range of the birds and their young.

There are other ways to enjoy the water other than speeding over the surface pushed by a monster, and I might add noisy, outboard engine. Some enjoy the quiet motion of the paddle in a kayak or canoe. The paddle sports have become very popular and kayaks can be purchased for nominal prices. Canoes can be somewhat more expensive but are a bit more stable for the average bird watcher or photographer.

Texas has a Paddling Trails Program that has been set up to develop public inland and coastal paddling trails throughout the state, and it supports these trails with maps, signage, and other information. Lists of birds that may be encountered are handy, and many rental businesses are happy to steer — excuse the pun — you in the right direction by providing a guide for your trip. The more adventurous may try paddling the trails on their own, using one of the maps printed just for that purpose.

These trails provide well-mapped accessible day trips in a variety of settings and for all levels of paddling experience. There are currently eight coastal paddling trails and twelve inland paddling trails, with several communities in the process of applying for participation in this program. To find out more about this great Texas program, go to the website at http://www.tpwd.state.tx.us/fishboat/boat/paddlingtrails.

Texas boasts of more than 3,700 named streams, 15 major rivers, and some 3,300 miles of tidal shoreline along the Gulf Coast, and offers myriad opportunities for paddling close to resting, feeding, and nesting birds. Stealth is the key, so quiet paddling is a must as is keeping your voice very low or being silent, speaking only when needed.

This brings me back to combining outdoor activities to increase the measure of enjoyment and pleasure from a day spent outdoors. For paddlers and birders, guided trips can be very productive and can allow access to areas others might only read about. I have added several species to my image catalog in just this manner.

As time has progressed and I have mentioned this book and its research to others, I have heard comments of surprise when I casually mention I am also a hunter, and a bird hunter at that.

"How can you be a birder and a hunter?" is the question most commonly heard from some.

American Avocet

My answer is really easy - "Hunters were the first conservationists". Hunters supported the passage of the Pittman-Robinson Act many years ago. The act added a ten percent federal excise tax to all hunting equipment, including firearms and ammunition. Hunters, through their purchases, have added millions of dollars for federal conservation because of this tax. Also, many millions of dollars have been added to the conservation effort in the form of money for Federal Wildlife Refuges by hunters with the purchase of a Federal Migratory Bird Stamp, better known as a Duck Stamp. Many states are now selling their own version of this stamp.

And taking a camera into my deer stand has resulted in many of my better bird images. Also my "Duck Stamp" is used to gain entrance to all federal wildlife refuges and some management areas.

So, after some thought, most will agree that hunters and birders meld nicely and even complement other species. It is a real shame that the comments heard the most are from either the radical hunter or the radical anti-hunter. There must be some common ground.

Dollars spent on hunting licenses help all wild species in a management area, not just the ones that can be hunted. Every birder should have in their possession a current federal waterfowl stamp and help support the work done on wildlife refuges; in many cases to improve the birding on that refuge. It all helps.

So as you will learn as you venture around the northern portion of Texas visiting some of the better birding locations in the Panhandle and Prairies & Pineywoods, Texas is just another way to spell birding.

Continuing this series of books, the next volume will cover the well known as well as some of the more obscure and out of the mainstream birding locations along the Texas Gulf Coast and the counties of West Texas.

In my travels I have visited many of the locations listed in this volume, but by no means do I tend to imply I have visited them all. It was also not my intention to say the locations listed are all of the birding places in Texas. As many will learn as they travel the state, Texas is a really big place and birds can be found everywhere.

It must be mentioned that Texas was the largest state until Alaska joined the union. Even today, Texas could be the largest state if someone would put all of Alaska's ice in plastic bags to be sold in the many convenience stores across the state – or melted and piped in to end a drought.

It is my hope you will enjoy using this book while exploring the many fine birding locations Texas has to offer and join me again when I venture along the Texas Gulf Coast and the expanses of West Texas along more Texas Birding Trails.

Jim Foster

Ethical Practices For Birdwatchers

Traveling throughout the state of Texas, birdwatchers will find that every place is unique and should be respected with all care possible.

Here are just a few of the ideas and practices that should occur while birdwatchers are in the field observing the many species of bird life Texas has to offer.

It is best if birders will learn the patterns of bird behavior so as not to interfere with life cycles or nesting practices of the species observed. This can be hard to accomplish because we, as a group, are always looking for something new, something special and unique.

Using the best equipment like binoculars and spotting scopes, we should try to not distress the birds while visiting their habitat – taking care to blend in with the environment while moving as little as we can and being quiet.

Respect and do your best not to interrupt the routine of the birds you're watching. Don't move into their feeding area just for a better view or a closer photograph.

Photographers should use the appropriate lens to photograph wild birds from a distance so as not to disturb or frighten the bird.

If while you are watching a bird and it starts to show stress, it is advised that you move farther back or use a longer lens to photograph the subject. This is also where spotting scopes and a good pair of binoculars will aid in observing and not disturbing the species.

Before entering any type of habitat you should acquaint yourself with the area and the fragility of any ecosystem. Stay on the trails that were put there to help lessen the impact on the area. In areas of endangered species, do not frighten or try to get too close. Texas has several endangered birds, so please observe all regulations and area rules.

If possible or appropriate, inform the managers or other authorities of your presence and the purpose of your visit. Most places will be aware of birders, their equipment, and the activities needed to pursue a certain birder species.

Birders should familiarize themselves with the rules and regulations of the areas where they will be, and abide by these rules strictly. In areas where fees are required, birders should pay these fees in advance before entering an area, or put money in the appropriate boxes. In the absence of any authority, birders should always use good judgment.

Birders should remember that they are the guests in these locations, and should treat them as if they are the homes of people they visit.

In regard to other birders and area visitors - the golden rule applies to birds as well as the people watching the birds.

Treat others courteously, and remember to ask before joining others in an area where they are already photographing or observing wildlife. This is an important issue, because at times birders and those photographing birds have spent considerable time gaining that position slowly and cautiously in order not to stress the bird. The appearance of a new individual could cause the bird to either leave the area or move farther away. You will disturb the bird and birder if you move in quickly or ask loudly.

Try to be a good role model, both as a photographer birdwatcher and as a person. Try to educate others by your actions in order to enhance their understanding of the situations and rules of the area.

Regarding state parks and wildlife management areas, these are special places offering people a chance to explore the outdoors and enjoy the wildlife. They have special rules and regulations covering their individual locations. In most state parks and wildlife management areas, the rules are easily understood and mostl are strictly enforced.

It is also true that state parks are places where families gather and give their youngsters a pleasing outdoor experience. Kids will be kids, so if some are too loud or boisterous, take it in stride and temper you comments, remembering you were once that age and all was fresh and new.

BIRDING TRAILS: TEXAS

PANHANDLE REGION

THE PANHANDLE REGION IS NOT ONLY A VERY HISTORIC AREA OF TEXAS, IT CAN AND WILL PROVIDE HOURS OF CONTINUOUS BIRDING ADVENTURES, AS WELL AS STEPS BACK IN TIME.

This region of Texas is made up of the northernmost 26 counties in the state, known for years as the "Staked Plains" (or the Llano Estacado) and part of the Indian Territories before state boundaries were drawn.

The Panhandle is a rectangular area bordered by New Mexico to the west and Oklahoma to the north and east. The southern border of Swisher County is considered by many to be the southern boundary of the region, though some consider the region to extend as far south as Lubbock County.

The Panhandle area's population as of the 2000 census was 402,862 residents, or 1.932 percent of the state's population (2010 numbers were not available at this writing.) This would place the average population concentration for the region at 16 persons per square mile. The region of the Panhandle counties although located in the most northern part of the state differs from North Texas, which is more to the southeast. Does this make since to anybody?

West of the Caprock Escarpment and north and south of the Canadian River breaks, the surface of the Llano Estacado is rather flat. South of the city of Amarillo, the level terrain gives way to Palo Duro Canyon, the second largest canyon in the United States. This colorful canyon is still being carved by the Prairie Dog Town Fork of the Red River.

It was in this canyon, sometimes called the Grand Canyon of Texas, that the Comanche Indians under the leadership of Quanah Parker evaded the army for years until their stronghold in the canyon and the route into the canyon was traded to the army by another Indian for an unknown amount.

North of Amarillo lies Lake Meredith, a reservoir created by the Sanford Dam on the Canadian River. The lake, along with the Ogallala Aquifer, provides drinking water and irrigation for this moderately dry area of the high plains.

Visitors should know the lake level is falling due to the conflict between Texas and New Mexico over water rights on the Canadian River. As of this writing,

Common Tern

New Mexico has cut off most of the water and Lake Meredith is quite low and getting lower.

Interstate Highway 40 (old Route 66) passes through the Panhandle, through Amarillo, and through Deaf Smith, Oldham, Potter, Carson, Gray, Donley, and Wheeler Counties.

Because the Act of Admission of Texas into the Union allows the state to divide itself, a bill was introduced to the Texas legislature in 1915 in order to create a State of Jefferson, made up of the Texas Panhandle. As all know now, this did not happen.

The Texas Panhandle has been identified as one of the fastest-growing wind-power-producing regions in the nation over the past decade because of its strong, steady winds. This fact could also be the reason that many of the migrating bird species pass through the area. Whether these wind farms will or will not produce power for the future is yet to be seen, as is the windmills' effect on local and migrating bird populations.

The Texas Panhandle has been the location of the successful stocking of the ring-necked pheasant. The large and colorful birds may be seen in many areas of the region, especially near agricultural crop fields. These pretty birds can be seen feeding along the roads or out in the planted or harvested fields. Many times, viewing these large, beautiful birds will be much easier than photographing them, due to their learned habit of moving away from any slowing or stopping vehicle. But it can be done, so be stealthy and give it your best shot.

There are many excellent birding locations in the Panhandle region. Due to the overall dryness of the area, many of the better locations are closely coupled to the availability of water in the region's lakes, streams, and rivers.

Here is a listing of some of the more popular, as well as some of the lesser-known, locations in the Panhandle region of Texas. Please keep in mind that some of these locations are on private property, some of these locations require a guide, and some will also charge a fee for entrance or for a guided tour.

Panhandle

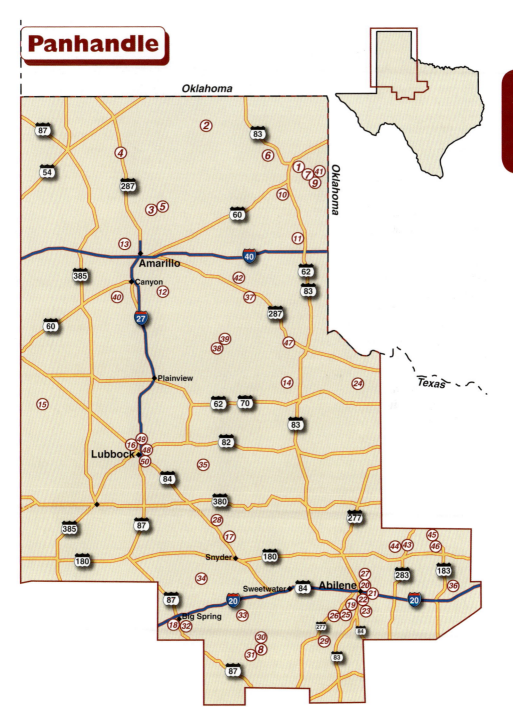

Oklahoma

Texas

Amarillo

Canyon

Plainview

Lubbock

Snyder

Sweetwater

Abilene

Big Spring

Panhandle Locations

#1 Lake Marvin Unit
#2 Lake Palo Duro
#3 Lake Meredith National Recreation Area
#4 Cactus Playa
#5 Alibates Flint Quarry National Monument
#6 North Canadian River Road
#7 Gene Howe Wildlife Management Area
#8 Dripping Springs Grotto
#9 Anderson Ranch
#10 Arrington Ranch
#11 Bob Weatherly's Home Place
#12 Palo Duro Canyon & State Park
#13 Wildcat Bluff Nature Center
#14 Matador Wildlife Management Area
#15 Muleshoe National Wildlife Refuge
#16 Lubbock Lake Landmark
#17 Wagon Wheel Ranch
#18 Big Spring State Park
#19 Perini Ranch
#20 Will Hair Park
#21 Abilene Zoological Garden and Nelson Park
#22 Kirby Lake
#23 Cedar Gap Farm
#24 Copper Breaks State Park
#25 Abilene State Park
#26 Lake Abilene
#27 Lake Fort Phantom Hill / Abilene
#28 Lake Alan Henry
#29 Fort Chadbourne
#30 Lake Spence-Humble Crossing
#31 Walnut Creek Ranch
#32 Comanche Trail Lake
#33 Fisher Park/Champion Creek
#34 Lake J. B. Thomas
#35 White River Lake
#36 Texas Adventure Trails – Ringling Lake
#37 Playa Lakes Wildlife Management Area, Taylor Lakes Unit
#38 Caprock Canyons State Park and Trailway
#39 Texas Highway 256 Scenic Drive
#40 Buffalo Lake National Wildlife Refuge
#41 Lake Marvin, Black Kettle National Grasslands Recreation Area
#42 Greenbelt Lake
#43 Fort Griffin State Park and Historic Site
#44 Stasney's Cook Ranch
#45 North Roadside Park
#46 Hubbard Creek Lake-North Campground
#47 Baylor Lake/Childress Lake
#48 Mackenzie Park
#49 Yellow House Canyon - Lakes
#50 Lubbock Cemetery

A FEW WORDS ABOUT PLAYA LAKES IN TEXAS

Playa lakes are arguably the most significant ecological feature in the Texas High Plains, even though they cover only two percent of the region's landscape. Playas are shallow, circular-shaped wetlands that are primarily filled by rainfall; although some playas found in cropland settings may also receive water from irrigation runoff. Playas average slightly more than 15 acres in size. Although larger playas may exceed 800 acres, most (around 87 percent) are smaller than 30 acres. Approximately 19,300 playas are found in the Texas High Plains, thus the highest density of playas in North America.

Compared to other wetlands, playas go through frequent and unpredictable wet/dry cycles. In wet years, they support the production of annual plants, such as smartweeds and millets. These plants produce a tremendous crop of seeds that are favored by dabbling ducks and other seed-eating birds. The wet/dry nature of playas, along with their high plant production, means they produce an abundance of invertebrates. This productivity makes playas a haven for birds throughout the year.

During migration periods, playas are often besieged with spectacular numbers of cranes, waterfowl, and shorebirds. Playas are critical "refueling points" for shorebirds making their way to wintering areas on the Gulf Coast. Some of the species of migrating shorebirds using playa lakes include American avocets, lesser yellowlegs, long-billed curlews, long-billed dowitchers, stilt sandpipers, and Wilson's phalaropes among the most abundant.

Most North American dabbling and diving ducks also use playas during migration. Blue-winged teal, green-winged teal, gadwall, and northern pintails are common during early autumn. During spring, gadwall and blue-winged teal often linger long after most mallards and northern pintails have departed for their more northerly breeding grounds. The Playa Lakes Region is second only to the Gulf Coast in providing habitat for wintering waterfowl in the Central Flyway.

The most conspicuous species during winter are Canada geese and snow geese. Recent estimates suggest that 300,000 geese are found in the Playa Lakes Region. Mallards and northern pintails are the most abundant wintering ducks.

Playa lakes can be a harsh environment for wintering birds and are subject to periodic drought and hard freezes during winter. In a recent January waterfowl survey, it was estimated that more than 90 percent of the available playas (those with water) were frozen. During these extremely cold periods, waterfowl are forced to move to large reservoirs or rivers. Additionally, waterfowl wintering in the playa region continually move to find suitable wetlands and food. Daily flights for ducks and geese foraging in agricultural fields can cover many miles.

FOR MORE INFORMATON – many times these agencies have maps of playa lakes that are viewable for birders: The U.S. Fish and Wildlife Service, the U.S.D.A. Natural Resources Conservation Service (NRCS), and the Playa Lakes Joint Venture at http://www.pljv.org.

PANHANDLE

PANHANDLE REGION
Lake Marvin Unit

#1

LOCATED NEAR PERRYTON, WHEELER, AND CANADIAN ON HEMPHILL COUNTY ROAD K, JUST OFF FM 2266

KEY BIRDS
Bald eagle, ferruginous hawk, northern shrike

BEST SEASON
Best mid-April through May for spring migrants and nesting activities; December through February for winter birds

AREA DESCRIPTION
Panhandle plains – some low rolling hills

The 576-acre Lake Marvin Unit, including a 63-acre lake, is part of the 31,399-acre Black Kettle National Grasslands. An additional 30,724 acres are located in nearby Oklahoma. Birding, hiking, fishing, picnicking, and camping are available.

Wild turkeys are present year round.

June - September: Mississippi kite, least tern, Chuck-will's-widow, red-headed woodpecker, scissor-tailed flycatcher, warbling vireo, indigo and painted buntings, and dickcissel occur.

December – March: Tundra swan, hooded and common mergansers, bald eagle, ferruginous hawk, northern shrike, and American tree, fox, and Harris's sparrows can usually be found in winter.

Camping is permitted at Lake Marvin and there are plenty of hotels and eating establishments in Canadian and Perryton, as well as additional camping around the main Gene Howe Wildlife Management Area.

For new birding strategies for this specific location, as well as directions to each birding spot and helpful general information contact the Perryton Chamber of Commerce.

Bald Eagle

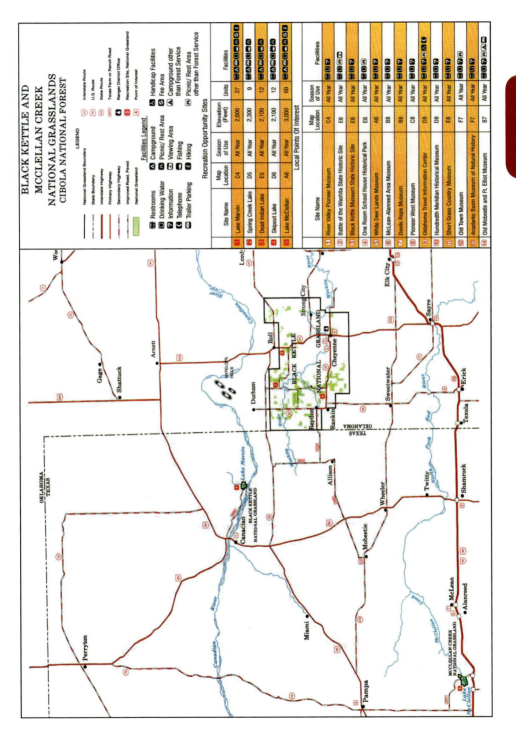

BLACK KETTLE AND McCLELLAN CREEK NATIONAL GRASSLANDS
CIBOLA NATIONAL FOREST

LEGEND

National Grassland Boundary	Interstate Route
State Boundary	U.S. Route
Interstate Highway	State Route
Primary Highway	Texas Farm or Ranch Road
Secondary Highway	Ranger District Office
Improved Road, Paved	Recreation Site, National Grassland
National Grassland	Point of Interest

Facilities Legend

Restrooms	Campground	Handicap Facilities
Drinking Water	Picnic/ Rest Area	Fee Area
Information	Viewing Area	Campground other than Forest Service
Telephone	Fishing	Picnic/ Rest Area other than Forest Service
Trailer Parking	Hiking	

Recreation Opportunity Sites

	Site Name	Map Location	Season of Use	Elevation (Feet)	Units	Facilities
1	Lake Marvin	C4	All Year	2,000	27	
2	Spring Creek Lake	D5	All Year	2,300	9	
3	Dead Indian Lake	E5	All Year	2,100	12	
4	Skipout Lake	D6	All Year	2,100	12	
5	Lake McClellan	A6	All Year	3,000	60	

Local Points Of Interest

	Site Name	Map Location	Season of Use	Facilities
1	River Valley Pioneer Museum	C4	All Year	
2	Battle of the Washita State Historic Site	E6	All Year	
3	Black Kettle Museum State Historic Site	E6	All Year	
4	One Room School House Historical Park	E6	All Year	
5	White Deer Lands Museum	A6	All Year	
6	McLean-Alanreed Area Museum	B8	All Year	
7	Devils Rope Museum	B8	All Year	
8	Pioneer West Museum	C8	All Year	
9	Oklahoma Travel Information Center	D8	All Year	
10	Hundreth Meridian Historical Museum	D8	All Year	
11	Short Grass Country Museum	E8	All Year	
12	Old Town Museum	F7	All Year	
13	Anadarko Basin Museum of Natural History	F7	All Year	
14	Old Mobeetie and Ft. Elliot Museum	B7	All Year	

PANHANDLE

This location offers birders several areas to search out their next addition to their life list.

SITE INFORMATION

Gene Howe WMA
806-323-8642
website:http://www.tpwd.state.tx.us/huntwild/hunt/wma/find_a_wma/list/?id=8

Perryton Chamber of Commerce:
806-435-6575
website: http://www.perryton.org/

White Ibis

PANHANDLE REGION
Lake Palo Duro

#2

SIX MILES NORTH OF SPEARMAN

KEY BIRDS
Bald and golden eagles, northern mockingbird, marsh wren, red-cockaded woodpecker

BEST SEASON
Winter through spring

AREA DESCRIPTION
Flat plains

This little lake is many times confused with water farther south in the Palo Duro Canyon. This area is much smaller and is actually near the Oklahoma border in northern Hansford County. Located only a short drive – less than 10 miles – from the Panhandle town of Spearman.

Lake Palo Duro has been called one of the best birding locations in the area. Construction of Lake Palo Duro was sponsored by Hansford and Moore Counties and by the city of Stinnett. Completed March 1991, the lake and surrounding property takes in a total of 8,983.5 acres with the lake having 2,413 surface acres of water.

This diminutive man-made lake is also one of the best locations to see wintering bald and golden eagles. This should be a prime Texas location for any birder. Bird the south boat ramp as well as all the trees and snags along Texas Highway 207. Wintering flocks of both snow and Canada geese spend time here but tend to raft near the middle of the lake, sometimes making identification hard. Bring out the spotting scope and add hours of birding to your day by viewing the distant geese and ducks. Have your ID books handy for verifying what you see. Another spotting scope species might be the common loon. Listen for their call in the morning and evening for the "sound of the wild" as a good friend called the cry of the loon.

Northern Mockingbird

Near and along the entrance to the lake, wintering numbers of mountain bluebird are found in small to medium flocks, feeding on small seeds in the ditches and fields.

Other birds that may be seen here are northern cardinal, blue jay, indigo bunting, ruby-throated hummingbird, red-headed woodpecker, wood thrush, eastern bluebird, rose-breasted grosbeak, horned lark, cedar waxwing, mourning dove, nuthatch, dark-eyed junco, northern mockingbird, marsh wren, red-cockaded woodpecker, yellow-billed cuckoo, purple martin, barn swallow, pine warbler, pine siskin, and the American robin.

The year-round birding experiences are in braggable proportions as are the many species of birds that frequent the lake, in addition to the four species of longspur that winter in this area.

Birders should also be aware of many species of birds including waterfowl on the way to the lake.

DIRECTIONS

From Apple Springs, take FM 357 south for approximately 6-8 miles. A series of Forest Roads will head east through the area. A large sign along the road will tell you that you are entering the Wildlife Management Area; however, there are a few tracks of private land interspersed, so only go within areas marked by the small yellow signs. From the intersection of FM 2501 and FM 2262 in Nigton, travel for 1.2 miles to a roadside sign and map for the area. Holly Bluff Road is located 2.0 miles from the intersection and provides access to the Neches River. Access can be gained all along the east and west side of FM 2262. When FM 2262 meets FM 357, you can travel west on FM 357 and there will be several other access points including FR 541 and 531.

SITE INFORMATION

Area information can be found at the Spearman, Texas website: http://www.spearman.org/ 806-659-5555

Birding in Hansford County: http://www.spearman.org/birding.html

PANHANDLE REGION
Lake Meredith National Recreation Area

#3

FRITCH, TEXAS - 35 MILES NORTH OF AMARILLO

KEY BIRDS
Rock wren, Mississippi kite, cinnamon teal, American kestrel, burrowing owl, canyon wren, curve-billed thrasher, and rufous-crowned sparrow, many species of migrating waterfowl, white pelicans, woodpeckers, flycatchers, and wrens. Scan carefully for water birds, particularly during migration.

BEST SEASON
Year-round plus migrating species during the spring and fall

AREA DESCRIPTION
The geographic center of the Panhandle

Driving around Lake Meredith, it is very obvious that rain has not fallen in this area of the Panhandle in quite some time; hence the lake is very low. Adding to the water shortage is the continuing water dispute with the state of New Mexico over water rights on the Canadian River.

This could change at any time but, at the time of this writing, there is much more land out of the water than in past years. However, there were many migrating waterfowl concentrated on the lake and several species of shore birds.

Lake Meredith lies on the dry and windy plains of the Texas Panhandle near the town of Fritch, Texas. The lake was created to supply water for 11 cities and to create recreational opportunities. The lake is one of three lakes on the Canadian River, and its roads and trails are conducive to some great birding. Access points to the lake are numerous, and making a slow drive around the lake and watching the lake's edge and trees will produce many species of both shore, water, and land birds for watching and photography.

The 45,000-acre national recreation area offers extensive birding opportunities for the traveling birder. It would be wise to spend time driving slowly along the access roads to the lake.

Imagine yourself standing where an ancient civilization once lived, surrounded by colorful flint that was used to make weapons and tools. This area has a place in history, as many of the Native American nations lived or traveled through the area hunting or gathering for their living and collecting material for their weapon points and tools.

Weather in this part of Texas is known for its changeability. A common saying in Texas is, "If you don't like the weather, just wait a few minutes, and it will change!" Summer

PANHANDLE

temperatures can reach 100 degrees Fahrenheit or more; winters are usually mild, but may bring snow, sleet, or hail. Tornadoes, windstorms, and lightning can also occur.

Some of the birds this location has to offer are migrant species in spring and fall waterfowl, grebes, as well as several species of song birds near and around the boat launch areas. Take your time and use your binoculars to spot birds along and ahead of your route. Please keep in mind that during the summer the boat ramp areas may be quite busy with anglers and boaters.

Pied-billed grebe and common merganser are expected here in winter, and mallards and other lingering waterfowl during spring and summer. Scoters or loons may also be seen during winter.

Other birds are the golden eagle, scaled quail, chukar, greater roadrunner, rock and canyon wrens, curve-billed thrasher, and rufous-crowned sparrow that are present year round. Mississippi kite, Swainson's hawk, Virginia rail, burrowing owl, red-headed woodpecker, scissor-tailed flycatcher, and Cassin's sparrow occur in summer. Common goldeneye, common merganser, ferruginous and rough-legged hawks, bald eagle, long-eared owl, mountain bluebird, Townsend's solitaire, Lapland longspur, and American tree, fox, and Harris's sparrows and can usually be found in winter.

SITE INFORMATION
Superintendent, P.O. Box 1460, Fritch, Texas 79036
806-857-3151 / website: http://www.nps.gov/lamr/

American Kestrel

PANHANDLE REGION
Cactus Playa

#4

EAST OF ETTER, TEXAS

KEY BIRDS
Waterfowl, snowy plover, least tern

BEST SEASON
Winter and during migrations

AREA DESCRIPTION
Typical Panhandle flat plains playa

One of the many features of the Panhandle region of Texas is its great number of playa lakes. Cactus Playa is one of these, and covers a substantial area that will hold water in many places much of the year.

Birding this area is quite interesting due to the large number of birds attracted during wet as well as dry periods. Observation shows that birders with stealth and the ability to spend some time searching the area will be rewarded.

The Cactus Playa Lake attracts many species of waterfowl during migration periods, and makes for excellent birding during much of the year. This lake, at times, will attract and hold thousands upon thousands of birds, not just waterfowl but shore birds like the snowy plover and least tern. On my visit, I did see two species of tern – both common and least – which I understand according to many visitors are quite rare. However, several photographers have recorded their presence.

The Cactus Playa Lake is like many of the others in this region as it allows viewers as well as photographers a good chance to get close to the birds.

The entrance to Cactus Playa is very narrow, so birders are asked to avoid blocking the entrance and to park along the roadsides and out of the traffic lanes.

Cactus Playa is the winter home to hundreds of thousands of geese and ducks every winter, which also serves as a magnet for eagles and other raptors. Spring and fall shorebirds find Cactus Playa irresistible as well. Check out the playa one mile south of Cactus Playa as well.

Don't let the abundance of waterfowl keep you from enjoying this property. Use your spotting scope to find other species along the banks of this playa. Closer observation reveals several species that are missed by the casual observer.

DIRECTIONS
On FM 28, go 11.5 miles east of Etter, Texas. Etter is 11 miles north of Dumas, Texas on Highway 287.

Greater Roadrunner

PANHANDLE REGION
Alibates Flint Quarries National Monument

#5

PANHANDLE

LAKE MEREDITH NATIONAL RECREATION AREA

KEY BIRDS
Bullock's oriole, blue grosbeak, greater roadrunner, Cassin's and lark sparrows

BEST SEASON
All seasons

AREA DESCRIPTION
Rocky terrain with some areas of steep walking

This site provides guided tours of the ancient flint quarry that served as a major source of tool material for Native Americans over a period of several thousand years. If you continue past the park ranger building to the boat ramp, lakefront habitat that includes reeds and trees provides good cover for migrating and resident birds. The reed beds and the salt cedars and willows adjacent to the boat ramp form a habitat that is very different from the surrounding rocky, juniper-covered slopes.

McBride Canyon is a great place to watch birds. To reach the canyon, instead of taking the right fork to the flint quarry and boat ramp, go left for 2.6 miles, at which point the paved road becomes dirt and a sign announces your arrival at this scenic and historic site. The avifauna of this site is quite different from what you'll find elsewhere on the lakeshore.

In spring, look for Brewer's and clay-colored sparrows, as well as lark sparrows and lark bunting. Painted bunting is a common nester here; great blue heron, mallard, American crow, and a variety of migrants including yellow-breasted chat, Swainson's thrush, and ovenbird occur here. Also red-headed woodpeckers, Carolina chickadees, blue Jays, yellow warblers, northern flickers, ash-throated flycatchers, Bewick's and rock wrens, painted buntings, blue grosbeaks, and northern cardinals all occur here.

DIRECTIONS
From I-40 drive east 2.9 miles to TX 136. Take TX 136 north 26.4 miles, turn left on Cas Johnson Road and enter Bates Canyon. At the Y, take the right fork to the flint quarry and drive about 2.5 miles.

SITE INFORMATION
This site is restricted and birders must call for reservations at 806-857-3151. A fee is charged.

Great Crested Flycatcher

PANHANDLE REGION
North Canadian River Road

#6

NEAR CANADIAN, TEXAS

KEY BIRDS
Pinyon jay

BEST SEASON
All seasons

AREA DESCRIPTION
Flat country

Driving slowly along this road will produce the best viewing results. It never fails to amaze me that there are people who will drive hundreds, maybe thousands of miles to visit an area and then drive faster than they can possibly see anything, much less make a good identification. I have witnessed this speedy driving in many states and locations, including Yellowstone National Park.

This road is a great place to put those binoculars and spotting scopes to work. Spotting birds several hundred yards down the road, then setting up to watch, is quite rewarding. Most times the traffic on the road is spotty, so be observant of others on the road and give them room. Do your best not to scare away the birds they are watching.

A basic rule of courtesy is not to barge in, or even close to, another birder either on foot or in a stopped car watching or photographing birds or other wildlife. I can attest to the fact that a lot of time has been wasted moving close to a subject only to have the subject leave due to another driver – either rude or uneducated – pulling up too close.

The first 20 miles of this road are quite scenic and supports several bird species. At about 12 miles the road climbs into limestone mesas, where the pinyon jay may be seen.

This road is excellent for birders as well as photographers because birds and wildlife spotted are many times close to the road - so drive slowly and enjoy this area.

DIRECTIONS
Located off US 83 on County Road F. Actually, County Road F is the North Canadian Road.

Northern Bobwhite

PANHANDLE REGION
Gene Howe Wildlife Management Area

#7

SEVEN MILES EAST OF CANADIAN, TEXAS IN HEMPHILL COUNTY

KEY BIRDS
Northern bobwhite, scaled quail, Rio Grande turkey, lesser prairie chicken, great crested flycatcher

BEST SEASON
Year-round, except during special and announced hunts conducted by Texas Parks and Wildlife

AREA DESCRIPTION
Sandsage, an open rangeland, then cottonwood bottomland

The Gene Howe Wildlife Management Area (GHWMA) consists of 5,387 acres located along the Canadian River in the northern rolling plains of Hemphill County. Using Pittman-Robertson funds, Texas Parks and Wildlife Department purchased the first parcels in 1950 and 1951 for the purposes of wildlife management, public use, and research.

The WMA is comprised of roughly two-thirds of the land consisting of sandsage and mid-grass rangeland and one-third of the land in cottonwood and tall grass bottomland.

Numerous bird species include northern bobwhite, scaled quail, Rio Grande turkey, lesser prairie chicken, great crested flycatcher, burrowing owl, and mourning dove.

Use special care while walking around the area because students, teachers, and scientists use the area for instructional, educational, and research purposes. Do not disturb any markings, flags, traps, etc. that you encounter, because this may affect research results.

Included within the managed area is the "McQuiddy Hide-a-way" located off FM-2266. It consists of a 40-acre tract of private land. This area has a grove of soapberry trees that attract several species of birds in the fall and winter. When allowed, walk lightly and quietly for the best viewing.

Gene Howe is the only wildlife management area in Texas to have its own prairie dog town. Spend some quiet time around the town and you will have a good chance of seeing a burrowing owl sitting on one of the dog holes.

There are two observation blinds for wildlife viewing. The blind in the south area sits on the edge of the marsh in the West Bull Pasture. A nature trail begins there and winds through the riparian bottomland for a fourth of a mile. The second viewing blind overlooks the prairie dog town in the Middle Pasture in the north area. This is a good place to see burrowing owls and northern mockingbirds. Please remember this place is private property and birders should stay on the roads and trails as they are marked.

SITE INFORMATION

Area supervisor James B Baker / 806-323-8642 / website: http://www.tpwd.state.tx.us/ huntwild/hunt/wma/find_a_wma/list/?id=8

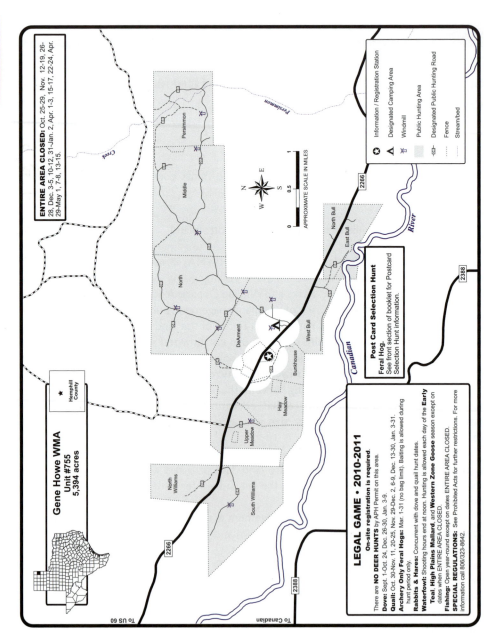

ENTIRE AREA CLOSED: Oct. 25-29, Nov. 12-19, 26-28, Dec. 3-5, 10-12, 31-Jan. 2, Apr. 1-3, 15-17, 22-24, Apr. 29-May 1, 7-8, 13-15.

Gene Howe WMA
Unit #755
5,394 acres

Hemphill County

Post Card Selection Hunt
Feral Hog.
See front section of booklet for Postcard Selection Hunt information.

LEGAL GAME • 2010-2011

On-site registration is required.

There are **NO DEER HUNTS** by APH Permit on this area.

Dove: Sept. 1-Oct. 24, Dec. 26-30, Jan. 3-9.

Quail: Oct. 30-Nov. 11, 20-25, Nov. 29-Dec. 2, 6-9, Dec. 13-30, Jan. 3-31.

Archery Only Feral Hogs: Mar. 1-31 (no bag limit). Baiting is allowed during hunt period only.

Rabbits & Hares: Concurrent with dove and quail hunt dates.

Waterfowl: Shooting hours end at noon. Hunting is allowed each day of the **Early Teal, High Plains Mallard,** and **Western Zone Goose** season except on dates when ENTIRE AREA CLOSED.

Fishing: Open year-round except on dates ENTIRE AREA CLOSED.

SPECIAL REGULATIONS: See Prohibited Acts for further restrictions. For more information call 806/323-8642.

APPROXIMATE SCALE IN MILES
0   0.5   1

Information / Registration Station
Designated Camping Area
Windmill
Public Hunting Area
Designated Public Hunting Road
Fence
Streambed

PANHANDLE REGION
Dripping Springs Grotto

#8

OFF TEXAS ROAD 158 WEST ON DRIPPING SPRINGS ROAD

KEY BIRDS
Brown thrasher, verdin, and canyon wren

BEST SEASON
All seasons

AREA DESCRIPTION
Acacia, mesquite, willow, and oak woodlands

This is one of the best birding venues in the region and has a tremendously picturesque grotto, with steep canyon walls and beautiful bluffs. It stays wet even in the driest conditions, and provides lush habitat for turtles, aquatic insects, and an excellent variety of birds. Brown thrasher, verdin, canyon wren, Bewick's wren, and cactus wren have all been seen here, as have Nashville warbler, McGillivray's warbler, and black-and-white warbler during migration. Scissor-tailed flycatchers abound in summer, and the acacia, mesquite, willow, and oak woodlands provide dense cover farther up the creek.

The Dripping Springs Grotto is one of those places where time spent is well rewarded. The wet areas will be home to several of the smaller species of bird. Watch the edges and the low brush for the small birds near the water. Birders need to check at the gate to see if the areas are open to visitors.

DIRECTIONS
Take TX 158 for 8.7 miles to the town of Edith in Coke County. Continue on TX 158 west for about 0.3 mile to Dripping Springs Road. Turn right/north and follow the road to the left, go about 200 yards to the low-water crossing, and park on the right. The grotto is over the edge. Observe only from the roadside.

SITE INFORMATION
The grotto may be open for visitors on a limited basis. No contact information available.

Puddle Ducks and Shore Birds

PANHANDLE REGION
Anderson Ranch

#9

CALL FOR DIRECTIONS: 806-323-6234

KEY BIRDS
Lesser prairie chicken, puddle ducks

BEST SEASON
Spring, summer, and fall

AREA DESCRIPTION
Short-grass prairie

The ranch offers tours to lesser prairie chicken booming grounds or leks, where the chickens provide an incomparable display of the rites of spring. One of the greatest concentrations of the dwindling lesser prairie chicken is in Hemphill, Wheeler, and Lipscomb counties. Intensive efforts to stabilize and restore the population are underway, and the Anderson Ranch has a significant tract of land that is in excellent range condition. Anderson Ranch has an estimated 26 lesser prairie chicken breeding leks and, depending on the year, good populations of northern bobwhite. The ranch also has prairie dog towns and well-managed native grasslands that include big bluestem, little bluestem, switchgrass, and yellow Indiangrass.

The lesser prairie chicken is a ground-nesting bird native to the mixed grass prairies of the Texas Panhandle, Colorado, Kansas, New Mexico, and Oklahoma. Two distinct populations occur in the Panhandle – one in the sand hills country of the High Plains west of Lubbock and the other in the Rolling Plains region in the northeast.

Although once common, the chicken's numbers have steadily declined across its range due to alteration of habitat for agricultural purposes. A related bird, the Attwater's prairie chicken, once abundant on coastal prairies, is currently the most endangered bird in Texas with only 42 wild birds recorded in the last census.

A blind near the riverbank provides ideal opportunities for wildlife photography or observation. Wild turkeys roost in the cottonwood stands along the river at night. The ranch provides an excellent venue for viewing the Canadian River breaks by kayak, which can be rented at the ranch when water levels permit. Look for a plethora of wildflowers in the spring, as well as raptors that can be found hunting above the grasslands.

A golden eagle has been seen by the large pond as you enter the ranch, and numerous puddle ducks and geese spend the winter here.

CONTACT INFORMATION
This is private property and the access to the site is restricted. Call ahead to 806-323-6234. A fee is charged.

Burrowing Owl

PANHANDLE REGION
Arrington Ranch

LOCATED SOUTH OF CANADIAN, TEXAS ON HIGHWAY 83 AND COUNTY ROAD 5

KEY BIRDS
Burrowing owl, ring-necked duck, wild turkey

BEST SEASON
Spring, summer, fall

AREA DESCRIPTION
Wetland area, very scenic

The ranch is very happy to have people come and enjoy the beauty of the great outdoors, the ranching lifestyle, and the comforts of the lodge.

Captain George Washington Arrington, a Texas Ranger stationed at nearby Fort Elliot, built the home that is just down the road from the wild and wooly frontier town of Mobeetie, where he also served as sheriff. The house was ordered from the Van Tein catalog, delivered by railroad, moved in pieces by wagon the last ten miles, and set up on the prairie in 1919. Today the house welcomes birding visitors to the remote ranch. The house was featured in the Tom Hanks movie "Cast Away".

The area seems completely flat but does present its great canyons and towering mesas around and close by the Canadian River.

Birders visiting the Canadian River and surrounding areas should always keep watch out for the golden eagles and beavers. In summer, watchers may also observe several species of dragonfly.

Prairie dogs and their abandoned holes provide shelter and nesting places for burrowing owls. Due to the variety of weather patterns, visitors should keep an eye out for rattlesnakes that will also den and hunt throughout prairie dog towns and vicinities.

Other species to watch for are a variety of wrens and meadowlarks, red-tailed hawks, northern harriers, ferruginous hawks, and rough-legged hawks hunting over and near the prairie dog holes.

It must be noted that a Texas law has been passed making the Canadian River bottoms off-limits to four-wheel off-road traffic. Birders should check before entering any of the access points to the river bottom. The birding is good here, but should be accomplished by walking the areas closed to traffic.

CONTACT INFORMATION
This is a private ranch, please call for directions – 806-323-6924.

Panhandle

Northern Flicker

PANHANDLE REGION
Bob Weatherly's Home Place

LOCATED JUST NORTH OF SHAMROCK ON HIGHWAY 83

KEY BIRDS
Several species of woodpecker and eastern & western forms of northern flicker

BEST SEASON
All seasons

AREA DESCRIPTION
The area is very flat, except around the Canadian River bluffs.

The Weatherly property includes four tracts, each of which offers a different view of the various ecosystems in the region. The area is open all year, however access is restricted and a fee is charged for entry.

The property features creek-fed ponds that run about two miles down the length of the property. The area is excellent habitat for woodpeckers, as numerous snags have been left standing. Some of the species that may be seen are golden-fronted woodpecker, downy woodpecker, hairy woodpecker, as well as eastern and western forms of northern flicker. These birds are common here in the fall and winter.

A one-mile tree line on the far edge of the property is excellent habitat for woodland birding. Wild Rio Grande turkey sub-species are found here in good numbers. If a roost is spotted, remain a distance away. There is a Texas law that forbids disturbing an active turkey roost, as turkeys will abandon a roost if disturbed too many times.

The property provides a cabin for overnight stays, making this a convenient place to wake up in the middle of habitat. The Sammons tract has a small, conveniently-located prairie dog town with a viewing blind to observe prairie dogs, burrowing owls, and raptors. The beautiful sand sagebrush rangeland of the Mitchell tract also provides opportunities for observing a variety of native grasses and wildflowers. This is a photographer's dream with the blinds, as well as beautiful sunsets.

CONTACT INFORMATION
Fee charged. Call for directions: 806-256-5042.

PANHANDLE

Painted Bunting

PANHANDLE REGION
Palo Duro Canyon & State Park

#12

LOCATED APPROXIMATELY 12 MILES EAST OF CANYON, TEXAS ON STATE HIGHWAY 217

KEY BIRDS
Prairie falcon, golden eagle, painted bunting

BEST SEASON
All seasons, but summers can be crowded and quite warm.

AREA DESCRIPTION
Rocky canyon country; loose rocks with steep landscape including grass prairies, and mesquite and juniper trees along the riverbanks and lower regions of the park.

Palo Duro Canyon State Park opened on July 4, 1934 and contains 29,182 acres of the scenic, northern-most portion of the Palo Duro Canyon. The Civilian Conservation Corp of the 1930s constructed most of the buildings and roads still in use by park staff and visitors.

The canyon is 120 miles long, as much as 20 miles wide, and has a maximum depth of more than 800 feet. Its elevation at the rim is 3,500 feet above sea level. It is often claimed that Palo Duro Canyon is the second largest canyon in the United States. The largest – the Grand Canyon – is 277 miles long, 18 miles wide, and 6,000 feet deep.

Palo Duro Canyon was formed by water erosion from the Prairie Dog Town Fork of the Red River. The water deepens the canyon by moving sediment downstream. Wind and water erosion gradually widen the canyon.

Early Spanish explorers are believed to have discovered the area and dubbed the canyon "Palo Duro" which is Spanish for "hard wood" in reference to the abundant mesquite and juniper trees.

Humans have resided in the canyon for approximately 12,000 years. The Apache lived in the canyon, but were replaced by Comanche and Kiowa tribes who resided in the area until 1874, when Col. Ronald Mackenzie was sent into the area to transport the Native Americans to Oklahoma.

One of the many sad parts of this event was the capture of more than 1,400 horses belonging to the tribe by the 4th Cavalry. The army kept the best of the herd and then took the remainder to Tule Canyon, where the rest of the horses were destroyed.

The Comanche were the southernmost tribe of the Native American horse culture and so, denied of their only means of transportation, the Comanche soon surrendered.

In 1876, Charles Goodnight entered the canyon and opened the JA Ranch. At its peak, the ranch supported more than 100,000 head of cattle. Goodnight operated the

PANHANDLE

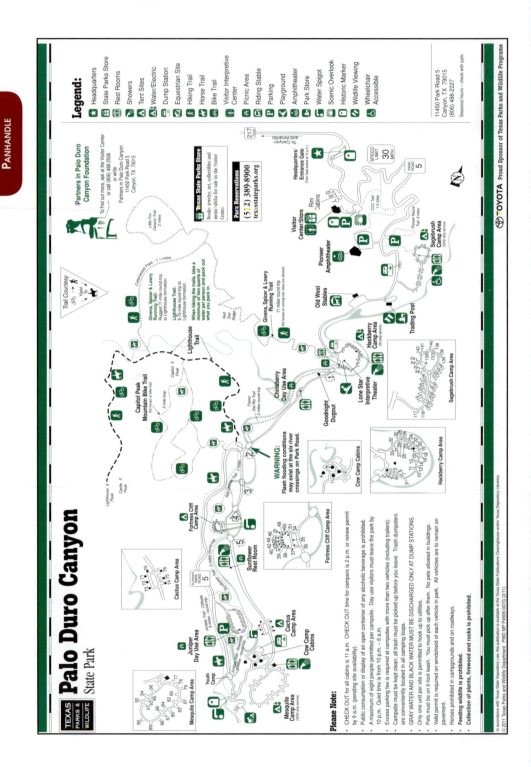

Palo Duro Canyon
State Park

Legend:

Headquarters		Visitor Interpretive Center	
State Parks Store		Picnic Area	
Rest Rooms		Riding Stable	
Showers		Parking	
Tent Sites		Playground	
Water/Electric		Amphitheater	
Dump Station		Park Store	
Equestrian Site		Water Spigot	
Hiking Trail		Scenic Overlook	
Horse Trail		Historic Marker	
Bike Trail		Wildlife Viewing	
		Wheelchair Accessible	

Partners in Palo Duro Canyon Foundation

To find out more, ask at the Visitor Center or call (806) 488-2506 or write
Partners in Palo Duro Canyon
11450 Park Road 5
Canyon, TX 79015

Texas State Parks Store

Books: jewelry, art, collectibles and memorabilia for sale in the Visitor Center.

Park Reservations

(512) 389-8900
texasstateparks.org

To Canyon and Amarillo 217

Headquarters/Entrance Gate
(Park Gate locked at 10 p.m.)

SPEED LIMIT 30 MPH

PARK ROAD 5

Rim Cabins

Visitor Center/Store

Pioneer Amphitheater

Sagebrush Camp Area
(50% amp service)

Pioneer Nature Trail .6 miles

Trail Courtesy
Yield To

Little Fox Canyon Trail 2 miles

Cottonwood Flats - 1.1 miles

Givens, Spicer & Lowry Running Trail
Rugged 11-mile round-trip to Lighthouse formation.

Lighthouse Trail:
5.75-mile round-trip to Lighthouse formation.

When hiking the trails, take a minimum of two quarts of water per person and pack out what you pack in.

Red Star Ridge

Givens, Spicer & Lowry Running Trail
11 miles round-trip
(No horses or running trail; bikes are allowed)

Old West Stables

Trading Post

Hackberry Camp Area
(30 amp service)

Sagebrush Camp Area

Chinaberry Day Use Area

Lone Star Interpretive Theater

Goodnight Dugout

Cow Camp Cabins

Hackberry Camp Area

WARNING:
Flash flooding conditions may exist at the six river crossings on Park Road.

Capitol X Peak

Capitol Peak Mountain Bike Trail
(No horses on bike trail)

3 mile loops

Castle X Peak

Lighthouse Trail

Lighthouse X Peak

Paseo Del Rio Trail 2 miles

Paseo Del Rio Trail 2 miles round-trip

Rojo Grande Trail 1.6 miles

Fortress Cliff Camp Area

Sunflower Rest Room

Fortress Cliff Camp Area

Juniper Day Use Area

Juniper Trail - campsite 6 miles / round-trip

Youth Camp

Cactus Camp Area

Cow Camp Cabins

Mesquite Camp Area
(50% amp service)

PANHANDLE ROAD 6

Please Note:

- CHECK OUT for all cabins is 11 a.m. CHECK OUT time for campers is 2 p.m. or renew permit by 9 a.m. (pending site availability).
- Public consumption or display of an open container of any alcoholic beverage is prohibited.
- A maximum of eight people permitted per campsite. Day use visitors must leave the park by 10 p.m. Quiet time is from 10 p.m. – 6 a.m.
- Excess parking fee is required at campsites with more than two vehicles (including trailers).
- Campsite must be kept clean; all trash must be picked up before you leave. Trash dumpsters are conveniently located in all camping loops.
- GRAY WATER AND BLACK WATER MUST BE DISCHARGED ONLY AT DUMP STATIONS.
- Only one unit per site is permitted to hook up to utilities.
- Pets must be on 6-foot leash. You must pick up after them. No pets allowed in buildings.
- Valid permit is required on windshield of each vehicle in park. All vehicles are to remain on pavement.
- Horses prohibited in campgrounds and on roadways.
- **Feeding wildlife is prohibited.**
- **Collection of plants, firewood and rocks is prohibited.**

11450 Park Road 5
Canyon, TX 79015
(806) 488-2227

Seasonal hours – check with park.

TOYOTA Proud Sponsor of Texas Parks and Wildlife Programs

TEXAS PARKS & WILDLIFE

ranch until 1890. Although only a fraction of its original size, the JA Ranch remains a working ranch today.

The Palo Duro Canyon State Park consists of over 16,000 acres of very diverse bird-watching habitats, including grass prairies, mesquite and juniper trees, riverbanks, the low, wet vegetation of the canyon floor, and the high elevations of the canyon rim. The Palo Duro Canyon is the second largest canyon in America, topped only by the Grand Canyon for its size and spectacular vistas. You can hike, bike, ride horses, and camp while bird watching at the park. Look for wild turkeys, red-headed woodpeckers, and painted buntings.

Here are some tips on finding some of the species found at the park's bird-watching hot spot. Park naturalist, Mark Hassell, has birded all over the park and suggests that birders try several of the many hiking trails. A slow walk along these will present more for birders.

Located behind the park trading post is a photo blind, where I spent an hour and saw and photographed a dozen species of birds. The site features bird feeders and a water feature to bring in the varied species. There are both high and low shoot-through holes for the birder or photographer.

As a special note, there is no signage showing the location of the blind. The trail to the blind begins to the right of the trading post building.

According to Hassell the lower end of the park has been having a "water problem", meaning the river has been trying to change its course. The park has been working on the problem but, at last report, the river is winning. Several of the lower campgrounds have been closed to camping but are still excellent birding locations.

One of the largest birds of prey in North America, the golden eagle, can be seen soaring over the prairies and trees of the park searching for prey. Look for the golden sheen of its large head, as well as its very long and broad tail and wings. This bird is dark brown in coloring all over, and has a large hooked bill.

Another large predator is the prairie falcon. It likes the grassy prairies of Palo Duro and can be found hunting for birds and mammals in the park. Look for long, pointed wings with brown spots and bars on its large, white chest. It has a dark mustache and dark ear patches as well.

Some other species are also found in the park. The mountain bluebird is found mostly in the open areas of the park. Watch grassy and brushy areas and water features, where this pretty bird will be hunting for small bugs and insects. The Townsend's solitaire will be in and around the junipers, feeding on its berries. The northern shrike – a songbird as well as a predator – will be found hunting small birds, mammals, and insects. The fox sparrow will be at the feeders as well as in the scrubby areas of the canyon.

CONTACT INFORMATION

For more information go to:
    http://palodurocanyon.com
    http://www.tpwd.state.tx.us/spdest/findadest/parks/palo_duro/
    http://www.allaboutbirds.org

Entrance is $4.00 per person. Reservations are not required for the photo blind.

Scissor-tailed Flycatcher

PANHANDLE REGION
Wildcat Bluff Nature Center

#13

2301 NORTH SONCY ROAD, AMARILLO, TEXAS 79124

KEY BIRDS
Burrowing owl, great horned owl, American kestrel, roadrunners, scissor-tailed flycatcher, western meadowlark

BEST SEASON
All seasons

AREA DESCRIPTION
Mostly flat, with easy walking trails

A special place, where you can step out of the daily routine and imagine a different time, is located just a few minutes from downtown Amarillo. More than 600 acres of rolling grasslands are threaded with nature trails offering a sense of isolation and tranquility. Discover delicate wildflowers amidst knee-high grasses, huge cottonwoods, and a magnificent bluff. Slow down enough to spot a horned lizard cross the trail, a hawk circling overhead, or a quail's nest hidden beneath a bush.

This is a place where you can reconnect with the timeless rhythm of the natural world and ponder the impact of civilization. At the same time, consider whether your great grandchildren will be able to experience first hand the wonders of nature and some excellent birding.

The place is Wildcat Bluff Nature Center. Named by early cowboys for a den of wildcats that lived under the bluff, it is also the site of a branch of the historic Santa Fe Trail, where wagon ruts are still visible today. It is a place of inspiration, a place for people to embrace the spirit of the land by exploring the natural magic of the Texas Panhandle.

CONTACT INFORMATION
PO Box 52132 Amarillo, TX 79159
Phone: (806) 352-6007
Fax: (806) 352-2274
email: info@wildcatbluff.org

Pyrrhuloxia

PANHANDLE REGION
Matador Wildlife Management Area

#14

3036 FM 3256, PADUCAH, TEXAS 79248

KEY BIRDS
Vermilion flycatcher, pyrrhuloxia

BEST SEASON
Year-round, with the exception of when the entire area is be closed for Special Permit Hunts. Permits are required for area entry and use.

AREA DESCRIPTION
The terrain here is made up of mostly mesquite uplands, shinnery oak rangeland, and gravelly hills consisting of red berry juniper and mesquite mix, with some bottomland areas.

The Matador Wildlife Management Area (MWMA) is located in the central Rolling Plains of Cottle County, Texas. Using Pittman-Robertson funds, the 28,183-acre MWMA was purchased by the Texas Parks and Wildlife Department in 1959 for the purposes of wildlife research, wildlife management, and public use.

Habitat types include mesquite uplands, shinnery oak rangeland, and gravelly hills consisting of red berry juniper and mesquite mix, and bottomland. Average annual rainfall is 22 inches, with the greatest precipitation normally occurring in May and June.

Public use activities include bird watching, camping, nature study, and photography. All visitors must register upon arrival at the registration building (open 24 hours) and check out when leaving.

All visitors, 17 years old and older, must possess a permit. These permits are available from any license vendor. Visitors under 17 years old must be accompanied by a person 18 years of age or older in possession of one of the permits. Tours of the area can be arranged for groups by contacting the Area Manager. Tours are not available during public hunts.

Numerous species occur on the area, including northern bobwhite, Rio Grande turkey, scissor-tailed flycatcher, Bullock's oriole, Mississippi kite, roadrunner, mourning dove, and painted bunting. Rare species sighted on the area include the vermilion flycatcher and the pyrrhuloxia.

Students, teachers, and scientists use the MWMA for instructional, educational, and research purposes. Do not disturb any markings, flags, traps, etc. that you encounter, as this may affect results.

Some areas on the WMA are inaccessible with two-wheel drive vehicles. Therefore, four-wheel drive vehicles are recommended to gain access to these remote areas. Signs are posted on roads where four-wheel drive vehicles are required.

All visitors are encouraged to bring plenty of drinking water. Those wishing to camp should bring camp stoves, since drought conditions often prohibit open fires. Electrical hookups and showers are not available. Foot protection for dogs is often recommended due to grass burs. It is also recommended that dogs have a collar and tag with the owner's name, address, and phone number in the event the dog is lost.

CONTACT INFORMATION

Chip Ruthven, manager. Phone: (806) 492-3405, Annual Public Hunting (APH) Permit or a Limited Public Use (LPU) Permit is required.

PANHANDLE REGION
Muleshoe National Wildlife Refuge

#15

PANHANDLE

LOCATED 20 MILES SOUTH OF MULESHOE ON STATE HIGHWAY 214 IN BAILEY COUNTY

KEY BIRDS
Waterfowl, sandhill crane, and raptors

BEST SEASON
October to February for cranes and waterfowl, spring and fall for migratory songbirds, and late summer for shorebirds

AREA DESCRIPTION
Sandy, short grass with two caliche outcroppings

Muleshoe National Wildlife Refuge, the oldest national wildlife refuge in Texas, was established by an executive order of October 24, 1935, and is administered by the United States Fish and Wildlife Service. The refuge is a unit in the national system of refuges in the Central Flyway.

The refuge serves as a wintering area for migratory waterfowl and sandhill cranes. Three saline lakes – White, Goose, and Paul's – each divided into upper and lower, are located within the refuge. At one time most of the lakes went dry annually, but in the 1930s this situation was remedied.

Muleshoe has three sink-type lakes that have no outlets, depend entirely on runoff for water, and are periodically dry. When the lakes are full, 600 acres of water are available for wildlife.

This enhances the value of the area as a migratory waterfowl refuge and as a habitat for resident birds and animals. The full lakes offer 600 acres of water for wildlife, though they usually are not full. In years of sufficient water, the refuge hosts tremendous numbers of sandhill crane and a variety of waterfowl.

Wintering sandhill cranes normally begin arriving around the end of September for a half-year stay. The sandhills' numbers peak between December and mid-February, often at 100,000 or more. In February, 1981 a record 250,000 sandhill cranes were sighted. When water is sufficient large numbers of migrating waterfowl begin arriving at the refuge during August, and their numbers peak by the end of December.

Small flocks of snow geese visit the refuge during the spring and fall migrations, and a few Canada geese winter there. The most common species of duck seen at the refuge is the pintail, but American wigeons, mallards, green-winged teals, and ruddy ducks also frequent the Muleshoe Preserve. Others are seen during migration.

The refuge comprises 7,089 acres, and the land is broken by two caliche outcroppings in the form of rim rocks near the northern and western boundaries. The outcroppings come alive with wildflowers in the spring, attracting hummingbirds. Trees and shrubs planted behind the refuge headquarters attract large numbers of songbirds, especially wood warblers in migration. Such raptors as red-tailed and Swainson's hawks can be seen, and in mid-winter it may be possible to see eight or more species of raptors in one day, including bald and golden eagles. Burrowing owls share homes with the local prairie dogs in their towns.

The refuge is open 24 hours a day all year.

CONTACT INFORMATION

Call the refuge at 806-946-3341 or visit the refuge website at www.fws.gov/southwest/refuges/texas/muleshoe.

Sandhill Cranes

PANHANDLE REGION
Lubbock Lake Landmark

#16

2401 LANDMARK DRIVE, LUBBOCK, TEXAS 79409

KEY BIRDS
Dark-eyed junco, fox sparrow, and ring-billed gull

BEST SEASON
All seasons depending on the weather, which may be severe during the winter months.

AREA DESCRIPTION
This is an area consisting of grassy plains and lakeside habitats with scattered hardwoods and mesquite brush.

The Lubbock Lake Landmark has historical records from people who roamed the plains up to 12,000 years ago! If you visit in the summer, you can see archaeologists excavating the site and discovering new treasures. Both self-guided and guided tours are available for you to fully understand and explore exactly what the Landmark has to offer. The Learning Center is a great place for both children and adults to reinforce the concepts and information present around the Landmark. Galleries exploring the past are also present at the site.

Lubbock has more of a northern birding feel than other parts of Texas. Dark-eyed juncos, fox sparrows, ring-billed gulls, and the cedar waxwing can be found with some frequency. Also expect burrowing owls, the marsh wren, the American kestrel, and the sharp-shinned and ferruginous hawks.

Some birds common to other parts of Texas but uncommon to the Panhandle Plains do show up at the Lubbock Lake Landmark, such as hummingbirds, the common nighthawk, and the common gallinule. The mountain plover also occurs at the Landmark on a somewhat uncommon basis.

CONTACT INFORMATION
806-742-1116
http://www.depts.ttu.edu/museumttu/lll
email: lubbock.lake@ttu.edu

Dark-eyed Junco

Goldenfronted Woodpecker

PANHANDLE REGION
Wagon Wheel Ranch
#17

PANHANDLE

Just outside Snyder, Texas

Key Birds
Swainson's hawk, great horned owl, common nighthawk, greater roadrunner, golden-fronted woodpecker, vermilion flycatcher, Bewick's wren, blue grosbeak, painted bunting, Cassin's and lark sparrows, common grackle, and Bullock's oriole

Best Season
Spring and fall migrations

Area Description
Ranchland with ponds and playa lakes

This guest ranch encompasses 800 acres, with the adjacent 1,200 acres — once part of the ranch still available to birders and naturalists.

Several loop roads, including one that encircles an 80-acre buffalo wallow (Playa Lake) provide access to the property and its birds, wildflowers, reptiles, and invertebrates.

Five ponds provide habitat for killdeer, wading birds, and several species of large showy dragonflies. In winter, these ponds attract wintering ducks and a few shorebirds.

Directions
Go to Snyder, then drive north on US 84 for 6.5 miles to FM 1142. Go 2.5 miles and turn left at the large white sign for the ranch. Follow this road for 1.2 miles to the Wagon Wheel Ranch on the right side of the road.

Contact Information
Phone: 915-573-2348

PANHANDLE

PANHANDLE REGION
Big Spring State Park

#18

#1 SCENIC DRIVE
BIG SPRING, TEXAS 79720

KEY BIRDS
Scaled quail, wild turkey, roadrunners, golden-fronted woodpecker, western scrub jay, and canyon towhee

BEST SEASON
April and May bring migrants and nesting activities, November through March for winter birds.

AREA DESCRIPTION
Mostly open and rolling areas with sparse trees and underbrush, with an area dedicated to a small prairie dog town.

Big Spring State Park is 382 acres located within the city limits of Big Spring in Howard County. Both city and park were named for a natural spring that was replaced by an artificial one. The park was deeded by the city of Big Spring in 1934 and 1935, and was opened in 1936.

Comanche and earlier Indian groups frequently visited the park area in the past, probably attracted by the permanent source of spring water. Spaniards may have first visited the area as early as 1768.

The Civilian Conservation Corps was created during the "Depression" to employ young men unable to find jobs. Using limestone quarried on the site and quality workmanship, the CCC built the pavilion, headquarters, residence, pump house, and restroom. Their biggest project was the three-mile drive that loops around the mountain, following the ledge of limestone rim rock capping the bluff.

In addition to some great birding, activities include picnicking, nature study, and sightseeing. Common wildlife such as cottontails, jackrabbits, ground squirrels, and roadrunners can often be seen, particularly early or late in the day.

There is also a small prairie dog town that lies in a little valley on the south side of the park. Many of the area's numerous and varied bird species can also be observed. Watch for wildlife near the ponds. A burrowing-owl population can be observed at a nearby airpark. Ask park workers for exact locations for these interesting little birds of prey.

Other species include curve-billed thrasher, white crowned sparrow, lesser goldfinch, Mississippi kite, Swainson's hawk, scissor-tailed flycatcher, western grebe, osprey, and western and mountain bluebirds.

CONTACT INFORMATION
Phone: 432-263-4931 / email: bigsprsp@sbcglobal.net

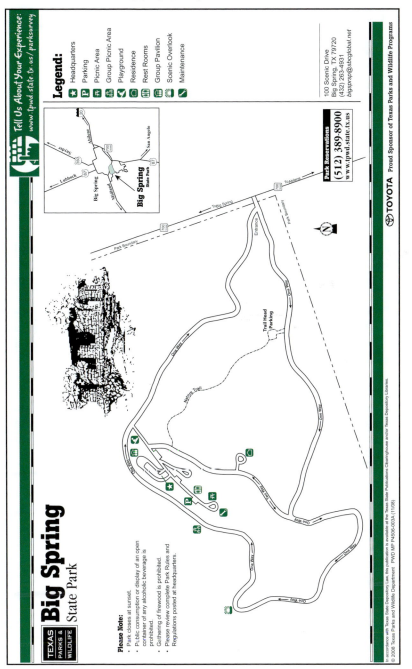

In accordance with Texas State Depository Law, this publication is available at the Texas State Publications Clearinghouse and/or Texas Depository Libraries.
© 2008 Texas Parks and Wildlife Department   PWD MP P4506-003A (11/08)

PANHANDLE REGION
Perini Ranch

#19

NEAR BUFFALO GAP, TEXAS

KEY BIRDS
Swainson's hawk, canyon towhee, northern bobwhite

BEST SEASON
All seasons

AREA DESCRIPTION
This ranch typifies the Abilene country with open areas broken up by stands of oak trees with some planted fields and wildflower areas and small man-made ponds or small lakes.

The Perini Ranch is a commercial operation offering accommodations, and meals at their steakhouse. The ranch is just beginning its operation for birders and many of the areas are still under construction. Located a short distance from the town of Buffalo Gap, this is a great area for birding and observing nature.

The Perini Ranch plans to have nature trails that will allow visitors to walk through stands of oak, viewing white-tailed deer, wild turkey, northern bobwhite, armadillos, raccoons, and migrating songbirds in spring. Wildflowers in the open fields attract an impressive diversity of butterflies.

The agricultural fields that border the ranch are known to attract migrating Swainson's hawks, which feed on small rodents and insects in the fields. The canyon towhee is one of the more interesting western birds that reside here. Several small ponds on the property provide good viewing opportunities for wildlife in general and odonata dragonflies and damselflies in particular.

The ranch also runs a steakhouse, which is open to the public.

DIRECTIONS
Enter Buffalo Gap, then turn right on FM 613, turn right 0.3 mile to FM 89 and turn left before the First Baptist Church in Buffalo Gap. After 0.7 mile, turn right at the sign for the Perini Ranch.

CONTACT INFORMATION
Birders need to call. Site access restricted. A small fee is charged.
Phone: 915-572-3339
www.periniranch.com

PANHANDLE REGION
Will Hair Park

#20

ABILENE, TEXAS

KEY BIRDS
Harris's sparrow, white-crowned sparrow, song sparrow, white-throated sparrow, field sparrow, and vesper sparrow

BEST SEASON
All seasons

AREA DESCRIPTION
Creek with hardwood trees.

This small 25-acre park is a top spot for birders and can produce good numbers and varieties of birds. A creek runs through the park and the hardwoods that line the creek banks provide roosting and nesting locations for several species.

In spring, check the mini fruiting mulberries in this riparian corridor. Harris's, white-crowned, song, white-throated, field, vesper, and Savannah sparrows are easy finds in winter, and flocks of American goldfinch and clay-colored sparrow are also here in early spring. During migrations, check the hardwoods for migrating songbirds.

Cedar Creek meanders through Will Hair Park, making this local park ideal for a quick birding stop. As with all urban parks, birding is best early in the morning before the locals put it to use. A favorite spot to watch for passerines and migrants is behind the houses on Cedar Crest Drive where frisbee golf is played.

When there is water running in the creek, birding can get interesting. A good location in all seasons, the birding is especially good during the winter along the creek and in the adjoining trees.

Mississippi kites nest here along with cardinals, mockingbirds, blue jays, and mourning, white-winged, Eurasian, and Inca doves. During winter northern flicker, downy woodpecker, and white-crowned, white-throated, Lincoln's, swamp, song, and Harris's sparrows are seen. Migration brings Nashville, orange-crowned, yellow-rumped and yellow warblers. Painted redstarts and thrushes put in a quick appearance before moving elsewhere. The creek attracts herons and egrets when the water is running and fish are swimming in the stream.

DIRECTIONS
From I–20 go south for 1.1 miles on FM 600 (West Lake Road). Turn left at the T-intersection, TX 351/Ambler Avenue. The park is on the right at 0.1 mile.

White-crowned Sparrow

PANHANDLE REGION

Abilene Zoological Garden And Nelson Park

#21

PANHANDLE

2070 ZOO LANE
ABILENE, TX 79602

KEY BIRDS
Waterfowl – including resident whistling-ducks and Bullock's oriole

BEST SEASON
All seasons

AREA DESCRIPTION
An urban landscape, but good birding.

In the truest since of the word, this location is a birder's zoo and contains a wetland as well as a small area planted to native grasses. Resident black-bellied whistling-ducks can be seen in relative proximity and, during spring migration, the wetland attracts a variety of shorebirds. Check the two large ponds in Nelson Park for uncommon species, among these are ring-billed gull and Forster's tern.

Waterfowl also inhabit both ponds during the two migration periods, and the cottonwoods that surround the edge of the second lake provide good cover for spring migrants, as well as nesting habitat for Bullock's oriole, woodpeckers, and flycatchers.

Black-bellied Whistling-duck

Black-crowned night-herons nest in the willow and cottonwood groves along the edge. White-faced ibis and yellow-headed blackbirds have been recorded during migration. Surf scoter and peregrine falcon, both rarities for Abilene, have occurred here.

DIRECTIONS
Follow TX 351/Ambler Avenue east from Will Hair Park to I-20 East, exit Loop 322 South (Exit 390). Go 1.7 miles and exit at TX 36 West. Follow signs to the zoo.

CONTACT INFORMATION
A fee is charged and the site is open daily. Developed camping is available. Phone: 915-676-6086

PANHANDLE REGION
Kirby Lake

SOUTH SIDE OF ABILENE, TEXAS

KEY BIRDS
Pyrrhuloxia, scarlet tanager, waterfowl and other migrating birds during the spring and fall

BEST SEASON
All seasons

AREA DESCRIPTION
Lakeshore terrain

A favorite birding spot in the Abilene area, Kirby Lake provides habitat for a variety of birds and for occasional rarities such as long-tailed jaeger, red knot, and red phalarope.

Just a short drive around Kirby Lake produced several sightings on my last trip there. Many of the side roads are dirt and, during wet weather, caution is advised.

During winter a good day can produce seven or eight species of sparrow, cactus wren, curve-billed thrasher, and pyrrhuloxia.

Spring migration fills the mesquite brush that surrounds the lake with passerines, and the shallow lake itself hosts migrants such as Baird's sandpiper, pectoral sandpiper, Wilson's phalarope, and Franklin's gull. Eared grebes in breeding plumage also occur here in spring.

During my visit there was quite a bit of construction going on at both entry points and may be going on for a while. Birding is good in the early morning and late afternoons after the workers have quit for the day.

A scarlet tanager was spotted and photographed in several locations, and approaching the little bird was good to within spotting scope and camera range.

Use your spotting scope to scan the cattails bordering the lake for the yellow-headed blackbird, which migrates through this region in dense flocks. Snowy plover and, less commonly, black-bellied plover can be seen at the lake during migration. Bell's vireo and verdin nest here, and merlin are occasionally seen.

DIRECTIONS
Follow Loop 322 South for about 3.5 miles and exit on Maple Street, turn left, and go 0.9 mile to the entrance on your right. The sign is small and easily missed; watch for the ball fields on your right.

CONTACT INFORMATION
Site open daily – park in designated areas. Developed camping available. Phone: 915-676-6217

PANHANDLE REGION
Cedar Gap Farm

TUSCOLA, TEXAS

KEY BIRDS
Migrating hummingbirds, towhee, and brown thrasher

BEST SEASON
All seasons

AREA DESCRIPTION
Private land with trees and brush and a comfortable house with a large window to see the birds.

My visit to Cedar Gap Farm was very rewarding, and an opportunity to meet several of the birders from the Abilene Audubon Society. While sitting in the climate-controlled birdhouse, several species of birds were observed. For photographers it may be necessary to move to the outside of the building and shoot around the corners. This is because of the large glass window separating the birders from the birds, where glare and reflections may occur. Normal bird watching is not affected in any way.

Rufous Hummingbird

Cedar Gap Farm is operated by the Hutto Family with their own finances, and offers birders a hummingbird viewing house from which visitors can get intimate views of large numbers of black-chinned hummingbirds.

Cedar Gap Farm is a great place to bird year round. There is a large climate-controlled building with huge windows for observing birds and wildlife. Food and water is provided year round at the birdhouse and several other locations along trails. Several trails loop through oaks, mesquite, junipers, and other native vegetation providing opportunities to see wildlife in its natural setting. Trails vary in length and difficulty. The trails are designed to please most skill levels of hikers.

Birders may see a mix of western and eastern birds in all seasons.

Records show that the following species have been seen at this site by drive– in birders and by the Abilene Audubon Chapter members: White-crowned sparrow, white-throated sparrow, eastern and spotted towhee, scrub jay, gray catbird, red-breasted nuthatch, yellow-bellied sapsucker, canyon towhee, brown thrasher, as well as painted, indigo, and lazuli buntings.

The spring and summer months bring hundreds of black-chinned hummingbirds to this area and in the fall rufous, ruby-throated, and an occasional Allen's hummingbird will put in an appearance. A small pond is located near the observation room and birds can be seen coming to the water here.

Hummers arrive around the middle of March and stay through November. Painted and indigo buntings arrive around mid-April and leave around the first of September. Wild turkeys put on a show with their spring mating rituals.

The farm also provides drinks and light snacks, as well as a variety of interpretive material for people interested in hummingbirds. Landscaping around the viewing area includes native plants favored by hummingbirds and butterflies.

The half-mile nature trail winds through the juniper and oak woods, and provides habitat for migrating warblers, vireos, and flycatchers.

As mentioned, no fee is charged but donations are appreciated. The daily cost of birdseed, nectar, and suet is expensive. It can't be stressed enough that Cedar Gap runs on donations, please give what you can.

DIRECTIONS
From Abilene drive south on 83/84. Turn left onto CR 150 and take the first dirt road to your left (CR 563). Watch for the sign to the Bird House.

CONTACT INFORMATION
Site access restricted. Call ahead. Donations are needed. The Bird House is open all day, every day from dawn to dusk. Call Homer, Earlene, or Mark Hutto at 325-572-4738 or 325-669-2879 / e-mail: cedargapfarm@aol.com.

PANHANDLE REGION
#24 Copper Breaks State Park

ON STATE HIGHWAY 6 BETWEEN THE TOWNS OF CROWELL AND QUANAH

KEY BIRDS
Virginia rail, roadrunners, golden-fronted woodpecker, canyon towhee, and rufous-crowned and black-chinned sparrow

BEST SEASON
Mid-April through June for migrating species and some nesting activities.

AREA DESCRIPTION
Lake, pond, river, marsh, mesquite grassland, and prairie pasture.

The park features rugged, scenic beauty with mixed grass/mesquite-covered mesas and juniper breaks. North Texas wildlife abounds at Copper Breaks State Park.

Roadrunners, great blue herons, many species of ducks, meadowlarks, quail, doves, cardinals, owls, flickers, bluebirds, kites, hawks, and mockingbirds are just a few of the many species of birds found in the park. Less commonly seen species in the park are eastern phoebe, painted bunting, and yellow-billed cuckoo. Most species of mammal in the park are best viewed during the early morning and late evening hours.

Prior to the arrival of the early white settlers, this region was the realm of the Comanche and Kiowa tribes. It remained so until the pressures of a new civilization forced the Indian onto reservations in nearby Oklahoma.

It was near the present park area where Cynthia Ann Parker was recaptured from a band of Comanche Indians and subsequently reunited with her relatives. Cynthia Ann had been captured as a small child by a raiding party near Mexia and grew up among the Indians.

Her son, Quanah Parker, was to become the last great war chief of the Comanche nation. After being reunited with her relatives, Cynthia Ann Parker did not adjust well to the ways of the settlers and longed for the free life style of the Comanche. She died in a relatively short period after being returned to her relatives.

DIRECTIONS
In Paducah, turn east on US 70 to Crowell — 36.3 miles. Turn north/left on TX 6 for 8.9 miles and enter the state park on your left.

CONTACT INFORMATION
777 Park Road 62 Quanah, Tx 79252-7679 / Phone 940-839-4331 / website: http://www.tpwd.state.tx.us/spdest/findadest/parks/copper_breaks/

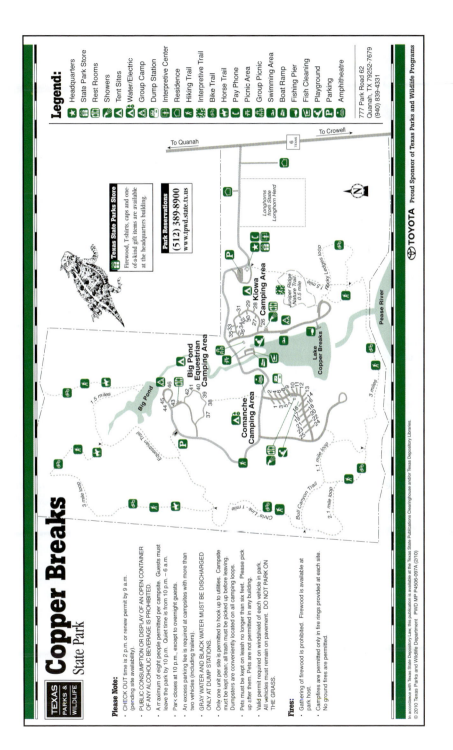

Copper Breaks
State Park

TEXAS PARKS & WILDLIFE

Please Note:

· CHECK OUT time is 2 p.m. or renew permit by 9 a.m. (pending site availability).

· PUBLIC CONSUMPTION OR DISPLAY OF AN OPEN CONTAINER OF ANY ALCOHOLIC BEVERAGE IS PROHIBITED.

· A maximum of eight people permitted per campsite. Guests must leave the park by 10 p.m. Quiet time is from 10 p.m. – 6 a.m.

· Park closes at 10 p.m. except to overnight guests.

· An excess parking fee is required at campsites with more than two vehicles (including trailers).

· GRAY WATER AND BLACK WATER MUST BE DISCHARGED ONLY AT DUMP STATIONS.

· Only one unit per site is permitted to hook up to utilities. Campsite must be kept clean; all trash must be picked up before leaving. Dumpsters are conveniently located on all camping loops.

· Pets must be kept on leash no longer than six feet. Please pick up after them. Pets are not permitted in any building.

· Valid permit required on windshield of each vehicle in park. All vehicles must remain on pavement. DO NOT PARK ON THE GRASS.

Fires:

· Gathering of firewood is prohibited. Firewood is available at park host.

· Campfires are permitted only in fire rings provided at each site.

· No ground fires are permitted.

Legend:

- Headquarters
- State Park Store
- Rest Rooms
- Showers
- Tent Sites
- Water/Electric
- Group Camp
- Dump Station
- Interpretive Center
- Residence
- Hiking Trail
- Interpretive Trail
- Bike Trail
- Horse Trail
- Pay Phone
- Picnic Area
- Group Picnic
- Swimming Area
- Boat Ramp
- Fishing Pier
- Fish Cleaning
- Playground
- Parking
- Amphitheatre

To Quanah

To Crowell

6 TEXAS

Texas State Parks Store
Firewood, T-shirts, caps and one-of-a-kind gift items are available at the headquarters building.

Park Reservations
(512) 389-8900
www.tpwd.state.tx.us

Longhorns from State Longhorn Herd

N

Pease River

Juniper Ridge Nature Trail 0.5 mile

Rocky Ledges loop

Kiowa Camping Area

Big Pond Equestrian Camping Area

Big Pond

Equestrian Trail

1.5 miles

3 mile loop

Comanche Camping Area

Lake Copper Breaks

3 miles

Chris Link 1 mile

Bull Canyon Trail

2.1 mile loop

1.1 mile loop

777 Park Road 62
Quanah, TX 79252-7679
(940) 839-4331

TOYOTA Proud Sponsor of Texas Parks and Wildlife Programs

PANHANDLE

PANHANDLE REGION
Abilene State Park

#25

LOCATED ON FM 89, SOUTH OF ABILENE, TEXAS

KEY BIRDS
Three species of wren — cactus, Carolina, and Bewick's

BEST SEASON
All seasons

AREA DESCRIPTION
Grassland, mesquite, and other trees of the Rolling Plains

Abilene State Park marks a point where the grasses and mesquite of the Rolling Plains meet the oak and juniper characteristic of the Edwards Plateau, resulting in a diverse mix of habitats and wildlife. Plant and bird species of xeric western ecosystems integrate with those that occur more commonly in eastern locations. Elm Creek adds a riparian pecan-elm-black willow mix, as well as the wetland features normally associated with a stream.

Plan to arrive at the park early before campers and hikers are out. The best place to bird is along the riparian habitat in the day use/picnic area. Elm Creek runs through the entire state park. As might be expected when there is water in the creek, many of the area's birds are feeding and bathing.

Warblers and vireos can be found in the spring and fall. Summer breeders are Mississippi kite, summer tanager, painted bunting, pyrrhuloxia, cactus wren, Bewick's and Carolina wrens, Bell's vireo, blue grosbeak, Bullock's oriole, scrub jay, and the usual suspects. Most winters you can find several different sparrows, house wren, winter wren, brown thrasher, white-throated sparrow, golden-crowned kinglet, and brown creeper. Eastern bluebirds breed in the area and mountain bluebirds and western bluebirds have been seen occasionally "across the street" at Lake Abilene during the winter months.

Near the water tower (black vultures hang out here in winter) on Eagle Trail is a good spot to bird. Seepage from Lake Abilene trickles down to this area and if you just stand and watch for awhile, you should see some birds. In the spring we found Chihuahuan ravens nesting on the water tower.

Mississippi kite, yellow-billed cuckoo, blue-gray gnatcatcher, and three species of wren - cactus, Carolina, and Bewick's - commonly nest here during summer, as do painted bunting and summer tanager.

In addition, the park offers wildlife observation and photographic opportunities for white-tailed deer, raccoons, armadillos, foxes, squirrels, cottontail rabbits, and a large variety of birds.

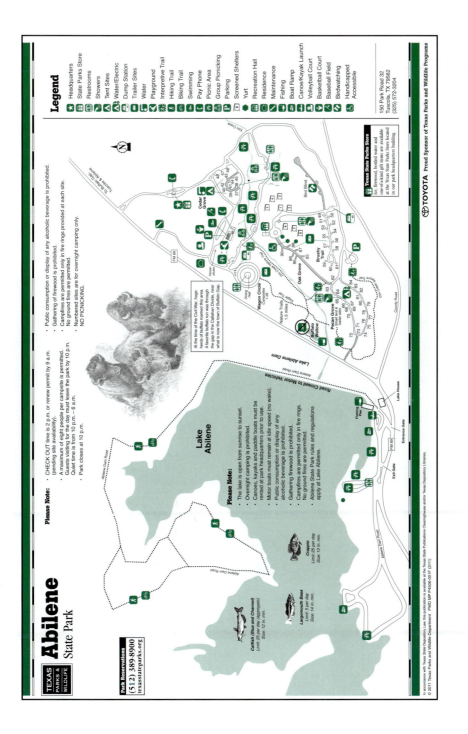

Abilene
State Park

Park Reservations
(512) 389-8900
texasstateparks.org

Please Note:
- CHECK OUT time is 2 p.m. or renew permit by 9 a.m. (pending site availability).
- A maximum of eight people per campsite is permitted. Guests visiting for the day must leave the park by 10 p.m. Quiet time is from 10 p.m.—6 a.m.
- Park closes at 10 p.m.

- Public consumption or display of any alcoholic beverage is prohibited.
- Gathering of firewood is prohibited.
- Campfires are permitted only in fire rings provided at each site. No ground fires are permitted. NO PICNICKING.
- Numbered sites are for overnight camping only.

At the time of the Civil War, huge herds of buffalo roamed this area. A favorite buffalo run was through the gap in the Callahan Divide, near what is now the town of Buffalo Gap.

Lake Abilene

Please Note:
- The lake is open from sunrise to sunset.
- Overnight camping is prohibited.
- Canoes, kayaks and paddle boats must be rented at park headquarters prior to use.
- Motor boats must remain at idle speed (no wake).
- Public consumption or display of any alcoholic beverage is prohibited.
- Gathering firewood is prohibited.
- Campfires are permitted only in fire rings. No ground fires are permitted.
- Abilene State Park rules and regulations apply at Lake Abilene.

Catfish (Blue and Channel) Limit 25 per day (aggregate). Size: 12 in. min.

Crappie Limit 25 per day. Size: 10 in. min.

Largemouth Bass Limit 5 per day. Size: 14 in. min.

Legend
Headquarters, State Parks Store, Restrooms, Showers, Tent Sites, Water/Electric, Dump Station, Trailer Sites, Water, Playground, Interpretive Trail, Hiking Trail, Biking Trail, Swimming, Pay Phone, Picnic Area, Group Picnicking, Parking, Screened Shelters, Yurt, Recreation Hall, Residence, Maintenance, Fishing, Boat Ramp, Canoe/Kayak Launch, Volleyball Court, Basketball Court, Baseball Field, Birdwatching, Handicapped Accessible

Texas State Parks Store
Ice, firewood, bottled water and one-of-a-kind gift items are available at the Texas State Parks Store located in our park headquarters building.

150 Park Road 32
Tuscola, TX 79562
(325) 572-3204

TOYOTA Proud Sponsor of Texas Parks and Wildlife Programs

In accordance with Texas State Depository Law, this publication is available at the Texas State Publications Clearinghouse and/or Texas Depository Libraries.
© 2011 Texas Parks and Wildlife Department PWD MP P4506-001F (2011)

PANHANDLE

The photo blind located on the main park road is very well built and convenient for photographers with both short or long lenses. Casual bird watchers will find the blinds and area conducive to spotting many species of birds. Volunteers from the Abilene Audubon Chapter maintain the feeders and water feature.

DIRECTIONS

Abilene State Park is located in southern Taylor County near Buffalo Gap, Texas. From the intersection of the Winters Freeway (Hwy. 83/84) take the Buffalo Gap Exit (Hwy. 89) which runs by the mall. Travel south on 89 approximately 10 miles until you come to Buffalo Gap. Highway 89 makes a right turn in Buffalo Gap, so watch for the sign. Then proceed south for another 3.9 miles to the entrance of the state park.

CONTACT INFORMATION

Site open for day use only. Fee charged. No reservations required for the photo blind. Phone: 915-572-3204 / website: http://beta-www.tpwd.state.tx.us/state-parks/parks/maps/abilene-state-park/

Bewick's Wren

PANHANDLE REGION
Lake Abilene

#26

LOCATED ON **FM 89 SOUTH. THE LAKE IS ON THE RIGHT.**

KEY BIRDS
Bluebirds — eastern, western, and mountain

BEST SEASON
All seasons

AREA DESCRIPTION
Woodland areas around lake

Lake edges are productive habitat for migrating shorebirds such as American avocet, semipalmated sandpiper, Wilson's phalarope, and great blue heron. The lake's appeal to migrant waterbirds depends on water levels. The lower the water levels, the greater the area's appeal. Dowitchers and sandpipers begin showing up as early as late February.

After you cross the dike, there is a nice pullout from which you can set up a spotting scope. Farther along the road there are numerous places to stop, get out, and walk closer to the edge of the lake for better viewing. The hills that surround the lake contain dense, mature stands of juniper, providing good habitat for woodland birds. All three bluebirds — eastern, western, and mountain — have been seen here. Common and hooded mergansers winter here and painted bunting and blue grosbeak nest here in summer.

Lake Abilene provides an excellent opportunity to see both woodland species and shorebirds that are attracted to the wetlands areas. Waterfowl can also be seen here throughout the fall and winter, then again in the spring.

CONTACT INFORMATION
Site open for day use only. Fee charged.

Eastern Bluebird

Curve-billed Thrasher

PANHANDLE REGION
Lake Fort Phantom Hill / Abilene

#27

PANHANDLE

LOCATED NORTH OF ABILENE

KEY BIRDS
Golden-crowned kinglet and pine warbler (in winter) and painted bunting, curve-billed thrasher

BEST SEASON:
All seasons

AREA DESCRIPTION
This is an open area with many of the old buildings and chimneys still standing and some old wagons.

Both sides of the lake are good for birding; just pick your side according to which way the sun is shining. Nothing's worse than trying to bird across the water when the sun's reflection is bouncing off the water right back into your eyes. Photographers will find the shooting better on the east side and from the access (dirt) roads on the west.

Great places to stop along West Lake Road are Seabee Park and Johnson Park. Passerines and shorebirds hang out at Seabee, and to a lesser extent at Johnson Park. Johnson Park has a boat launch, picnic tables, and wading area so it gets lots of use. Golden-crowned kinglet and pine warbler (in winter) and painted bunting, curve-billed thrasher, cactus wren, Bullock's oriole, and Bell's vireo are found in the spring and summer.

The places to stop along East Lake Road are the boat ramp — look for the sign — to scope the lake and the mesquite scrub habitat area around the lake for passerines. Sandhill cranes lift off early in the morning during the winter, and the south end of the lake is an excellent area to see them rise into the air.

Drive the public residential roads for hawks and passerines. Toward the north end of the lake, you will find several places to pull off and go to the water's edge to look for shorebirds and other waders.

Off of FM 1082, go around one curve, and before you curve again, pull off right after the low water crossing. The chances are good to see whimbrel, godwits, plovers, dowitchers, peeps, and a reddish egret (2003).

Just two miles north on FM 600 are the Fort Phantom Hill ruins. This is a great place to bird for passerines – especially sparrows – in the winter. There were several hawks there during my visit, and we also saw a peregrine falcon hunting the lake.

DIRECTIONS

Lake Fort Phantom Hill is located just north of I-20, between West Lake Road FM 600 and East Lake Road FM 2833.

CONTACT INFORMATION

No fees are charged and there are no attendants at the park. For more information, contact the Abilene Convention and Visitors Bureau at 800-727-7704 or 915-677-7241.

Yellow-headed Blackbird

PANHANDLE REGION
Lake Alan Henry

PANHANDLE

2706 BOAT RAMP ROAD
JUSTICEBURG, TX 79330

KEY BIRDS
Loggerhead shrike, yellow warbler, indigo bunting, and yellow-headed blackbird

BEST SEASON
All seasons

AREA DESCRIPTION
Lakeshore and rocky open areas

Lake Alan Henry is a reservoir built by the City of Lubbock that provides an outstanding recreational area for people to enjoy nature and birding.

Camp on primitive sites that overlook the lake, and birders would be well rewarded hiking the rugged trails.

Situated on the South Fork of the Double Mountain Fork of the Brazos River, the lake extends 11 miles between the rocky sides of the river channel and has 56 miles of shoreline.

Birders visiting the lake have produced documented sightings of solitary sandpiper, a wood pewee, western and scissor-tailed flycatchers, verdin, loggerhead shrike, a yellow warbler, indigo bunting and a yellow-headed blackbird. In addition to birds, there are a number of mammal species, as well as the butterflies and wildflowers.

DIRECTIONS
On US 84, go 65 miles south of Lubbock, through Post to Justiceburg. The lake is four miles east of Justiceburg, on the Double Mountain Fork of the Brazos River.

CONTACT INFORMATION
City of Lubbock Parks and Recreation Department oversees Lake Allen Henry.
For more information, phone: 806-775-2673.

PANHANDLE

PANHANDLE REGION
Fort Chadbourne

#29

LOCATED HALFWAY BETWEEN ABILENE AND SAN ANGELO, TX AND IS 12 MILES NORTH OF BRONTE ON HWY 277

KEY BIRDS
Bullock's oriole, painted bunting, and dickcissel

BEST SEASON
All seasons

AREA DESCRIPTION
Ranchland and wet areas

Fort Chadbourne sits on 10,000 acres of private ranch land. This historic fort was officially open from 1852-1867. In 1876, Thomas L. Odom and his son, Garland, drove cattle into the fort, establishing the O-D Ranch. Today, Thomas's great-great-great grandson, Garland Richards, continues to operate the working ranch, and has preserved, stabilized, and restored the ruins to their original structure.

Oak Creek Lake provides habitat for great blue herons, and in the winter, for a variety of migrating waterfowl and shorebirds. Sparrows abound in winter. Scissor-tailed flycatcher, lark sparrow, red-tailed hawk, eastern and western meadowlarks, and Cooper's hawk are common breeders that are easily seen in the summer. Also look for Bullock's oriole, painted bunting, and dickcissel. Both northern bobwhite and scaled quail occur here.

CONTACT INFORMATION
Fort Chadbourne
Foundation, 651 Fort
Chadbourne Road, Bronte,
TX 76933.
The site is restricted;
please call ahead for
directions.
Phone: 915-743-2555 or
325-743-2555
www.fortchadbourne.org
fortchad@taylortel.com

Bullcock's Oriole

PANHANDLE REGION
#30 Lake Spence-Humble Crossing

BETWEEN ABILENE AND SAN ANGELO

KEY BIRDS
Sandhill crane, bald eagle, and osprey

BEST SEASON
Spring, summer, and winter

AREA DESCRIPTION
Riparian areas and river frontage

This multi-use park has boating, fishing, and picnic facilities, as well as riparian areas on the Colorado River. This location attracts wintering sandhill crane, bald eagle, and osprey. Greater roadrunner, northern bobwhite, rattlesnakes, jackrabbits, and deer are abundant here. The monarch butterfly migration in October brings large numbers of these colorful insects through the park, where they nectar on large milkweed plants.

DIRECTIONS
Located 8.4 miles north on TX 208, look for the turn sign for Lake Spence. Turn left and go 4.0 miles to the entrance. Veer off to the right at the public toilets for riverfront access.

CONTACT INFORMATION
Fee charged. Site open for day use only. Phone: 915-453-2061

Osprey

PANHANDLE

Osprey

PANHANDLE REGION
Walnut Creek Ranch

#31

LOCATED IN WEST TEXAS BETWEEN STERLING CITY AND WATER VALLEY

KEY BIRDS
Black-capped vireo, eastern and western bluebirds

BEST SEASON
All seasons

AREA DESCRIPTION
Rocky with cactus, then grasslands, a creek-side landscape, and riparian woodlands

This ranch is located along both sides of Walnut Creek, where the Hill Country and Rolling Plains landscapes of Texas merge. Having over 10,000 acres of varied habitat makes this an excellent site for wildlife enthusiasts, as well as historians and archaeologists. Prehistoric burial sites are visible from most hillsides. Flint chips, arrowheads, and handmade Indian tools litter the land. This ranch offers evidence of human occupation for over 12,000 years.

Mixed riparian woodlands, canyons, and limestone ledges in grassland scrub and mesquite savannahs constitute the outlying areas of the ranch. Habitats on the ranch support a wide variety of birds, such as black-capped and Bell's vireos, Scott's and Bullock's orioles, vermilion flycatcher, canyon and cactus wrens, canyon towhee, greater roadrunner, northern bobwhite, scaled quail, wild turkey, and painted bunting. Look for black phoebe along the creek. Mountain, eastern, and western bluebirds are common. In addition to the many wintering sparrows and woodpeckers, Walnut Creek Ranch is a wintering home to bald eagles and, occasionally, golden eagles.

Bird enthusiasts have marveled at the multiple arrays of birds that inhabit the area. The black-capped vireo, a highly endangered and protected bird, has been banded and observed on the ranch. Management for this species is meticulously followed because of its fragile ties to the environment.

The vermilion flycatcher is a must-see and the magnificent bald eagle winters at Walnut Creek Ranch. The ranch itself was cited by the National Audubon Society as an important bird area (IBA).

CONTACT INFORMATION
Site access is restricted. A fee is charged. Call ahead.
Contact: Kathi Johnson, PO Box 163, Water Valley, TX 76956
Phone: 877-690-6400
website: www.walnutcreekranch.com
email: walnutcreekranch@gmail.com

PANHANDLE

PANHANDLE REGION
Comanche Trail Lake

#32

NEAR BIG SPRING, TEXAS

KEY BIRDS
Several species of wren and sparrow

BEST SEASON
Spring and summer

AREA DESCRIPTION
Mostly open low grass areas, low brush with mesquite and other low trees surrounding lakeshore habitat.

Follow the signs to Comanche Lake to reach the spring from which Big Spring got its name. A traditional watering hole for the Comanches, the spring has various wren and sparrow activity in the morning. The area also provides good habitat for dragonflies in summer. This multi-use park provides full visitor facilities, as well as a nature trail and a hike-and-bike trail, so take your time and walk and explore this very "birdy" area.

DIRECTIONS
From the city of Big Spring from the south on US 87, turn left at the sign to Comanche Trail Lake. Site open for day use only.

White-throated Sparrow

PANHANDLE REGION

Fisher Park/Champion Creek Reservoir

#33

PANHANDLE

NEAR COLORADO CITY, TEXAS

KEY BIRDS
Spotted sandpiper and other shorebirds, sandhill crane

BEST SEASON
All seasons

AREA DESCRIPTION
Open areas with lakeside and shoreline habitat. Some camping is available.

On the way to the reservoir, check the roadsides for large flocks of sandhill crane in winter. White pelicans are present during migration and some winters. Watch for spotted sandpiper and other shorebirds. Horned grebe, scarce inland, has occurred among the more common eared grebes. Trilling rock wrens may be seen flitting about the rocks around the lakeshore.

DIRECTIONS
Return to FM 2836 South for 0.7 mile. Turn north onto TX 163 for 6.8 miles. Turn right on Business 20/208 and go 1.5 miles to TX 208. Turn right on TX 208 South for 7.8 miles, and right again onto County Road 123, following signs to the lake.

CONTACT INFORMATION
Site open daily, with only primitive camping available and some fees are charged. For information, call 325/728-5331 for present pricing.

Sandhill Crane

PANHANDLE

PANHANDLE REGION
Lake J. B. Thomas

#34

ON THE COLORADO RIVER, 12 MILES SOUTHWEST OF SNYDER

KEY BIRDS
White pelican

BEST SEASON
All seasons

AREA DESCRIPTION
The lake takes in 7,282 acres

The South Side Park has excellent views of this large reservoir on the Colorado River, and provides good lakeshore habitat. Look for a variety of waterfowl in winter, with shorebirds during migrations.

Return to FM 1298 South and go west on County Road 3236 for 2.4 miles to White Island Park. White pelicans have been seen here in winter. This part of the lake also has good lakeshore habitat, with nice scenery from the rocks that overlook the lake.

DIRECTIONS
From Colorado City, take TX 208 North to Dunn and FM 1606, 13.7 miles. Turn left on FM 1606 and continue for 7.1 miles to Ira. Go straight ahead on FM 1606 West for 4.9 miles to the junction of FM 2085 West. At 2.4 miles, go left onto FM 1298 South for 2.2 miles to the lake entrance on the right.

CONTACT INFORMATION
Site open daily. Developed campsites are available. Fee charged. Call 915-574-6853.

White Pelican

PANHANDLE REGION
White River Lake

#35

LOOP 289 IN LUBBOCK

KEY BIRDS
Horned grebe (in winter), hooded merganser

BEST SEASON
All seasons

AREA DESCRIPTION
Lakeside habitats with scattered trees and some low brush moving into the open areas

During winter, the lake attracts gulls, grebes, and waterfowl such as hooded merganser along with a variety of other diving and puddle ducks. The trees along the edge of the lake provide good cover for migrating songbirds in spring and fall. Winter provides a good chance to scout for uncommon birds on the lake, such as the horned grebe, which has become a regular visitor in the region.

DIRECTIONS
From Post, take FM 651 north 23.7 miles to FM 2794. Take FM 2794 east/right 7.1 miles to the entrance of the lake on the left. Go north on FM 651 for 13.5 miles to Crosbyton. Go west/left on US 82 for 35 miles to Loop 289 in Lubbock.

CONTACT INFORMATION
The site is open for day use only and fees are charged, call for more information. White River Municipal Water District 2, Box 141, Spur, TX 79370 / 806- 263-4240.

White Pelican

Common Ground Dove

PANHANDLE REGION

Texas Adventure Trails — Ringling Lake

#36

LOCATED 0.6 MILE TO THE NORTH OF RINGLING LAKE ON CR 536

KEY BIRDS
Migrating Mississippi kite, Inca dove

BEST SEASON
All seasons

AREA DESCRIPTION
Post oak country, some areas are very thick with thorns and brush

The trails meander through post oak woodlands. Vegetation is dense in some areas. Look for blue-gray gnatcatcher, ladder-backed and golden-fronted woodpeckers, Inca and mourning doves, and great horned owl.

In brushy grasslands, look for northern bobwhite and greater roadrunner. Red-tailed and red-shouldered hawks are common, and migrating Mississippi kite can be seen in season in large flocks overhead.

Along the lake, look for summer tanager, white-eyed vireo, painted and indigo buntings. Dragonflies are abundant, so look for black saddlebags, eastern pondhawk, widow skimmer, roseate skimmer, and russet-tipped clubtail. Butterflies flit throughout the park, including little yellow, common buckeye, pearl crescent, and pipevine swallowtail. The ponds are good places to find southern leopard frog, Blanchard's cricket frog, and gray tree frog. Waterfowl and shorebirds can be seen in winter.

DIRECTIONS
From I-20 in Cisco, go east 11.6 miles to Exit 343/TX 112. Take a left onto TX 112 North, go 1.7 miles to the intersection of TX 6 and TX 112. Turn right on TX 112 North for 0.6 mile to Ringling Lake/ CR 536. Go left at Ringling Lake/CR 536 and follow for 1.1 miles to entrance.

CONTACT INFORMATION
The site open for day use only. Call 254-629-8321.

Blue-winged Teal

PANHANDLE REGION

Playa Lakes WMA, Taylor Lakes Unit

#37

LOCATED 7 MILES EAST OF CLARENDON ON US 287

KEY BIRDS
Waterfowl, wild turkey, roadrunner, painted bunting, eastern bluebird, and northern bobwhite

BEST SEASON
Fall and spring migrations

AREA DESCRIPTION
Playa lakes and open grassland with small trees

The Taylor Lakes Unit is located in the Rolling Plains of the Panhandle in north Texas, Donley County, near Clarendon. Clarendon was one of the first settlements in the area. The WMA was part of a family farm and purchased by Texas Parks and Wildlife in 1993 to preserve and provide the playa lakes wintering habitat for migratory waterfowl and shorebirds.

The existing low-level lakes provide good conditions for plant growth.

Habitat conditions at this WMA provide a place for waterfowl as well as upland game. Throughout the year the area is an excellent location for observing North American birds in a rich native environment.

Wintering Canada and snow geese, as well as puddle ducks, congregate here in large numbers. Over 200 species of birds have been recorded here. Some of these are wild turkey, roadrunner, painted bunting, eastern bluebird, and northern bobwhite.

Habitats also include tallgrass prairie and riparian woodlands, offering opportunities to observe grassland and woodland species. Sunset spectacles of these lakes and marshes as they fill up with birds provide wonderful photo opportunities.

There are three viewing blinds offering an outstanding opportunity to observe and photograph migratory waterfowl and shorebirds. These blinds are available on a first-come first-served basis – early arrivals are recommended. One of the blinds is wheelchair accessible. There are no drinking water or restroom facilities.

DIRECTIONS
From US 287, go east through Clarendon for 7.0 mile. The WMA is on the right. Leila Lake is 0.3 mile past the WMA.

CONTACT INFORMATION
Michael Janis, 3036 FM 3256, Paducah, TX 79248 / Phone: 806-492-3405. This unit is open year round, except closed for special permit hunts. Please call the WMA office to check on hunt dates. Birders will need a $12.00 dollar Limited Use Permit available where Texas hunting and fishing licenses are sold.

Greater Yellowlegs

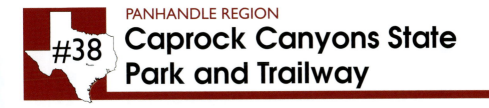

PANHANDLE REGION
Caprock Canyons State Park and Trailway

ON FM 1065 NEAR QUITAQUE

KEY BIRDS
Greater and lesser yellowlegs, willet, spotted, least, Baird's, and pectoral sandpipers

BEST SEASON
Spring and fall migrations

AREA DESCRIPTION
Sparse badlands, bottomlands

The red rocks of Caprock Canyons are stunning, especially at dawn and sunset. Vegetation communities vary from the sparse badlands, with their juniper, mesquite, and cacti, to the abounding bottomlands with tall grasses, cottonwoods, plum thickets, and hackberries.

Over 175 species of birds have been seen at this location with a variety of shorebirds during spring migration, including avocet, greater and lesser yellowlegs, willet, spotted, least, Baird's, and pectoral sandpipers, as well as a variety of warblers.

Caprock Canyons State Park is also home to the largest herd of bison in the Texas state park system.

As a suggestion, those wishing to experience solitude, hike, bike, or take a guided tour along the Caprock Canyons Trailway, there is a 64-mile route crossing three counties in what is one of the finest nature routes in the state.

In addition to area birds, look for the occasional bald eagle and other wildlife that may appear along this route, providing wonderful viewing and photographic opportunities. Park headquarters will have more trail information and a checklist of the park's many species.

DIRECTIONS
From the intersection of TX 86 and FM 1065 in Quitaque (pronounced "Kit-a-quay"), go north on FM 1065; the park is on the left after 3.0 miles.

CONTACT INFORMATION
The site is open daily and the entry cost for one day is $4.00. Call Park Headquarters at 806-455-1492.

PANHANDLE

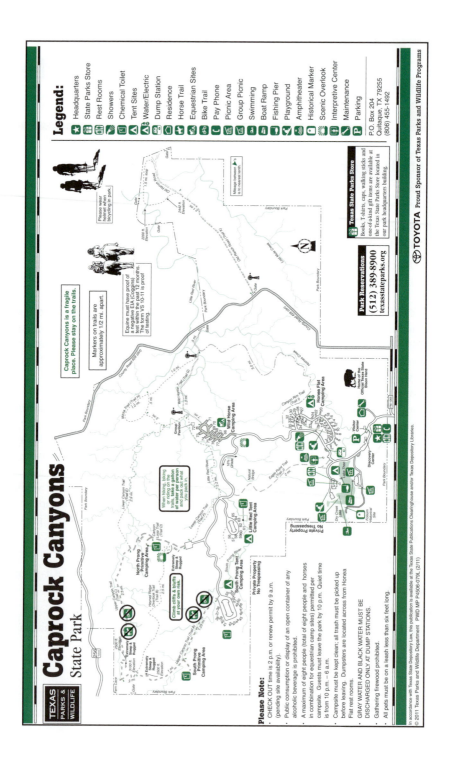

TEXAS PARKS & WILDLIFE

Caprock Canyons
State Park

Legend:

- Headquarters
- State Parks Store
- Rest Rooms
- Showers
- Chemical Toilet
- Tent Sites
- Water/Electric
- Dump Station
- Residence
- Horse Trail
- Equestrian Sites
- Bike Trail
- Pay Phone
- Picnic Area
- Group Picnic
- Swimming
- Boat Ramp
- Fishing Pier
- Playground
- Amphitheater
- Historical Marker
- Scenic Overlook
- Interpretive Center
- Maintenance
- Parking

Caprock Canyons is a fragile place. Please stay on the trails.

Markers on trails are approximately 1/2 mi. apart.

Equine must have proof of a negative EIA (Coggins) test within the past 12 months. The form VS 10-11 is proof of testing.

When hiking, biking or riding on the trails, take a gallon of water per person and pack out what you pack in.

Please wear helmet when bicycling in park.

Mileage between is to nearest tenth.

Texas State Parks Store

Books, T-shirts, caps, walking sticks and one-of-a-kind gift items are available at the Texas State Parks Store located in our park headquarters building.

Park Reservations
(512) 389-8900
texasstateparks.org

P.O. Box 204
Quitaque, TX 79255
(806) 455-1492

Please Note:

- CHECK OUT time is 2 p.m. or renew permit by 9 a.m. (pending site availability).
- Public consumption or display of an open container of any alcoholic beverage is prohibited.
- A maximum of eight people (total of eight people and horses in combination for equestrian camp sites) permitted per campsite. Guests must leave the park by 10 p.m. Quiet time is from 10 p.m. – 6 a.m.
- Campsite must be kept clean; all trash must be picked up before leaving. Dumpsters are located across from Honea Flat rest rooms.
- GRAY WATER AND BLACK WATER MUST BE DISCHARGED ONLY AT DUMP STATIONS.
- Gathering firewood prohibited.
- All pets must be on a leash less than six feet long.

In accordance with Texas State Depository Law, this publication is available at the Texas State Publications Clearinghouse and/or Texas Depository Libraries.
© 2011 Texas Parks and Wildlife Department   PWD MP P4506-079L (2/11)

TOYOTA Proud Sponsor of Texas Parks and Wildlife Programs

PANHANDLE REGION
#39 Texas Highway 256 Scenic Drive

PANHANDLE

HIGHWAY 256 – DRIVE SLOW FOR THE BEST VIEWING

KEY BIRDS
Mountain bluebird, pinyon jay

BEST SEASON
Winter

AREA DESCRIPTION
Highway viewing

The highway route follows the northern border of Caprock Canyons State Park and, when connected to TX 70 South and TX 86 East, makes a loop that terminates at the park entrance. The red rock scenery provides some of the best scenic views in the Southwest.

Fight the desire to drive faster and get back to the park. One birder I spoke with told me he and his wife will sometimes make the loop three of four times before leaving the highway or entering the park.

Watch the juniper that is found throughout the hillsides for flocks of mountain bluebirds, and the much rarer – but similarly colored and larger – pinyon jay.

DIRECTIONS
From Quitaque, follow TX 86 east for about 10 miles to Turkey. Follow TX 70 north 13.2 miles to TX 256. Go west on TX 256. The scenic route continues until the intersection with TX 86.

Mountain Bluebird

PANHANDLE

PANHANDLE REGION
#40 Buffalo Lake National Wildlife Refuge

APPROXIMATELY 30 MILES SOUTHWEST OF AMARILLO

KEY BIRDS
Burrowing owls are year-round residents while Cooper's hawk, goshawk, and Mississippi kite are the occasional visitors here

BEST SEASON
All seasons

AREA DESCRIPTION
Shortgrass prairies spill into marshes, woodlands, riparian habitat, croplands, and water-carved canyon walls

The large lake and surrounding prairie provide excellent winter habitat for bald eagle and prairie falcon, as well as wintering geese and ducks. The common raven has been seen on the farmland adjacent to the refuge. The refuge has a very good driving loop with interpretive signage that explains the ecology of the area. Golden eagle, osprey, Swainson's hawk, and northern harrier are common in the spring.

We know that the buffalo/bison in their mind-boggling numbers are gone forever from the plains. At one time, history says there was a lake here reflecting the clouds in the big Texas sky – that lake is now dry. A new lake has replaced it — formed behind Umbarger Dam — attracting migrating waterfowl by the thousands.

There was a time, now passed, when bison grazed these shortgrass prairies that today are empty of bison at the Buffalo Lake National Wildlife Refuge. But here today the shortgrass prairie remains as one of the best in the high plains grassland ecosystem.

In fact, this prairie is so important that 175 acres of it carries the designation of National Natural Landmark. Over 4,000 acres of grasslands are the best you'll see anywhere in the area.

The prairie dog town is located on FM 168, 1.7 miles south of FM 1714. The site includes an interpretive trail onto the prairie. In spring/summer this area offers most of the same birds listed for the prairie habitat; look for burrowing owls and horned larks. Watch for prairie dogs sitting near their holes watching for danger. This is the same area where the burrowing owls make their homes in abandoned prairie dog holes.

There is a larger prairie dog colony near the town of Canyon along Pandeseta Road. The various roads between the refuge and US 87 are mostly cropland and pasture. Some birds are seen in this area, including longspurs, such as McCown's, Lapland, and chestnut-collared longspurs.

The refuge has a total of 7,664 acres of habitat for migratory as well as year-round birds and wildlife.

DIRECTIONS
From Tulia go north on I-27 for 13.4 miles to US 87/Exit 88B in Happy. Take US 87 north 13.4 miles to FM 1714. Turn left/west and proceed 10.5 miles to FM 168. Turn right/north and continue 1.5 miles to the refuge entrance.

CONTACT INFORMATION
Site open for day use only and there is a fee of $2.00 per day per car.
Mailing address: PO Box 179, Umbarger, TX 79091 / 806-499-3382
Website: http://southwest.fws.gov/refuges/texas/buffalo.html

Mountain Bluebird

PANHANDLE

#41 Lake Marvin, Black Kettle National Grasslands

EAST OF CANADIAN, TEXAS

KEY BIRDS
Mountain bluebird, brown creeper, ruddy duck, and both hooded and common mergansers

BEST SEASON
All seasons

AREA DESCRIPTION
Panhandle plains and grassland with lakeshore birding areas

This is one of the best birding locations in the Panhandle, and the best part of this area is there is no entry fee to enter and use the area. Most of the roads within the area are dirt, so caution must be taken during bad weather. I had conflicting reports about cell phone use, so let someone know where you are planning to be birding.

In winter, check the lake for numerous ducks including ring-necked, common goldeneye, bufflehead, ruddy, and both hooded and common mergansers. A group of tundra swan was seen here in 2002. Watch for eared grebe and the less common horned grebe. Bald eagles will be spotted in small numbers but no nesting has been discovered. Check the woods along the edge of the lake for other raptors like the red-tailed hawk;

Common Merganser

also mountain bluebird and brown creeper are common during migrations.

In spring and summer, woodpeckers, yellow-billed cuckoo, great crested flycatcher, brown thrasher, northern mockingbird, Carolina chickadee, tufted titmouse, warbling vireo, northern cardinal, blue grosbeak, indigo bunting, yellow warbler, as well as house, Bewick's, and Carolina wrens occur here. Watch the reed beds at the end of the boardwalk for marsh wren and common yellowthroat.

Bird slowly along the unpaved roads leading into Lake Marvin. Sand sagebrush habitat dotted with thickets of wild plum, cottonwoods, and roadside ponds provide habitat for great blue heron, ducks, a few shorebirds in season, warbling vireo, Mississippi kite, northern flicker, red-headed woodpecker, and hooded merganser. Cassin's lark and field sparrows are very common.

Birders will be extremely fortunate to see the lesser prairie chicken due to the extremely secretive nature of the bird, and virtually impossible to see off the booming grounds during spring. Remember these birds are endangered and should not be crowded or bothered. Grasshopper sparrow is quite common, as are eastern and western kingbirds, western meadowlark, roadrunner, and common nighthawk.

DIRECTIONS

From US 60/83, take FM 2266 east for 12 miles and bear to the right where the road forks once you've entered Black Kettle. The road leads directly to Lake Marvin.

CONTACT INFORMATION

This site is for day use only and no fees are charged. Black Kettle Ranger District, Route 1, Box 55-B, Cheyenne, Oklahoma 73628 / 580-497-2143.

PANHANDLE

PANHANDLE REGION
Greenbelt Lake

#42

NORTH OF CLARENDON, TEXAS ON TX 70

KEY BIRDS
Cassin's sparrow, western kingbird, black tern

BEST SEASON
All seasons

AREA DESCRIPTION
Lakeshore habitat, low brush, mesquite

Birders first arriving at the lake should watch the trees near the boat ramp area for birds resting in the trees, as well as some nesters in the spring. At times, shore birds are numerous along the banks during times not conducive to boating. From the parking area near the boat ramp, first watch the lake for water birds. This large reservoir provides an opportunity to see loons, grebes, ducks, geese, and other wintering waterfowl. Cottonwood trees at several boat ramps hold nesting western kingbird, scissor-tailed flycatcher, warbling vireo, common grackle, Bullock's oriole, and other songbirds.

During summer, listen for dickcissel and western meadowlark. At other times, check any flooded fields for shorebirds and puddle ducks. When the road turns to mesquite and low brush, watch for additional species such as Bewick's and house wrens, Cassin's sparrow, and western kingbird. As you reach the southern side of the lake's western arm, continue west on the dirt roads that access additional shallow coves. Yellow-billed cuckoo, orchard and Bullock's orioles, blue-gray gnatcatcher, eastern and western kingbirds, and red-headed woodpeckers occur here. Watch for an area where small snags protrude from the water. Terns and woodpeckers roost here and black terns have been seen flying over these shallows.

DIRECTIONS
From I-40, turn south on TX 70 for 12.1 miles and turn right at the sign directing you to the public boat ramp. Take TX 70 for 4.7 miles to US 287 then take FM 3257 for about 3.2 miles until it ends at the lake.

CONTACT INFORMATION
The site is open all season for day use only. Those persons 15 years old and over pay a recreation fee of $5.00 per day. Phone 806-874-3650

PANHANDLE REGION
#43 Fort Griffin State Park and Historic Site

ABOUT 15 MILES NORTH OF ALBANY

KEY BIRDS
Grasshopper and Cassin's sparrows, cactus wren, curve-billed thrasher, and eastern phoebe

BEST SEASON
Spring, summer, and fall

AREA DESCRIPTION
Historic ruins and grasslands to the west, and to the east is the riparian habitat next to the Clear Fork of the Brazos River

Fort Griffin once held the command of the southern plains and saw the end of both the great herds of bison and those who hunted them. The fort was home base to a rugged group of men. Fort Griffin was constructed in 1867 by the army and deactivated in 1881.

The 506-acre park sits on an escarpment along the Clear Fork of the Brazos River. The 1.5-mile Wohaw Nature Trail follows along the Clear Fork of the Brazos and provides scenic and peaceful views of the park's creek bottom habitat. Both the black swallowtail and orange sulphur butterflies, as well as the black-chinned hummingbird are regular visitors to this site. Fort Griffin also has a herd of longhorn cattle and flocks of cattle egrets following the herd.

If you arrive before the headquarters opens at 8:00am, bird the riparian area first. More of the eastern birds of the area can be found there such as red-bellied woodpecker, eastern bluebird, lazuli bunting, painted bunting, indigo bunting, red-shouldered hawk, and barred owl.

In spring blue grosbeaks, warblers, and vireos can be found in the large trees around the RV and tent campsites. Be sure and bird the Mill Creek Trail as it winds through mature trees leading down to the river.

Don't forget to bring your sunscreen, bug spray, and drinking water in the warmer months.

To the west of Hwy 283 are the ruins of the fort. This is grassland habitat and, in spring, it attracts many seed eaters who feed off the grass sprigs and seeds.

DIRECTIONS
From Truscott, travel south on TX 6 through Benjamin, Rule, and Stamford to Albany – 97.0 miles. At US 283 in Albany, go north 14.9 miles to the park entrance on the right.

PANHANDLE

Fort Griffin
State Park and Historic Site

TEXAS PARKS & WILDLIFE

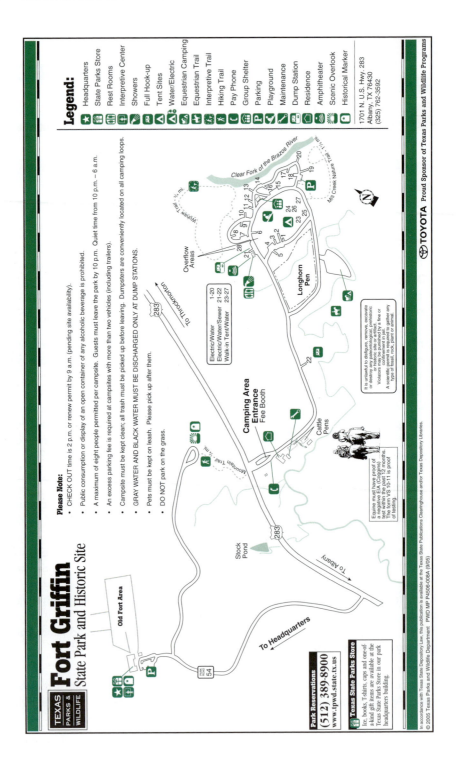

Park Reservations
(512) 389-8900
www.tpwd.state.tx.us

Texas State Parks Store
Ice, books, T-shirts, caps and one-of-a-kind gift items are available at the Texas State Parks Store in our park headquarters building.

Old Fort Area

To Headquarters

To Albany

Stock Pond

FARM ROAD 54

Please Note:
- CHECK OUT time is 2 p.m. or renew permit by 9 a.m. (pending site availability).
- Public consumption or display of an open container of any alcoholic beverage is prohibited.
- A maximum of eight people permitted per campsite. Guests must leave the park by 10 p.m. Quiet time from 10 p.m. – 6 a.m.
- An excess parking fee is required at campsites with more than two vehicles (including trailers).
- Campsite must be kept clean; all trash must be picked up before leaving. Dumpsters are conveniently located on all camping loops.
- GRAY WATER AND BLACK WATER MUST BE DISCHARGED ONLY AT DUMP STATIONS.
- Pets must be kept on leash. Please pick up after them.
- DO NOT park on the grass.

To Throckmorton

283

Camping Area
Entrance
Fee Booth

Mountain Trail ¼ mi.

Cattle Pens

Electric/Water   1-20
Electric/Water/Sewer 21-22
Walk-in Tent/Water   23-27

Overflow Areas

Wohaw Trail ¼ mi.

Clear Fork of the Brazos River

Mill Creek Nature Trail ¼ mi.

Longhorn Pen

Equine must have proof of a negative EIA (Coggins) test within the past 12 months. The form VS 10-11 is proof of testing.

It is unlawful to disfigure, remove, excavate or destroy any paleontological, prehistoric or historic site or artifact. Violators may be punished by a fine or confinement in jail. A scientific permit is required to gather any type of fossil, rock, plant or animal.

Legend:
Headquarters	Equestrian Camping
State Parks Store	Equestrian Trail
Rest Rooms	Interpretive Trail
Interpretive Center	Hiking Trail
Showers	Pay Phone
Full Hook-up	Group Shelter
Tent Sites	Parking
Water/Electric	Playground
	Maintenance
	Dump Station
	Residence
	Amphitheater
	Scenic Overlook
	Historical Marker

1701 N. U.S. Hwy. 283
Albany, TX 76430
(325) 762-3592

In accordance with Texas State Depository Law, this publication is available at the Texas State Publications Clearinghouse and/or Texas Depository Libraries.
© 2005 Texas Parks and Wildlife Department   PWD MP P4506-008A (9/05)

Contact Information

The site is open daily 8am to 5pm and the fees are as follows: Adults - $4.00 / Ages 6-18 and students with ID - $3.00 / 5 and under - free / School Groups - $1.00 per student with the required reservations.

Guided Tours are available and the fees are as follows: Adults - $7.00 / Ages 6-18 and students with ID - $6.00.

Phone: 915-762-3592

Vermilion Flycatcher

PANHANDLE REGION
Stasney's Cook Ranch

#44

LOCATED 5.5 MILES FROM ALBANY, TEXAS

KEY BIRDS
Ash-throated flycatcher, vermilion flycatcher, scrub jay

BEST SEASON
All seasons

AREA DESCRIPTION
Rolling ranchland, canyons, and a lake area with small draws

This is a 25,000-acre private ranch which abounds with spectacular habitat that includes canyons, rock cliffs, valleys, creeks, and limestone deposits full of fossils.

In addition to a good assortment of spring migrants, wintering sparrows, and waterfowl, there is a dazzling array of summer beauties such as painted bunting. The ranch's photo blinds will give the patient observer intimate views of many local and visiting birds, wild turkeys, and other wildlife.

An interesting mix of east and west avifauna occurs here, with both species of meadowlarks and eastern phoebes nesting around the lodge.

In wet years, grasshopper sparrows can be seen and heard, perched atop the taller weed stems. Throughout the year, several species of flycatcher can be found here, including ash-throated flycatcher and vermilion flycatcher; the scrub jay has been spotted here, as have several common poorwill.

Wildflowers are everywhere in wet years, producing superb opportunities for photography and botanical study. The ranch offers great history, beautiful scenery, lots of wildlife, and many activities for nature enthusiasts. Lodging is available in the main lodge and in cabins modeled after the officers' quarters at surrounding forts on the Texas Forts Trail.

CONTACT INFORMATION
Call or write for directions and the required reservations. Cabin costs range from $100.00 a night to $175.00. The ranch's photo blinds are for guests only and are on a first-come first-served basis.

P.O. Box 3190, Albany, TX 76430
325-762-3311 or 888-762-2999
Website: http://www.stasneyscookranch.com/

PANHANDLE REGION
North Roadside Park

SOUTH OF WOODSON, TEXAS

KEY BIRDS
Woodpeckers, warblers, and flycatchers, northern flicker, ruby-crowned and golden kinglets

BEST SEASON
Spring and winter

AREA DESCRIPTION
A roadside picnic area near a highway bridge, large hardwood trees

The park site is heavily wooded with pecan trees and dense shrubbery along the river's edge. Beneath the bridge, birders can see nesting northern rough-winged, barn, and cliff swallows. Close-distance viewing makes this a great opportunity to study these swallows in their various plumages.

Watch for woodpeckers, warblers, and flycatchers in the trees and – for winter birders – look for yellow-bellied sapsucker, northern flicker, ruby-crowned and golden kinglets, red-breasted nuthatch, and brown creeper.

Summer tanager, yellow-billed cuckoo, and painted bunting can be heard and seen here. Green heron and great egret can also be found along the river shore. Watch the shoreline for some of the smaller wading birds.

DIRECTIONS
From the intersection of US 283 and FM 209, take FM 209 to Woodson, 7.6 miles. Turn right on US 183 south 6.8 miles to Clear Fork of the Brazos River. The park is under the bridge, at the southwest corner of the river-road junction.

PANHANDLE

#46 Hubbard Creek Lake-North Campground

ON SANDY CREEK, HUBBARD CREEK, AND BRUSHY CREEK IN STEPHENS COUNTY – 51 MILES NORTHEAST OF ABILENE AND ABOUT FIVE MILES WEST OF BRECKENRIDGE

KEY BIRDS
Woodpeckers, nuthatches, creepers, and waterfowl

BEST SEASON
Winter

AREA DESCRIPTION
Lakeshore areas and low brush and mesquite, with wooded areas away from the lake

This is a large park with good access to the lake and habitats that support various mammals and birds. Greater roadrunner and wild turkey roam the area. In winter, look for chipping, field, lark, Savannah, song, and vesper sparrows. The mesquite and oaks host woodpeckers, nuthatches, and creepers.

Mammals you might expect to see are white-tailed deer, gray fox, bobcat, and the nine-banded armadillo. Watch the ground during the warmer months for the western diamondback rattlesnake. Stay well clear of the latter.

Scope the lake for rafting canvasback, redhead, northern pintail, lesser scaup, gadwall, American wigeon, green-winged and blue-winged teal, bufflehead, ring-necked duck, ruddy duck, hooded merganser, common goldeneye, and northern shoveler.

Watch the rocky shorelines and rip-rap for shorebirds like the great blue heron, snowy egret, and the great egret.

Northern Shoveler

DIRECTIONS
Go south on US 183 6.5 miles to CR 274, turn-off for Hubbard Lake Dam, signposted for Public Boat Ramp. Go right on this road for about 1 mile, turn left and continue for 0.7 mile to lake entrance.

CONTACT INFORMATION
West Central Texas Municipal Water District, 410 Hickory Street, Abilene, Texas 79601 / 325-673-8254 or 254-559-3677

PANHANDLE REGION
#47 Baylor Lake/Childress Lake

SOUTH OF WELLINGTON

KEY BIRDS
Common loons, flycatchers, tanagers, and wading birds

BEST SEASON
Winter, and during spring and fall migrations

AREA DESCRIPTION
Low panhandle brush and lakeshore

This was found to be one of the better "on-your-own" sites if you are in the area or just passing through. Several birders advised me I would be wasting my time visiting here due to the fact that these lakes are very susceptible to drought and can be very low. During times of drought the boat ramps are left high and dry. However, I did spot over 25 species of birds on my short visit in December.

Baylor Lake is in Childress County, Texas and is used for recreation purposes. Construction of Baylor Lake Dam was completed in 1950. At normal levels, it has a surface area of 1.1 square miles and is the property of city of Childress.

In spring, pay special attention to the wetlands along the edge of the entry road going to the lake for flycatchers, tanagers, and also several varieties of sparrow during the summers. These wet areas will also provide habitat for several shore and wading birds.

This site provides opportunity to view waterfowl during the winter and shorebirds during migrations. Common loons have been seen on both lakes during spring.

Shore Birds

DIRECTIONS
From the town of Wellington, go south on US 83 for 30 miles to US 287 in Childress. Go 4.7 miles north/right and head west/left on Loop 328 for 1.7 miles; then take FM 2466 west/left for 2.2 miles. Turn left at the stop sign and follow the signs to the lake. To reach Childress Lake, continue straight out of Baylor Lake onto the dirt road, which runs into Childress Lake.

CONTACT INFORMATION
This site is open for day use only. For additional information, call 940-937-2102

PANHANDLE

Mackenzie Park

#48

601 MUNICIPAL DRIVE
LUBBOCK, TEXAS

KEY BIRDS
Fox sparrow, dark-eyed junco, and waterfowl of many species

BEST SEASON
All seasons

AREA DESCRIPTION
Flat farmlands with grasslands, pasture, and some wooded areas

This is a large urban park with open, wooded savannah and thickets on the margin of the woods. Winter flocks include fox sparrow, dark-eyed junco and titmice. A variety of migrant ducks may be mixed in with the resident waterfowl.

There is also a resident population of black-tailed prairie dogs and their town that attracts several species of hawk as well as the small yellow-eyed burrowing owls nesting and living in abandoned prairie dog holes.

The stands of old deciduous trees and the stream that flows through them provide extensive habitat for migrating warblers and resident songbirds, such as several species of wren and the northern mockingbird.

DIRECTIONS
Driving on US 62/82 entering Lubbock from the east, exit north on Loop 289 and follow it for 1.3 miles. Exit on Municipal Drive and go left under the overpass and continue for 1.8 miles to the park on the left.

CONTACT INFORMATION
Site open for day use only. For more information, call 806-775-2687.

PANHANDLE REGION
#49 Yellow House Canyon — Lakes

JUST PAST MACKENZIE PARK, ACROSS US 62

KEY BIRDS
Migratory birds, waterfowl, burrowing owls

BEST SEASON
All seasons

AREA DESCRIPTION
Lakeside habitat and some trees

Lubbock is lucky to have over seventy parks within its city limits, with a large variety of wildlife including birds, reptiles, mammals, and fish.

Lubbock also falls within the Central Flyway, and throughout the year a large number of migratory birds fly through or winter in the region. This makes Lubbock's parks and lakes great places to view wildlife and to enjoy a birding experience with family and friends.

In the 1930s, a prairie dog town was established in Mackenzie Park, and has been enjoyed by residents and visitors alike throughout its history. This was where I first photographed a burrowing owl and began my lifelong interest in birds and photographing them. The prairie dog town recently underwent remodeling and is has now re-opened to the public.

This site consists of a long lake that runs along the roadside, and is excellent for photographing waterfowl and other birds that live in the reed beds. Mesquite, oak, elm, and grassland surround the lake, making it a good site to look for sparrows in winter. Below the dam, the creek provides good habitat for viewing migrating warblers and shorebirds.

DIRECTIONS
Follow Canyon Lake Drive through Mackenzie Park, then cross US 62 and see the lake on your right.

CONTACT INFORMATION
This site is open for day use only and no fees are charged. The lakes are owned by the city of Lubbock.

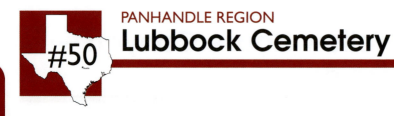

PANHANDLE REGION
Lubbock Cemetery

#50

2011 EAST 31ST STREET
LUBBOCK, TEXAS 79404

KEY BIRDS
Several species of owl in early mornings and evenings

BEST SEASON
All seasons, with spring and fall migrations sometimes the best

AREA DESCRIPTION
Cemetery landscape with large trees and open grassy areas

No, my friends this is not an Edgar Allen Poe tale of horror and slow demise, with maybe the exception of a wandering crow flying in every now and then to distract a visitor.

This is a quality birding location, if respect and care is taken and the nature of the location is taken into consideration. There are many open areas as well as large trees within the grounds that can and do provide habitat for several species of local songbirds as well as visitors.

The cemetery's good stands of trees attract a variety of species, particularly during fall and spring migrations. Owls are regularly seen in the park, and migrating warblers and vireos are attracted to the locust trees.

DIRECTIONS
Exit onto Martin Luther King, Jr. Street in Lubbock, between Lakes 5 and 6 then turn south to 31st Street, for 0.6 mile. Turn east on 31st Street and go two blocks to Teak Avenue. Follow the sign to the cemetery.

CONTACT INFORMATION
No contact information available and the site is only open for day use.

Great Horned Owl

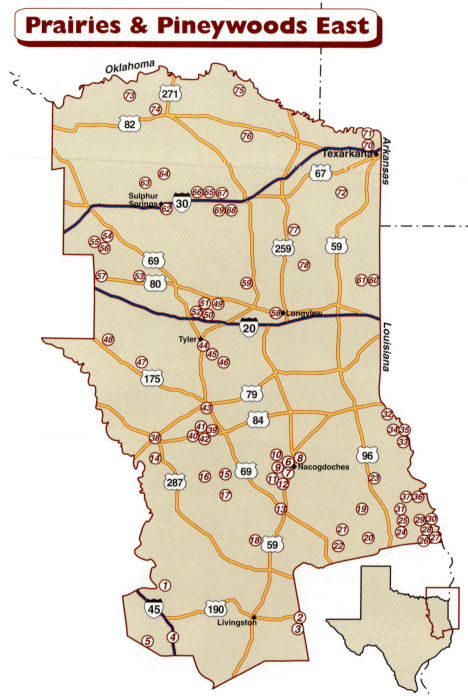

Prairies & Pineywoods East

Oklahoma

Arkansas

Louisiana

Texarkana

Sulphur Springs

Longview

Tyler

Nacogdoches

Livingston

Prairies & Pineywoods East Locations

#1-Trinity River Bridge - Hwy 19
#2- Woodlands Trail
#3- Big Sandy Trail
#4- Huntsville State Park
#5- Stubblefield Recreational Area
#6- Pineywoods Native Plant Center
#7- SFA Mast Arboretum
#8- La Nana Creek Trail & Pecan Park
#9 -Stag Leap Retreat/Country Inn & Bed and Breakfast
#10- Stephen F. Austin Experimental Forest and Interpretive Trail
#11- Alazan Bayou Wildlife Management Area
#12- Saint's Rest Road
#13- Texas Forestry Museum, Urban Wildscape Trail
#14- Ivy's Wildlife Refuge
#15- Neches Bluff Area
#16- Mission Tejas State Park
#17- Big Slough Wilderness and Four-C's National Recreation Trail
#18- Alabama Creek Wildlife Management Area
#19- Bannister Wildlife Management Area
#20- Ralph Mcallister Park
#21- Bird Islands - Lake Sam Rayburn
#22- Upland Island Wilderness and Longleaf Ridge Special Area
#23- Ayish Bayou
#24- Trail Between the Lakes
#25- Moore Plantation Wildlife Management Area
#26- Willow Oak Recreation Area
#27- The Stark Tract
#28- Hillside Inn & RV Park
#29- Lakeview Campground
#30- Indian Mounds Wilderness, Sabine National Forest
#31- Longleaf Roadside Pines Park
#32- North Toledo Bend Wildlife Management Area
#33- Robinson's Lodge on Toledo Bend Reservoir
#34- Haley's Ferry Recreation Area
#35- Ragtown Recreation Area
#36- Red Hills Lake
#37- Carrice Creek Bridge Area
#38- Community Forest
#39- Texas State Railroad State Park - Palestine Train Station
#40- I.D. Fairchild State Forest
#41- Cherokee Rose B&B
#42- Texas State Railroad Park - Rusk Train Station
#43- Nichol's Green Park
#44- Rose Rudman Park
#45- Camp Tyler

#46- Lake Tyler Concession Area #1
#47- Texas Freshwater Fisheries Center
#48- Purtis Creek State Park
#49- Little Sandy National Wildlife Refuge
#50- Tyler State Park
#51- Sabine Bottom Wildlife Management Area
#52- Mineola Preserve on the Sabine River
#53- Grand Saline Salt Marsh
#54- Tawakoni Wildlife Management Area
#55- Sweeney Environmental Center
#56- Lake Tawakoni State Park
#57- Wills Point Bluebird Trails
#58- Grace Creek Nature Area
#59- Lake Gilmer Park & Kelsey Creek Sanctuary
#60- Caddo Lake Wildlife Management Area
#61- Caddo Lake State Park
#62- Coleman Lake Park
#63- Cooper Lake State Park
#64- Cooper Wildlife Management Area
#65- Gibbs Rockin' G Ranch
#66- Dupree Park Nature Preserve
#67- Choctaw Trails / Bluebird Trails
#68- Lake Bob Sandlin State Park
#69- Lake Cypress Springs
#70- Bringle Lake
#71- Sparks Lane
#72- Atlanta State Park
#73- Caddo National Grasslands
#74- Gambill Goose Refuge
#75- Lennox Woods Preserve
#76- Terrapin Hill
#77- Daingerfield State Park
#78- Lake O' The Pines - Cedar Springs Park

BIRDING TRAILS: TEXAS

PRAIRIES AND PINEYWOODS

As we move away from the Panhandle counties and move to what is known as north and northeast Texas we add some outstanding birding and wildlife observation opportunities.

Traveling east and birding in the "Big Thicket" allows birders to watch the pileated woodpecker, a great variety of colorful warblers, and raptors such as the red-shouldered hawk and common nighthawk. Even many experienced birders don't know that the common nighthawk eats more "skeeters" in one night than a purple martin does in a lifetime.

Spotting these little birds during the day can be a challenge. Look on horizontal limbs for what might look like a bump, a knot, or just something that doesn't look quite right.

This is the area where Texas "brags" were born; like I said, this is Texas: the state of many lakes, rivers, and streams. These wet areas along shores and riverbanks are responsible for providing habitat for the many wading and shore birds. Most species are found here; birds such as the great blue heron, egrets, and several species of kingfisher.

However, this is also where you will learn the only natural lake – Caddo Lake – is the only one in the entire land mass of the state of Texas. All other impoundments are man made. Texas in its infancy somehow knew the importance of water to the growing country, and later to the Lone Star State.

During the winter months, Texas attracts many pairs of nesting bald eagles. There are scattered sightings of golden eagles, but these are restricted mostly to the western counties of Texas. As of late, several pairs of the national birds have taken up residence in the state and are spotted here at all times of the year. Birders and eagle watchers on Lake Buchanan have documented a nesting pair of bald eagles.

This is also the part of Texas where Texas "the country" was born; where it became a nation of its own; then a state of the United States; following that a part of both the Confederate States of America and finely, where we are today as a state within the United States of America.

Private ranches in the open grasslands and within hardwood forests are the places to see prairie birds such as grasshopper sparrow, dickcissel, and eastern meadowlark. Also look for woodland species such as indigo bunting and summer tanager and many more of this type of bird. Patient viewers will be rewarded to see bald eagles making seemingly lazy circles in the air or striking a regal pose on a tree close to the water.

While driving through some of the few remaining expanses of native blackland prairie habitat in northeast Texas, look for fields of native wildflowers and tall grasses. The open prairie is the natural home to scissor-tailed flycatcher, Cooper's hawk, and many more.

Don't count out the cities, as they are excellent viewing locations. There is much nature and bird life to be seen. McKinney is one of the smaller cities within the vast Dallas and Fort Worth mega-area. The small area offers birders many places to observe birds in their parks, zoos, and nature centers. It also offers birders much to see in the city as well as the outlying countryside. The Heard Natural Science Museum and Wildlife Sanctuary is one such place. The Heard offers birders many ways to watch birds, including nature trails and photo blinds where reservations are not required. Located near the center of the state, it is a great side trip and way to spend a day. There will be more information about the Heard later in this book.

Urban wildlife viewing is another great way to spend an afternoon or a weekend with family and friends. In other words, don't leave your binoculars and spotting scopes at home while taking a drive through the cities.

PRAIRIES AND PINEYWOODS - EAST

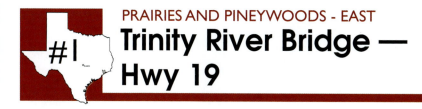

PRAIRIES AND PINEYWOODS - EAST
Trinity River Bridge — Hwy 19

#1

TRINITY, TEXAS

KEY BIRDS
Indigo bunting, great egret, and great blue heron

BEST SEASON
Winter and spring

AREA DESCRIPTION
River bottom landscape with large trees

A paved parking area and boat ramp at the south end of the bridge provides access to the Trinity River. Visitors can canoe or kayak to experience the serene environment of the river. An abundance of backwater and wetland areas, typically inaccessible on foot, allow visitors to view wading birds and other woodland and wetland wildlife.

If a day on the water is not for you, the riverbanks of the Trinity River are teeming with activity. Keep your eyes open for alligators warming on the bank or in search of a snack in the water.

During the spring and early summer, watch for piles of dead vegetation and stay well clear. This could be a nesting site for a momma gator. During their nesting times, females are very protective of their nests and will charge and sometimes attack those near the nest.

Spring and summer birders should watch for the cliff swallows around the water catching small insects during a hatch. Their nests can be found on the undersides of the bridges. Watch for the somewhat small and shallow mud nests. During the nesting season, watch for parents returning to the nests to feed their young.

There are two sloughs within walking distance of the parking lot. The first is visible from the pull-off entrance. Look for indigo buntings in the willows and great egrets and great blue herons feeding around the edges of the sloughs.

The second slough is the larger of the two; however you must be a bit more adventurous to reach it. As you walk under the bridge the second slough will become

visible. There are no facilities located at the bridge, but the towns of Riverside and Trinity, to the south and north of the bridge, are home to a variety of restaurants, shops, and other amenities.

DIRECTIONS

From the intersection of FM 230 and Hwy 19 in Trinity, drive south on Hwy 19 for 5.0 miles to the north end of the Trinity River Bridge. There is a paved parking area so please do not park on the bridge. The bridge is several miles long and a paved parking area is provided on the east side of the southern end of the bridge. The bridge can also be reached by going northeast on Hwy 19 for 16.0 miles from Huntsville.

CONTACT INFORMATION

The site is open only for day use. Phone 936-594-3595.

Great Egret

PRAIRIES AND PINEYWOODS - EAST
Woodlands Trail

LOCATED WITHIN THE BIG SANDY CREEK UNIT OF THE BIG THICKET NATIONAL PRESERVE

KEY BIRDS
Pileated and red-headed woodpeckers, blue grosbeak, painted and indigo buntings

BEST SEASON
Birding is good here year round, barring bad weather.

AREA DESCRIPTION
Hardwood forest with some low brush

The Woodlands Trail has trails for all levels of hiker. Photographers should give these trails some thought if you might be using super-lenses and tripods. The trails are in measured distances of 3.3, 4.5, and 5.4 miles. The trails start near an old pine plantation, and then wind through and into mature bottomland hardwoods located within the Big Sandy Creek floodplain.

Mature hardwoods such as water oak, basket oak, water tupelo, and sweetgum trees tower overhead. The ground cover is relatively open; consisting of American hornbeam, various hollies, loblolly pine, southern magnolia, and American beech.

Different bird species abound within the upland and bottomland habitats traversed by the trails. Look and listen for pileated and red-headed woodpeckers in the bottomlands and for blue grosbeak, painted and indigo buntings, and yellow-breasted chat in the open fields, with prairie warblers flying in and out of the pine stands.

DIRECTIONS
From the intersection of US 59 and US 190 in Livingston, go east on US 190 for approximately 12.5 miles. Turn right (south) on FM 1276 and follow 3.3 miles to the trailhead on the left.

CONTACT INFORMATION
Site access restricted. Please call ahead.
Phone 409-246-2337
Website: www.nps.gov/bith/

PRAIRIES AND
PINEYWOODS EAST

Indigo Bunting

PRAIRIES AND PINEYWOODS - EAST
Big Sandy Trail

#3

PRAIRIES AND PINEYWOODS EAST

LIVINGSTON, TEXAS

KEY BIRDS
Pileated woodpecker, red-headed and brown-headed nuthatches, wood thrush, greater roadrunner

BEST SEASON
All seasons, but best can be the spring nesting season

AREA DESCRIPTION
Hardwood and pine forest

The 18-mile round trip trail within the Big Sandy Unit of the Big Thicket National Preserve is open for birding and wildlife photography. The trail crosses upland pine forests with gradual slopes covered with American beech, southern magnolia, and loblolly pine. It then travels into bottomland hardwoods within the floodplains of Simons Branch and Big Sandy Creek.

Tree species include sweetgum, basket oak, hornbeam, and holly. Look for bald cypress trees at the wetland located at the 2.5-mile mark on the trail. Watch the branches overhead and listen for the variety of birds spending time in the higher branches.

The various habitats of the Big Thicket support a diversity of birds such as the greater roadrunner, red-headed and pileated woodpeckers, brown-headed nuthatch, and wood thrush. Look overhead for black vulture, turkey vulture, red-shouldered hawk, red-tailed hawk, and common nighthawk.

During the spring months nesting birds may include black and white, prothonotary, yellow-throated, pine, and Kentucky warblers.

DIRECTIONS
From US 190 Exit off of US 59 in Livingston, go east on US 190 for 12.3 miles and turn south on FM 1276 for 8.5 miles to Sunflower Road. Turn west on Sunflower Road for 2.0 miles to the trailhead on the left.

CONTACT INFORMATION
Site access is restricted. Backcountry primitive camping permits are required for overnight stays and can be obtained by calling 409-246-2337. Call ahead. Website: www.nps.gov/bith/

PRAIRIES AND PINEYWOODS - EAST
Huntsville State Park

PO Box 508
HUNTSVILLE, TX 77342-0508

KEY BIRDS
Eastern kingbird, northern cardinal, white and red-eyed vireos, and Carolina wren

BEST SEASON
Late April and early May, but birders are rewarded during all seasons

AREA DESCRIPTION
Pine forest with many hardwoods

Huntsville State Park covers 2,083.2 acres located six miles southwest of Huntsville, in Walker County.

Areas rich in hardwoods offer excellent birding opportunities during spring migration. Wood warblers, thrushes, and vireos can be common in the park during late April and early May. However, the most dynamic season is summer, when the forest is alive with the songs of the park's breeding birds. Fourteen species of warblers have been found in the park in summer.

The park's checklist — available at park headquarters - includes 230 species, 218 of which have been observed either within the park boundaries or have been observed overhead, and 14 species which are considered hypothetical. The latter are based on well-documented area records.

This state park offers considerable opportunities to enjoy birding and the outdoors. Woodlands dominated by loblolly and shortleaf pine, sweetgum, and water oak mostly cover the area. Yaupon, American beautyberry, sabal palm, and Virginia creeper are common plants. Birders should at least try to visit the sabal palm grove and observe the birds that are drawn to that area of the park.

Early morning or late evenings are excellent for chances to observe bird life such as the pileated and red-headed woodpeckers, crow, eastern kingbird, northern cardinal, white and red-eyed vireos, and Carolina wren. Overnight campers will sometimes hear the calls of great horned owls.

During the summer months, birders can try out their identification skills by searching and listening for one of the 14 species of warblers common in this location.

Lake Raven winds through the park and provides a variety of opportunities for even the most experienced birder. Exploring the lake in a canoe or kayak is a great way to get close-up sightings and full frame photographs of wading birds. Watch for grebes, coots, and ducks on the open water. Chimney swifts and swallows are common winter visitors flying overhead. An experienced as well as lucky birder, especially one with a spotting scope, may see bald eagles in trees or in the air.

DIRECTIONS

In Huntsville, take Exit 109 from I-45 to PR 40. Go west on PR 40 for 1.5 miles to the park.

CONTACT INFORMATION

Site open daily. Developed camping available. A fee of $4.00 is charged. Camping fees depend on whether camping is by tent or RV. Campers must have a reservation. Phone 936-295-5644.

Greater Roadrunner

PRAIRIES AND PINEYWOODS - EAST
Stubblefield Recreational Area

#5

ABOUT ONE HOUR NORTH OF HOUSTON OFF I-45

KEY BIRDS
Red-cockaded woodpecker

BEST SEASON
Spring and summer

AREA DESCRIPTION
Pine forest and bottomland hardwoods

Located in the Sam Houston National Forest, this recreation area was built in 1937 by the Civilian Conservation Corps. Activities include fishing, birding, hiking, canoeing, and year-round wildlife viewing.

Visitors can enjoy a 1.1-mile interpretive trail and the more extensive Lone Star Hiking Trail, which weaves 140 miles through the Sam Houston National Forest. Trail access is located in the campground parking area.

Habitats include pine forest and bottomland hardwoods associated with Stubblefield Lake and the San Jacinto River. Wading birds of several varieties and bald eagles can be seen along the river. Other birds to watch for include eastern kingbird, summer tanager, eastern phoebe, and indigo bunting.

Careful observers and the very stealthy may have the chance to see an endangered species, the red-cockaded woodpecker. Spend time watching the open pine habitats scattered with large trees. Don't rush your time here. As the old saying goes, "Haste makes waste" or in this case, no woodpecker.

DIRECTIONS
Starting on I-45 outside of Houston, take Exit 102 and head west on FM 1375 for 9.6 miles. Turn north on FSR 215 for 3.0 miles to the campground entrance on the right. This area is about one hour north of Houston and can become very busy on summer weekends and holidays.

CONTACT INFORMATION
Site open daily. Developed camping sites are available. Sam Houston National Forest, West New Waverly, TX 77358 / 936-344-6205 / Toll free 888-361-6908.

PRAIRIES AND PINEYWOODS - EAST
Pineywoods Native Plant Center

#6

2900 RAGUET STREET
NACOGDOCHES, TEXAS 75962

KEY BIRDS
Red-bellied woodpecker and tufted titmouse

BEST SEASON
All seasons

AREA DESCRIPTION
Pine forests with hardwood groves along the creek

These lovely gardens are a wonderful place for wildlife viewing. Checklists of the many plants and birds are available on the center's web site.

Whether you admire plants for their beauty or appreciate the variety of adaptations to specific environments, these gardens are a wonderful place to relax and enjoy the outdoors. Portions of the gardens consist of mature hardwoods and pines in a park-like setting, while other portions are maintained in brushy thickets. There are a number of short trails located throughout the property. The center contains hundreds of species from families of conifers, ferns and fern-allies, and flowering plants.

A main trail takes visitors through Tucker Woods to join the La Nana Creek Trail. Look for resident birds such as the northern cardinal, Carolina chickadee, red-bellied woodpecker, and tufted titmouse or listen for the calls of summer residents such as the summer tanager and red-eyed vireo. Over 105 species of birds have been spotted in Tucker Woods and around the center. During spring and fall migration, the trees and shrubs are alive with colorful songbirds. While the fall migration brings less color in birds, it is a great time to check out the colors of fall foliage. During winter, look for mixed flocks of birds in the tree canopy. Be sure to stop along the wooden boardwalk to admire the bald cypress, American elder, willow, buttonbush, smartweed, and ash. Several snags and woody debris along the trail provide excellent places to look and listen for woodpeckers.

The trail joins the La Nana Creek Trail, where visitors can hike another 2.5 miles along the creek.

DIRECTIONS
From Hwy 59 Business in Nacogdoches, turn east onto Austin. Go two blocks and at the intersection of Austin and Raguet (a four-way stop), turn south on Raguet. The Pineywoods Native Plant Center is located on the east side of the street, just north of the Raguet Elementary School. Parking is available along the gravel drive.

CONTACT INFORMATION

The site is open for day use only. Open Monday through Friday 8am to 5pm. Phone: 936-468-4104 / website: pnpc.sfasu.edu/

Black-crested Titmouse

PRAIRIES AND PINEYWOODS - EAST
Stephen F. Austin Mast Arboretum

STEPHEN F. AUSTIN STATE UNIVERSITY

KEY BIRDS
Finches, and at least two species of oriole

BEST SEASON
Spring, summer, and fall

AREA DESCRIPTION
Planted gardens and walks

The SFA Mast Arboretum is a ten-acre garden along La Nana Creek at Stephen F. Austin State University, Nacogdoches, Texas. The gardens began in 1985 as a small garden project on the south side of the agriculture building, a project of the first Landscape Plant Materials class taught by Dr. Dave Creech. Over the years, the gardens expanded into one of the most diverse collection of plants in the South. The Mast Arboretum is dedicated to acquiring, testing, introducing, and promoting new plants for the landscape and nursery industry in the southern USA. This includes plants that will attract birds of all varieties.

The perennial border near the facility parking area is alive with a rainbow of colors and is an excellent place to watch for ruby-throated hummingbirds along with various butterflies, bees, and other insects.

The arboretum attracts a variety of migratory and resident birds including warblers, Carolina wren, cardinal, mockingbird, mourning dove, swallows, Carolina chickadee, sparrows, woodpeckers, finches, and at least two species of oriole.

DIRECTIONS
From Hwy 59 Business in Nacogdoches, the arboretum can be reached by taking Starr or College Avenue east off of Hwy 59/ North Street and turning onto Wilson Drive. The arboretum is next to the SFASU intramural fields on the campus of Stephen F. Austin State University.

CONTACT INFORMATION
Site open for day use only. Phone: 936-468-3705 / Website: arboretum.sfasu.edu

PRAIRIES AND PINEYWOODS EAST

Bird Watching in Nacogdoches County

The impressive variety of birds that call the surrounding forests, trails, lakes, and pasturelands home make the oldest town in Texas a bird-watcher's paradise. Favorite sightings to this region of the state are the red-cockaded woodpecker, brown-headed nuthatch, altamira oriole, and Bachman's sparrow.

PRAIRIES AND PINEYWOODS EAST

Altamira Oriole

PRAIRIES AND PINEYWOODS - EAST
#8 La Nana Creek Trail & Pecan Park

NACOGDOCHES, TEXAS

KEY BIRDS
Warblers and orioles

BEST SEASON
Spring and summer

AREA DESCRIPTION
Mostly wetland areas with large trees

Not widely known as a birding site, this is a walk that can be – it was for me – a birder's dream in spite of my visit being in the winter. Several species of wading birds were seen in addition to some colorful waterfowl.

The 3.5-mile trail starts from the soccer complex across from Liberty Hall and continues north through a variety of habitats and past several areas worth pausing for a look around. These include but are not limited to: the Eyes of Father Margil, Oak Grove and Zion Hill Cemeteries, New Orleans Greys' Campground, Pecan Park, SFA Mast Arboretum, Pineywoods Native Plant Center and Tucker Woods, and ending at the Jimmy Hinds Park. Pecan Park, a vast spread of pecan trees located near the university campus, has restrooms and water fountains.

Look high in the branches of the bald cypress, sycamore, willow, arrowhead, and ash, which are some of the plants that comprise this wetland vegetation. If this trail seems too long, then it can be broken up into several shorter walks.

Look for the massive water oaks along the creek banks. Look and listen for the characteristic call and plumage of the Louisiana waterthrush bobbing in and out along the stream's edges. The density of trees varies along the trail, as does the amount of understory vegetation, providing ample opportunities for viewing a whole host of wildlife species.

Spring migration brings colorful warblers and orioles, which adorn the trees with brightly-colored plumage and musical songs. Some of these birds nest during the spring and summer or live year round along the creek.

DIRECTIONS
The trail starts at 805 E. Main (TX 21 & Hwy 7) behind Liberty Hall and just off the east side of Loop 224.

CONTACT INFORMATION
Site is open for day use only. Phone: 936-559-2960 / Website: www.ci.nacogdoches.tx.us

PRAIRIES AND
PINEYWOODS EAST

PRAIRIES AND PINEYWOODS - EAST

Stag Leap Retreat/Country Inn & Bed and Breakfast

#9

2219 FM 2782
NACOGDOCHES, TEXAS 75964

KEY BIRDS
Pileated and red-bellied woodpeckers, red-eyed vireo, and tufted titmouse

BEST SEASON
All seasons

AREA DESCRIPTION
East Texas landscape with large trees and creekside vegetation

Stag Leap offers five private bed-and-breakfast cabins, each one uniquely furnished and surrounded by wildlife habitat. Several of the cabins have large decks that overlook the creek and surrounding forest. Hummingbird and seed feeders and flowering plants are located around the cabins. The views from the cabins provide wonderful opportunities for enjoying nature. The owners also offer golf carts, archery, horseshoes, volleyball, and basketball to their guests.

Birders can relax and enjoy southern hospitality while exploring the 200-acre retreat. Numerous trails throughout the property provide plenty of opportunities to hike and bike. Forested habitats include hickories, eastern red cedar, pine, water oak, sweetgum, post oak, American holly, winged elm, sassafras, dogwood, American beauty-berry, Virginia creeper, red buckeye, coral bean, American elder, and black walnut. Listen as Carolina wrens and white-eyed vireos call from the trees, while vultures and chimney swifts finish the day searching for a meal.

Bonaldo Creek runs through the property, providing a peaceful atmosphere and great habitat for birds as well as butterflies.

Pay special attention in the wooded areas and chances are good you may spot a pileated woodpecker's red flare or at least hear its call, in addition to its loud drumming in the trees. Zero in on the sound and watch this large and very special bird. A now widely understood fact is that the pileated woodpecker has been mistaken several times for the very extinct ivorybilled woodpecker that hasn't been seen since the 1940s, in spite of some reported but undocumented and skeptical "sightings".

Pileated and red-bellied woodpeckers, red-eyed vireos, and tufted titmice are just a few of the common birds that may be observed. Listen for the call of the red-tailed hawk or a wood thrush as you walk through the trees. Evening birders that are watching the tree tops can experience sightings of owls, flying squirrels, and other nocturnal animals.

DIRECTIONS

From Loop 224 heading west/south in Nacogdoches, travel west to the Hwy 7/Crockett Exit. Go west on Hwy 7 for 6.4 miles to FM 2782. Turn right onto FM 2782 and go 2.0 miles to Stag Leap Retreat.

CONTACT INFORMATION

This site has restricted access and reservations are required. Cabin and guesthouse rates start at $140.00 a night. Hosts are Mattie and Wayne Collins, and Kirby Collins, 936-560-0766 or Leslea Gardner at 936-715-9477 / Website: www.stagleap.com

Red-eyed Vireo

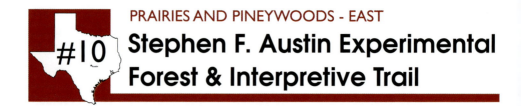

PRAIRIES AND PINEYWOODS - EAST

#10 Stephen F. Austin Experimental Forest & Interpretive Trail

LOCATED IN SOUTHERN NACOGDOCHES COUNTY, ON THE NORTH SIDE OF THE ANGELINA RIVER

KEY BIRDS
Yellow-billed cuckoo, red-eyed and white-eyed vireos, white-breasted nuthatches, brown creepers

BEST SEASON
All seasons

AREA DESCRIPTION
Both pine and hardwood forest and some flooded areas with marsh

This is an experimental forest consisting of 2,560 acres. The forest is made up primarily of mature bottomland hardwood habitat of about 1,600 acres that may be seasonally flooded. In addition there are mature upland hardwood pine and pine habitats. The habitat diversity is what accounts for more than 150 species of resident and migratory birds, and over 80 species of butterflies.

Two loops comprise 3.0 miles of nature trails with a viewing blind. The Jack Creek Loop is a 0.8-mile paved interpretive trail with a variable grade along Jack Creek. Flowing water adds to the tranquility of the forest and provides another habitat for visitors to explore. Notice the ferns, basket grass, and may apples growing on the forest floor.

The Management Loop, which serves as a demonstration site for forest and wildlife management practices, winds through five different management units of the forest. Signs along the trail correspond with a brochure available near the parking area.

Interpretative signs give both the casual observer and the well-studied nature enthusiast insights into the forest vegetation. Birds such as northern cardinal, Carolina wren, downy woodpecker, American crow, and tufted titmouse are sure to make their presence known. Summer tanager, yellow-billed cuckoo, red-eyed and white-eyed vireos, white-breasted nuthatch, brown creeper, yellow-bellied sapsucker, barred owl, screech owl, prothonotary warbler, and northern parula warbler are also often heard and seen.

Numerous benches, conveniently located along the trails, provide visitors a place to rest while watching the birds or just enjoying the surrounding beauty.

DIRECTIONS
From the intersection of Hwy 7 and FM 2782 just southwest of Nacogdoches, turn south on FM 2782 and proceed 2.3 miles to the entrance of the SFA Experimental Forest. Proceed past the entrance gate approximately 0.25 mile and then follow the signs to the

trail parking lot. From Lufkin, go north on Hwy 59 to FM 2782. Turn left and proceed 2.5 miles to the SFA Experimental Forest entrance.

CONTACT INFORMATION
Site open for day use only with no entry fees. Camping is not allowed.
Phone: 936-569-7981
Website: ww.srs.fs.usda.gov/wildlife/trail.htm

PRAIRIES AND PINEYWOODS EAST

Northern Cardinal

PRAIRIES AND PINEYWOODS - EAST
Alazan Bayou Wildlife Management Area

#11

1805 E. LUFKIN
LUFKIN, TX 75901

KEY BIRDS
Scissor-tailed flycatcher, sparrows, loggerhead shrike, dickcissel, blue grosbeak, great egret, little blue heron, white ibis, great blue heron, American bittern, and Indigo bunting

BEST SEASON
Spring and summer

AREA DESCRIPTION
Forestland and wetlands

This 2,063-acre WMA located in southern Nacogdoches County was purchased in 1991 to preserve mature bottomland hardwood forests adjacent to the Angelina River. In addition to the Angelina River, other significant drainages include Loco Bayou and Moral Creek. The bottomland forest typically begins to flood during mid-winter as the river and bayous overbank, with inundation continuing through early spring. For great wildlife viewing, visit the viewing deck at the end of the road on the west side, overlooking the wetland cells. Interpretive panels discussing bottomland hardwood forests, wetland habitat management, and birding opportunities are also found on the viewing deck.

Look for scissor-tailed flycatcher, sparrows, loggerhead shrike, dickcissel, and blue grosbeak in open grassland along the road. In wetland areas, look for great egret, little blue heron, white ibis, and great blue heron as well as camouflaged American bittern. Indigo buntings can be heard singing from the trees. Several wood duck boxes are mounted throughout the wetlands and, at times, the lucky birder will be in the right place at the right time to see young wood ducks leaving the boxes and dropping into the water.

The middle road winds through additional upland and wetland habitats before ending at the parking area. From here, three woods roads provide additional access to various habitats.

Look for birds such as yellow-billed cuckoo, blue-gray gnatcatcher, green heron, yellow-breasted chat, common yellowthroat, white-tailed kite, painted bunting, wood stork, and Le Conte's sparrow.

DIRECTIONS
The WMA is located approximately 6.2 miles south of Nacogdoches just off of Highway 59. Go west on FM 2782 approximately 1.1 miles to the WMA. There are three entrances along FM 2782 with information/registration stations.

CONTACT INFORMATION

Open year round, the site is open daily with developed campsites available. Users must have a $48.00 Texas Public Lands Permit available from TPW vendors. This one permit will allow entry to most Texas wildlife management areas. Contact: Ron Mize, Phone: 936-569-8547 or 936-639-1879.

House Finch

PRAIRIES AND PINEYWOODS - EAST
Saint's Rest Road

#12

NACOGDOCHES, TEXAS

KEY BIRDS
Louisiana waterthrush, solitary vireo, rusty blackbird, purple finch, and Kentucky, yellow-throated, prothonotary, and Swainson's warblers

BEST SEASON
All year, weather permitting

AREA DESCRIPTION
Pine forest to riparian bottomland hardwoods

Follow Doors Creek and drive down to the banks of the Angelina River to view the various habitat types and unique wildlife species along Saint's Rest Road.

Parking is limited to the county road right-of-way but because the road is a dead-end, traffic is light. As you drive down the road, the habitat changes from pine forest to riparian bottomland hardwoods, and finely to Angelina River bottomland. Look for Louisiana waterthrush, solitary vireo, rusty blackbird, purple finch, and Kentucky, yellow-throated, prothonotary, and Swainson's warblers. Watch the beaver pond area for belted kingfisher and various wading birds.

DIRECTIONS
From Nacogdoches, take FM 1275 South from Loop 224 for 6.3 miles to CR 538. Turn right on CR 538 for 0.4 mile then left on CR 539 which is Saint's Rest Road and continue 3.0 miles until it dead ends at the Angelina River. The site is restricted to viewing from the county road right-of-way.

CONTACT INFORMATION
Phone: 936-564-7351.

Great Crested Flycatcher

PRAIRIES AND PINEYWOODS - EAST
Texas Forestry Museum, Urban Wildscape Trail

1907 ATKINSON DRIVE
LUFKIN, TEXAS 75901

KEY BIRDS
Blue jay, pine warbler, Carolina wren, mourning dove, downy woodpecker

BEST SEASON
All seasons

AREA DESCRIPTION
Primarily a mixed pine-hardwood forest

The Texas Forestry Museum's exhibitions and collections tell the story of the forests of Texas. The complexity of the forests' natural resources, the legacy of the East Texas timber industry, and the current and future role of forest management is outlined here for visitors.

Birders will enjoy the Urban Wildscape Trail. Permanent exhibits include the Forest History Wing, where visitors can view logging tools and equipment and see a steam engine that powered a sawmill. The museum's website offers several virtual tours.

Hundreds of avian species make the Pineywoods their home, or visit the region during seasonal migrations. But the area's amazingly diverse habitats also support animals and plants of every description.

There are quite a variety of species using the habitat and the urban environment similes include chimney swift, northern cardinal, blue jay, pine warbler, Carolina wren, mourning dove, downy woodpecker, tufted titmouse, robin, chipping sparrow, and red-tailed hawk.

There is a 0.12-mile paved portion of the trail consisting of wood chip footing. This portion of the trail has three bridge crossings over low-lying areas with interpretive signs along the trail.

CONTACT INFORMATION
Hours: Monday - Saturday 10:00am to 5:00pm / Sunday 1:00pm to 5:00pm / Phone: 936-632-9535 / Website: www.treetexas.com

PRAIRIES AND PINEYWOODS - EAST
Ivy's Wildlife Refuge

#14

COUNTY ROAD 134
ELKHART, TX 75839

KEY BIRDS
Northern cardinal, pileated woodpecker, chickadee, and the great-crested flycatcher

BEST SEASON
Spring and fall migrations

AREA DESCRIPTION
Forested with brush and streamside vegetation

Visitors and birders are requested to check in at the house to let the caretakers know you are there. Camping is allowed near the pavilion where they have restrooms, a kitchen, and showers. As of this writing no entry fee is charged.

Take a walk through a woodland of pines and hardwoods, across a rustic bridge, to a beautiful creek. Have your binoculars and spotting scopes ready for unexpected sightings. The rock substrate of the creek is pitted and pocked and holds isolated pools of water very attractive to water striders.

Carefully pick up a few small rocks and look for the small aquatic invertebrates taking refuge under the rock. Although you shouldn't touch these sensitive creatures, a glance is rewarding enough. As water flows over the rock bluff into the large pool of water below, look for fish in the lower pools waiting for a snack to gulp down.

Walk or ride your bike on the many sand and red clay trails on the property. Forest vegetation includes water oak, sugarberry, winged elm, post oak, willow oak, redbud, mockernut hickory, black cherry, American basswood, dogwood, American holly, sassafras, blackjack oak, American beautyberry, and Virginia creeper.

Unique mushrooms and shelf fungus can be studied along several trails. Wood debris on the forest floor provides excellent habitat for reptiles, insects, and ground-feeding birds. Watch for snakes along your route - although not seen regularly, they are present.

Some of the birds to be seen are vultures, hawks, red-eyed vireo, American crow, northern cardinal, pileated woodpecker, chickadees, and the great-crested flycatcher as well as feral hogs. Birders may also see spring visitors such as the snoutnose and swallowtail butterflies.

The pipeline right-of-way that traverses the property grows abundant wildflowers, including Mexican hat, black-eyed Susan, and asters. When flowers are present watch for hummingbirds darting among the blooms.

PRAIRIES AND PINEYWOODS EAST

Bird feeders and nest boxes are located around the house and several Carolina wrens can be observed nesting during the spring and summer.

CONTACT INFORMATION
No fees are charged to bird on the refuge, but please call first for directions and to alert owners to your arrival Phone: 903-764-2605.

Downy Woodpecker

PRAIRIES AND PINEYWOODS - EAST
Neches Bluff Area

DAVY CROCKETT NATIONAL FOREST – WEST OF LUFKIN, TEXAS

KEY BIRDS
Hooded warbler, blue-gray gnatcatcher, red-eyed vireo, northern parula, downy woodpecker

BEST SEASON
All seasons

AREA DESCRIPTION
East Texas forest and bottomland

Located deep in the heart of the Davy Crockett National Forest, this site provides a large diversity of habitats including wetlands, marshes, ponds, hardwood bottomlands, and upland pine forest.

Bird songs are heard in the trees and the blue-gray gnatcatcher, red-eyed vireo, northern parula, downy woodpecker, and ruby-throated hummingbird are just a few of the species that can be seen. A trail crosses several small creeks, which are alive with water insects that will attract several species of small ground-feeding birds.

There are beautiful wetlands along the trail, including ponds with bald cypress and unique areas tucked back in the woods. These wetlands provide scenic stopping points and viewing locations for birders. Look for wading birds and waterfowl including herons, teal, and wood ducks. Several wood duck nest boxes are located on the ponds.

The spring breeding season is a great time for wetland wildlife, although a variety of species can be observed year round. Rushes, sedges, and a plethora of other wetland plants line the banks of the pond. Warblers are a common resident of the hardwoods and underbrush. Look for the jet black and canary yellow feathers of the hooded warbler as it calls from the brush. In September, be sure to look for the beautiful, large, white flowers of the rare Neches River rose-mallow around wetland edges.

DIRECTIONS
Between Crockett and Alto on Hwy 21, turn south on FR 511 that is about 1.0 mile southwest of the Neches River Bridge. Follow FR 511 for 0.6 mile, turn left on FR 511-A, and follow it for 0.3 mile. Turn right on FR 511 and follow it for 1.1 miles to the T-intersection at the power line. Turn right and park about 100 yards from the turn.

CONTACT INFORMATION
This site is open daily and has some developed camping available. Phone: 936-655-2299.

PRAIRIES AND PINEYWOODS EAST

PRAIRIES AND PINEYWOODS - EAST
Mission Tejas State Park

#16

120 STATE PARK RD. 44, GRAPELAND, TX 75844

KEY BIRDS
Ruby-throated hummingbird, summer tanager, pine warbler, and indigo bunting

BEST SEASON
During spring and fall migrations and late summer

AREA DESCRIPTION
Pine and hardwoods with some scattered hills

The Mission Tejas State Park is a 363.5-acre park. The park was constructed in 1934 by the Civilian Conservation Corps (CCC) and acquired in 1957 by legislative act from the Texas Forest Service, at which time it was opened to the public.

The park was built as a commemorative representation of Mission San Francisco de los Tejas, the first Spanish mission in the province of Texas, which was established in 1690.

Located near the northern end of the Davy Crockett National Forest, the park offers an atmosphere of rustic beauty and tranquility among the tall pines.

The trail from the picnic area traverses hilly terrain and winds through mixed pine/hardwood forest. Trees and shrubs are marked and an interpretive guide is available at the park entrance. Enjoy watching birds and other wildlife at the three-acre pond located adjacent to the trail. The diverse vegetation provides excellent habitat for several species of birds, including ruby-throated hummingbird, summer tanager, pine warbler, and indigo bunting. Migratory birds are plentiful during spring and fall. The trail continues to a boardwalk over a riparian area and pond, and offers an opportunity to view the area from an elevated vantage point.

DIRECTIONS
This location is in Houston County, 22 miles northeast of Crockett. The headquarters is approximately 100 feet off Hwy 21 on the right. Look for the brown State Park highway signs that will show the way.

CONTACT INFORMATION
Site is open daily and has developed camping areas. As with other state parks a $4.00 entry fee is charged. Phone: 936-687-2394.

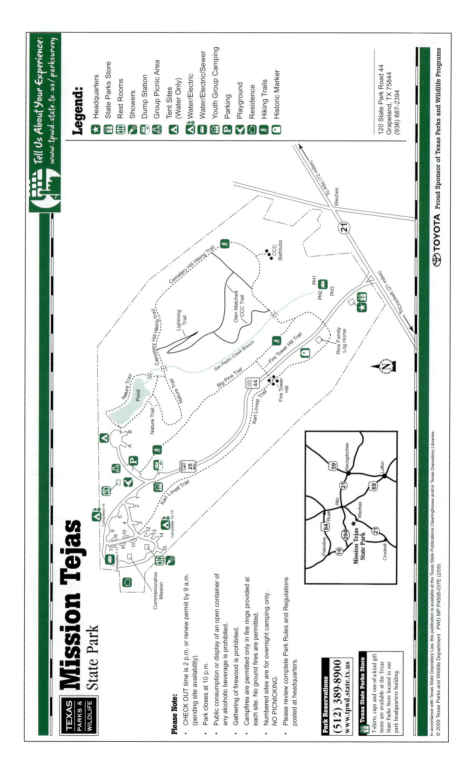

Mission Tejas

State Park

TEXAS
PARKS &
WILDLIFE

Please Note:

- CHECK OUT time is 2 p.m. or renew permit by 9 a.m. (pending site availability).

- Park closes at 10 p.m.

- Public consumption or display of an open container of any alcoholic beverage is prohibited.

- Gathering of firewood is prohibited.

- Campfires are permitted only in fire rings provided at each site. No ground fires are permitted.

- Numbered sites are for overnight camping only. NO PICNICKING.

- Please review complete Park Rules and Regulations posted at headquarters.

Park Reservations

(512) 389-8900
www.tpwd.state.tx.us

Mission State Parks Store

T-shirts, caps and one-of-a-kind gift items are available at the Texas State Parks Store located in our park headquarters building.

Tell Us About Your Experience:
www.tpwd.state.tx.us/parksurvey

Legend:

Headquarters		Water/Electric
State Parks Store		Water/Electric/Sewer
Rest Rooms		Youth Group Camping
Showers		Parking
Dump Station		Playground
Group Picnic Area		Residence
Tent Sites (Water Only)		Hiking Trails
Water/Electric		Historic Marker

120 State Park Road 44
Grapeland, TX 75844
(936) 687-2394

TOYOTA Proud Sponsor of Texas Parks and Wildlife Programs

PRAIRIES AND PINEYWOODS - EAST

#17 Big Slough Wilderness & Four-C's National Recreation Trail

DAVY CROCKETT NATIONAL FOREST
18551 STATE HIGHWAY 7
EAST KENNARD, TX 75847

KEY BIRDS
Parula warbler, Carolina wren, Carolina chickadee, vireos, and woodpeckers

BEST SEASON
Spring and fall

AREA DESCRIPTION
Primarily pine and hardwood

The U.S. Congress designated the Big Slough Wilderness as a land-managed area to allow the earth's natural processes to shape and influence the area.

The 3,639-acre Big Slough Wilderness was set aside under the Texas Wilderness Act of 1984 and since then, these areas have been managed to remain natural and provide opportunities for solitude and, of course, observing nature.

The forest cover in the area is primarily hardwood, including white oak, red oak, hickory, chestnut oak, cherry-bark oak, sweetgum, nutall oak, and willow. Hardwood areas account for 66 percent of the area; about 26 percent of the area is shortleaf and loblolly pine. Mixed hardwood and pine account for four percent, with water in the slough accounting for four percent of the wilderness area.

Known for its undisturbed, old growth bottomland hardwoods, Big Slough is located within the boundaries of the Davy Crockett National Forest. Four C's Recreational Trail crosses through the center of this area.

You may also take the Big Slough Canoe Trail to the interior. Like walking slow, a slow, quiet paddle will get you up close and personal with many species of the area's birds. Don't leave your binoculars and cameras in the car.

The hiking trail highlights some very large old pines and oaks. Portions of the trail have dense underbrush, including American beautyberry, a plant with excellent wildlife value.

The fluted, muscle-like trunks of the American hornbeam line the trail. You may notice the marks left by yellow-bellied sapsuckers on many of the trees. Rows and rows of tiny holes have been bored into many of the tree trunks. Parula warbler, Carolina wren, Carolina chickadee, vireos, and woodpeckers are a few of the forest birds that are most common to the area.

PRAIRIES AND PINEYWOODS EAST

DIRECTIONS

From the intersection of SR 7 and FM 227 in Ratcliffe, go north on FM 227 for 0.9 mile to CR 1165. Go north 3.4 miles on CR 1165, then east on CR 1165/1170. A faded sign at this intersection directs visitors to the right. Follow to CR 1175 where another faded sign directs visitors to turn left (west). Follow this road 1.2 miles to the Wilderness Area boundary. There is a parking area on the left and a trail map. The trailhead will be a few hundred yards down on the right and left. A detailed map of the area is available from the Forest Service.

CONTACT INFORMATION

Site open for day use only. Phone: 936-655-2299.

PRAIRIES AND PINEYWOODS - EAST
Alabama Creek Wildlife Management Area

#18

DAVY CROCKETT NATIONAL FOREST
SOUTHWEST OF LUFKIN, TEXAS

KEY BIRDS
Hawks, owls, vultures, kites, bald eagle, prothonotary warbler, and various waterfowl

BEST SEASON
Spring and fall migrations and summer months

AREA DESCRIPTION
Upland pine forest, mixed aged stands of hardwood and pine forest, bottomland hardwood forests, and Neches River frontage and adjacent wetlands

Spend an hour or spend the day exploring the 14,000-acre management area located within the 150,000-acre Davy Crockett National Forest.

Habitats include upland pine forest, mixed-aged stands of hardwood and pine forest, bottomland hardwood forests, and Neches River frontage and adjacent wetlands. The interspersion of vegetation types provides numerous levels of habitat – from the forest floor to the upper canopies – resulting in a profusion of wildlife and birds.

Holly Bluff Road is a great place to gain river access. Watch for hawks, owls, vultures, kites, bald eagle, prothonotary warbler, and various waterfowl and wading birds along the miles of river frontage within the management area. Several paths venture from the forest roads, but these are not designated or signed trails; so if you move into the interior, be careful not to get lost.

Red-cockaded woodpecker clusters are one of the many highlights of Alabama Creek. This endangered species prefers park-like stands of pines and an area relatively devoid of hardwoods and understory vegetation. The birds live in family groups and are most visible at dawn and dusk between April and June. A heavy white resin coating around the hole typically marks the active cavities.

These highly protected areas are marked by signs. When entering these areas, use common sense and keep your visits short. These birds are sensitive to disturbance and are protected by federal law. Drive along FR 541 and FR 531 for easy access to several clusters immediately adjacent to the roadway.

Either stay in or very near your car for watching or photographing these woodpeckers. Many times these birds are close enough for a smaller pair of binoculars or medium telephoto lens. Birders should not venture off the road for a closer look and disturb the birds.

PRAIRIES AND PINEYWOODS EAST

Notice the black burn marks along the bases of some of the pine trees. Forest thinning by the use of prescribed burning is a key management tool that is used to help maintain the required habitat of the red-cockaded woodpecker.

DIRECTIONS

From Apple Springs, take FM 357 south for approximately 6-8 miles. A series of Forest Roads will head east through the area. A large sign along the road will tell you that you are entering the Wildlife Management Area; however, there are a few tracks of private land interspersed, so only go within areas marked by the small yellow signs. From the intersection of FM 2501 and FM 2262 in Nigton, travel for 1.2 miles to a roadside sign and map for the area. Holly Bluff Road is located 2.0 miles from the intersection and provides access to the Neches River. Access can be gained all along the east and west side of FM 2262. When FM 2262 meets FM 357, you can travel west on FM 357 and there will be several other access points including FR 541 and 531.

CONTACT INFORMATION

Site open daily. Developed camping available. Birders are required to have a $48.00 Public Lands Permit covering all Texas Wildlife Management Areas. Contact Dick Pike, 415 S. First St., Suite 110, Lufkin, TX 75901 / 936-639-8544.

Bald Eagle (immature)

PRAIRIES AND PINEYWOODS - EAST
Bannister Wildlife Management Area

#19

TWENTY MILES EAST OF LUFKIN OFF FM 705

KEY BIRDS
Eastern wild turkey, wood duck, redheaded and pileated woodpeckers, brown-headed nuthatch, roseate spoonbill, wood stork, white ibis, sage wren, and rusty blackbird

BEST SEASON
All seasons

AREA DESCRIPTION
Bottomland hardwood forest, mixed pine, longleaf pine savanna, fields, pastures, and cropland

The Bannister Wildlife Management Area covers a 28,063-acre area of San Augustine County and part of the Angelina National Forest. It is located on a peninsula extending into Sam Rayburn Reservoir. It is separated from the lake by private land and national forest service land.

Texas Parks and Wildlife acts as an adviser concerning wildlife management. The area is a designated eastern wild turkey restoration site and closes certain sections during turkey brooding season.

The area provides habitat for a diversity of birds including, as mentioned, the restoration of the eastern sub-species of wild turkey and also the endangered red-cockaded woodpecker. The wide variety of native and migrating species of birds makes the area a special bird watching location all year long.

The area includes the Turkey Hill Wilderness. This habitat includes mature stands of loblolly and slash pine, along with hardwood trees such as sweetgum, red maple, laurel oak, and American elm occurring in the creek and streamside areas.

Primary management of the vegetation includes controlled burns necessary to maintain the open understory required by red-cockaded woodpeckers. Visitors are reminded to minimize noise and disturbance to the cavity trees, particularly during the nesting season.

The relatively open nature of these mature pine stands provides high visibility for viewing Bachman's sparrow and sedge wren in summer and grasshopper and Henslow's sparrows in winter.

DIRECTIONS
The area is accessed from Hwy 103 about 20 miles east of Lufkin by turning south on FM 1277, FSR 301, Hwy 147, or FM 705.

PRAIRIES AND PINEYWOODS EAST

CONTACT INFORMATION

Site open daily. Developed camping available. Only birders, hikers, and bikers are allowed in these areas at this time. Contact Dick Pike, 1342 S. Wheeler, Jasper, TX 75951 / 936-639-8544 or call the US Forest Service at 409-639-8620 or the Jasper office of Texas Parks and Wildlife at 409-384-6894.

Roseate Spoonbill

PRAIRIES AND PINEYWOODS - EAST

#20 Ralph McAllister Park

ON TX 103 – NORTH SHORE OF SAM RAYBURN RESERVOIR

KEY BIRDS
Yellow-billed cuckoo, eastern wood-pewee, Acadian and great crested flycatchers, brown-headed nuthatch, red-eyed and white-eyed vireos, as well as several warbler and woodpecker species

BEST SEASON
Migrations winter, spring, and fall

AREA DESCRIPTION
Mixed woods, pine forest, hardwood sloughs, and lakeshore

This small park offers a variety of habitats, including mature mixed woods, pine forest, hardwood sloughs, and lakeshore. The upland mixed woods and pine forest provide habitat for yellow-billed cuckoo, eastern wood-pewee, Acadian and great crested flycatchers, brown-headed nuthatch, red-eyed and white-eyed vireos, as well as several warbler and woodpecker species.

The shoreline and open lake provide great opportunities to observe wading shorebirds, eared and horned grebes, dabbling and diving ducks, common loons, and the occasional bald eagle. This compact site offers diverse wildlife viewing and pleasant surroundings.

DIRECTIONS
From the intersection of US 96 and TX 103 approximately 20 miles south of Nacogdoches, go west on TX 103 for 16.0 miles to the park entrance, which is to the south just after crossing the Sam Rayburn Reservoir Bridge.

CONTACT INFORMATION
Site open for day use only; no fees are charged. Phone 936-564-7351.

PRAIRIES AND PINEYWOODS EAST

PRAIRIES AND PINEYWOODS - EAST

Bird Islands - Lake Sam Rayburn

#21

ON THE SR 147 HIGHWAY AND BRIDGE OVERLOOKING THE LAKE

KEY BIRDS
Multitudes of waterfowl, common loon, horned grebe, American white pelican, Bonaparte's and ring-billed gulls

BEST SEASON
All seasons

AREA DESCRIPTION
Lakeshore and shallow water habitats

The Bird Islands are located on the east side of the highway, but birds — particularly waterfowl — are often on both sides of the road. The only parking available is on the shoulder of the road and at several pull-offs located on the north shoreline.

The shallow waters located at the north end of the SH 147 bridge over Lake Sam Rayburn provide excellent habitat for wintering waterfowl as well as resident water birds. The bridge offers excellent lake views. Water levels will often determine the species of birds present.

Resident species observed during all seasons include great blue and little blue herons, pied-billed grebe, and great and snowy egrets. During the summer months look for tricolored heron, geotropic cormorant, yellow-crowned night heron, white ibis, black-crowned night heron, roseate spoonbill, and wood stork. Winter is the best time to look for common loon, horned grebe, American white pelican, Bonaparte's and ring-billed gulls. Dabbling ducks such as green-winged and blue-winged teal, mallard, American wigeon, northern pintail, northern shoveler, and gadwall can be observed in the shallow water areas, whereas divers such as canvasback, redhead, ring-necked duck, greater and lesser scaup, bufflehead, common golden eye, hooded merganser, and ruddy duck are more common in deeper water.

One of the neat things about this site is that you won't need to move far to experience different species of bird life. When you find birds, set up your cameras and spotting scopes and spend time in that location. When things get quiet, more birds will show themselves. Take your time.

DIRECTIONS
From the intersection of Hwy 63 and SR 147 in Zavalla, go northeast on SR 147 approximately 6.0 miles to the SR 147 bridge as it crosses Lake Rayburn below Broaddus.

CONTACT INFORMATION
Phone: 936-897-1068

American White Pelican

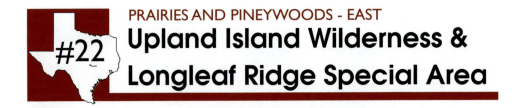

PRAIRIES AND PINEYWOODS - EAST

Upland Island Wilderness & Longleaf Ridge Special Area

#22

LOCATED ON FR 303 SOUTH OF SAM RAYBURN RESERVOIR

KEY BIRDS
Henslow's, Bachman's, and Le Conte's sparrows

BEST SEASON
Winter, spring, and summer

AREA DESCRIPTION
Forest, bogs, and hardwood bottomlands

The Upland Island Wilderness Area spans 13,331 acres of pine forest with bogs and hardwood bottomlands leading to the Neches River. The Longleaf Ridge Special Area is approximately 32,300 acres and is located east of the Upland Island Wilderness Area. Located within the Angelina National Forest System, the Longleaf Ridge Special Area is bordered by the Sam Rayburn Reservoir to the north, and includes two shoreline recreation areas: Sandy Creek and Caney Creek. The Longleaf Ridge Special Area is managed specifically for red-cockaded woodpecker and associated upland species such as eastern wild turkey. Boykin Spring and Bouton Lake are located within this area.

Birding in the area is excellent. The shorelines provide habitat for water birds such as pied-billed grebe, cattle and snowy egrets, Forster's tern, belted kingfisher, and various herons. Resident birds inhabiting the woodlands include American kestrel, blue jay, Carolina chickadee, tufted titmouse, Carolina wren, eastern bluebird, pine warbler, and red-bellied, downy, and pileated woodpeckers. Chuck-will's-widow, wood thrush, American redstart, Louisiana waterthrush, indigo and painted buntings, and eastern towhee occur in summer. In winter look for American woodcock, and grasshopper, Henslow's, Bachman's, and Le Conte's sparrows.

The mixed woods along riparian areas support yellow-billed cuckoo, eastern wood-pewee, Acadian and great crested flycatchers, brown-headed nuthatch, and red-eyed and white-eyed vireos. While driving south on FSR 313 and FSR 326 watch for red-cockaded woodpecker and the eastern wild turkey that are common; this will be one of the best chances to spot these species in this area of the forest.

DIRECTIONS
From the intersection of US 69 and SR 63 in Zavalla, go east on SR 63 for 7.1 miles to FR 303. Turn right (south) on FR 303 and follow it south to the site. This area can also be accessed to the east of Hwy 63 by FSR 308, 347 and 333.

CONTACT INFORMATION

The site is open daily with some developed camping available. There are no fees charged for using this area. Phone: 936-897-1068.

Song Sparrow

PRAIRIES AND PINEYWOODS - EAST
Ayish Bayou

#23

LOCATED NEAR SAN AUGUSTINE, IN THE UPPER REACHES OF THE AYISH BAYOU BEHIND THE TOURISM CENTER

KEY BIRDS
Northern cardinal, northern mockingbird, tufted titmouse, and cliff swallow

BEST SEASON
During migrations and in the early spring

AREA DESCRIPTION
East Texas pine and streamside hardwoods

The Ayish Bayou begins from deep and clear springs in the north-central part of San Augustine County. Ayish Bayou was named by early visitors for the Ais Indians. The bayou runs southward almost the entire length of the county and then empties into the Angelina River.

The San Augustine Civic and Tourism Center is located on the upper reaches of the Ayish Bayou. Although the Bayou at this location is only about 10 feet wide, the associated riparian vegetation provides exceptional habitat for a number of bird species.

Northern cardinal, northern mockingbird, tufted titmouse, and cliff swallow nest in the area. White-eyed vireo, painted and indigo buntings, rose-breasted grosbeak, and dark-eyed junco can be seen during migration and also occasionally nest nearby. Watch the skies overhead for red-tailed hawk and black vulture.

The long, planked walkway from the Tourist Center across Ayish Bayou to the Caboose offers excellent viewing opportunities for the traveling birder. Take your time here and see all there is to see.

The City of San Augustine operates the center. The grounds are open to the public year round. In just a short visit to the Tourism Center you will learn more about local history and see the beautiful gold leaf paintings and woodcarvings.

DIRECTIONS
From the intersection of TX 21 and US 96 in San Augustine, go east on TX 21 for 0.4 mile to San Augustine Civic and Tourism Center. Ayish Bayou is behind the center.

CONTACT INFORMATION
Site open for day use only.
Phone: 936-275-3610
Website: www.sanaugustinetx.com

PRAIRIES AND PINEYWOODS - EAST
Trail Between the Lakes

#24

A 28-MILE HIKING TRAIL FROM TOLEDO BEND RESERVOIR TO SAM RAYBURN RESERVOIR

KEY BIRDS
Red-cockaded woodpecker, prairie and pine warblers, Bachman's, grasshopper, and Henslow's sparrows, and several other species of woodpeckers

BEST SEASON
Spring for nesting birds along the whole trail

AREA DESCRIPTION
Pine forest, pockets of riparian, mixed woods

The trailhead for the Between the Lakes Trail is just south of the Devil's Ford Bridge. Step out into the wilderness as you trek down this 28-mile trail that takes you through a variety of east Texas habitats. The trail extends from Toledo Bend Reservoir to Sam Rayburn Reservoir, and is maintained by members of the Golden Triangle Group. While dominated primarily by pine forest, pockets of riparian mixed woods and deciduous forest are also encountered while traversing the trail. Multiple access points are available to allow hikers to decide the length of their trek.

The trail extends northward to the Moore Plantation Wildlife Management Area and crosses Devil's Ford and Curry Creek before intersecting FM 2426. The trail turns westward through the managed pine forest of Moore Plantation, intersecting Hwy 87, and continuing through the Sabine National Forest until its end at the Lakeview Recreational Area.

There are many opportunities to camp in the primitive and natural settings along the route. Camping is not allowed in the Moore Plantation Wildlife Management Area during deer hunting season or near the colonies of red-cockaded woodpeckers, which are an endangered species. Woodpecker colony boundaries are marked with aqua-green paint and boundary signs. An active red-cockaded woodpecker cluster is located just as the trail approaches FM 2426 in the Moore Plantation WMA. Other bird species likely to be observed include prairie and pine warblers, Bachman's, grasshopper, and Henslow's sparrows, and various woodpeckers.

DIRECTIONS
From Pineland, follow FM 2426 east for 10.0 miles to Hwy 87. Turn right (south) on Hwy 87 for 3.0 miles to FM 2928. Turn left (east) on FM 2928 for 3.5 miles to the end of the paved road, continue 4.0 miles to the campground.

CONTACT INFORMATION
Site open daily and developed camping is available.
Phone: 409-787-3870
Website: www.fs.fed.us/r8/texas/recreation/index.shtml

Northern Mockingbird

PRAIRIES AND PINEYWOODS - EAST

Moore Plantation Wildlife Management Area

#25

EAST OF PINELAND, TEXAS

KEY BIRDS
Painted and indigo buntings, prairie and pine warblers

BEST SEASON
Spring, winter, fall

AREA DESCRIPTION
Mixture of mature pine trees with an open understory that is being restored

Restoring the pine forest to its natural state has been the management goal for the Moore Plantation Wildlife Management Area. With recurring controlled burns on much of the property, the WMA is being restored to a healthy mixture of mature pine trees with an open understory – a habitat requirement for the endangered red-cockaded woodpecker.

The open understory also provides habitat for birds such as painted and indigo buntings, prairie and pine warblers, brown-headed nuthatch, American woodcock, Bachman's sparrow, sedge wren, and grasshopper and Henslow's sparrows. In addition to red-cockaded woodpeckers, pileated, downy, and red-bellied woodpeckers can also be observed in this habitat.

The Moore Plantation Wildlife Management Area covers 25,601 acres. Visitors can see the area by vehicle on the Forest Service roads. Trails for hiking and horseback riding are also available. White-tailed deer and eastern wild turkey are common in the area, and traveling south on FSR 114 provides a good opportunity to see wild turkeys. In the spring watch carefully for mating activities like strutting and displaying toms.

DIRECTIONS
From the intersection of Hwy 1/ FM 2426 in Pineland, travel east on FM 2426 for 3.8 miles to its intersection with FSR 152. Turn left and follow to the WMA.

CONTACT INFORMATION
Site open daily with some developed camping available. The $48.00 Public Lands Permit is required. Address: 1342 S. Wheeler, Jasper, TX 75951 / Phone: 936-639-8544 or 409-384-6894.

PRAIRIES AND PINEYWOODS - EAST
#26 Willow Oak Recreation Area

LOCATED 14 MILES SOUTH OF HEMPHILL ON TEXAS STATE HWY 87 ON TOLEDO BEND RESERVOIR

KEY BIRDS
Barred owl, yellow-billed cuckoo, eastern wood-pewee

BEST SEASON
Spring, fall, winter

AREA DESCRIPTION
Mixed pine/hardwoods, lakeshore, freshwater marshes, and hardwood sloughs

In the opinion of several birders interviewed, this is one of the best places to see and hear a variety of owls during the cooler times of the year, and early and late during the warmer months. Some calling has been successful here.

Willow oaks are a dominant feature at this recreation area. Habitats include mature mixed pine/hardwoods, lakeshore, freshwater marshes, and hardwood sloughs.

The upland forest provides habitat for birds such as barred owl, yellow-billed cuckoo, eastern wood-pewee, Acadian and great crested flycatchers, brown-headed nuthatch, red-eyed and white-eyed vireos, in addition to several warbler and woodpecker species. The shoreline and open lake area provide extensive opportunities to spot wading birds, eared and horned grebes, dabbling and diving ducks, and common loons.

DIRECTIONS
From Pineland, follow FM 2426 east for 10.0 miles to Hwy 87. Turn right (south) on Hwy 87 for 11.0 miles and follow to the entrance.

CONTACT INFORMATION
Site open daily. Developed camping available. There is a $2.00 day use fee and a $4.00 fee for camping and boat launching. Each site has a tent platform, table, and lantern post. Phone: 409-787-3870 or 409-565-2273.

Barred Owl

PRAIRIES AND PINEYWOODS - EAST
The Stark Tract

#27

LOCATED ON A STEEPLY SLOPED PENINSULA THAT EXTENDS INTO THE TOLEDO BEND RESERVOIR

KEY BIRDS
Little blue and great blue herons, and great and snowy egrets are found near the lake and pileated and downy woodpeckers

BEST SEASON
All seasons

AREA DESCRIPTION
Forest and lakeshore habitat

The Stark Tract is another east Texas tract being restored to open longleaf pine forest. At the time of this writing there are no active red-cockaded woodpecker clusters at this site, however management practices known to restore suitable habitat are now in progress. It is hoped that soon a cluster will be located in this area.

Pileated and downy woodpeckers are commonly seen here, along with eastern wild turkey, painted and indigo buntings, prairie and pine warblers, and various sparrow species.

Forest openings along the four miles of gravel road provide vistas of distant pine forests. The site is located on a steeply sloped peninsula that extends into Toledo Bend Reservoir. Frogs and turtles along with little blue and great blue herons, and great and snowy egrets frequent the coves.

DIRECTIONS
From Pineland, follow FM 2426 east for 10.0 miles to Hwy 87. Take Hwy 87 south approximately 10.0 miles to FM 255 East. Follow FM 255 East to FR 196 and head left for 4.0 miles to the park.

CONTACT INFORMATION
No fees are charged. Phone: 409-787-3870.

Snowy Egret

PRAIRIES AND PINEYWOODS - EAST
#28 Hillside Inn & RV Park

SOUTHEAST OF HEMPHILL, TEXAS ON THE TOLEDO BEND RESERVOIR

KEY BIRDS
American white pelicans, coot, crow, American kestrel, American robin, American woodcock, bald eagle, Brewer's blackbird, blue jay, Canada goose, cedar waxwing, eastern bluebird, roadrunner, mourning dove, cardinal, osprey, pine siskin, hummingbirds, tufted titmouse, yellow-crowned night heron

BEST SEASON
All seasons, barring weather

AREA DESCRIPTION
Lakefront and pine forest

This is an easy location for the traveling birder, and a good place to spend a few days while exploring the Toledo Bend Reservoir area. Facilities at this lakefront site include a seven-room inn, multiple RV slots, a boat ramp, pavilion, recreation room, and other amenities. The relaxed atmosphere of the facility invites you to sit on the porch swing and watch the birds at the feeders and near the water.

Wading birds can be observed in the cove and along the shoreline and a diversity of songbirds can be enjoyed during spring and fall migrations. Over 71 species of birds have been recorded at the site.

DIRECTIONS
From Hemphill, take Hwy 87 south 15.0 miles to FM 3315. Go east on FM 3315 for 6.0 miles to the T-intersection and turn right on Hickory Hills for 0.5 mile to the inn and RV park on the left.

CONTACT INFORMATION
Site access restricted. Call ahead. Phone: 409-579-3422
Website: www.toledo-bend.com/hillside
Email: cdillard78@gmail.com

House Finch

Gray Catbird

PRAIRIES AND PINEYWOODS - EAST
Lakeview Campground

#29

LOCATED ON TOLEDO BEND RESERVOIR

KEY BIRDS
Common nighthawk, Acadian flycatcher, gray catbird, red-eyed vireo, northern parula, broad-winged hawk, yellow-billed cuckoo

BEST SEASON
All seasons

AREA DESCRIPTION
Lakefront with mixed forest, pine forest, and cypress/willow sloughs

Toledo Bend Reservoir surrounds Lakeview Campground on three sides, providing visitors with unobstructed views of the lake year round. Operated by the Sabine River Authority, the campground is the eastern trailhead of the Trail Between the Lakes. Mixed forest, pine forest, and cypress/willow sloughs provide for a diversity of wildlife.

With lots of shoreline and coves, ample viewing of shorebirds and water birds is available year round. Resident woodland inhabitants include American kestrel, red-bellied, downy, and pileated woodpeckers, blue jay, Carolina chickadee, tufted titmouse, Carolina wren, pine warbler, and eastern bluebird. During the summer look for various warblers, thrushes, and buntings. Red-shouldered hawk, barred owl, common nighthawk, Acadian flycatcher, gray catbird, red-eyed vireo, northern parula, broad-winged hawk, yellow-billed cuckoo, summer tanager, and orchard oriole are particularly attracted to the area's sloughs. Look for migratory songbirds during the spring and fall months.

DIRECTIONS
From Pineland, follow FM 2426 east for 10.0 miles to Hwy 87. Turn right (south) on Hwy 87 for 3.0 miles. Turn left (east) on FM 2928 for 3.5 miles to end of paved road, continue 4.0 miles to the campground.

CONTACT INFORMATION
Site open daily. Developed camping available. An annual $30.00 day-use fee is charged, but birders should see if they are in possession of a Golden Age or Golden Access Pass. Phone: 409-787-3870 or 409-565-2273.
For more information about the usage permit go to:
http://www.fs.fed.us/r8/texas/passes/annual_day-use_pass_brochure_2011.pdf

PRAIRIES AND PINEYWOODS - EAST
#30 Indian Mounds Wilderness, Sabine National Forest

LOCATED EAST OF HEMPHILL, TEXAS ON TOLEDO BEND RESERVOIR

KEY BIRDS
American kestrel, blue jay, Carolina chickadee, tufted titmouse, Carolina wren, red-bellied, downy, and pileated woodpeckers

BEST SEASON
All seasons

AREA DESCRIPTION
This is a rough area and care should be taken before setting forth into this area

For the more adventurous naturalists, the 12,369-acre Indian Mounds Wilderness Area has a lot to offer. Be sure to bring your compass or GPS and carry a topographic map to get to the remote points of interest in this area. The trail system and old logging roads offer ideal hiking and birding opportunities for the more remote wildlife viewing. An active bald eagle nest can be observed in the Hurricane Bayou drainage.

Birding in the area is excellent. Birds observed year round include pied-billed grebe, little blue and great blue herons, cattle and snowy egrets, yellow-crowned night heron, Forster's tern, and belted kingfisher. Resident bird species include American kestrel, blue jay, Carolina chickadee, tufted titmouse, Carolina wren, red-bellied, downy, and pileated woodpeckers, eastern bluebird, and pine warbler. Chuck-will's-widow, woodthrush, American redstart, Louisiana water thrush, indigo and painted buntings, eastern towhee, and numerous warbler species frequent this area in summer. Other birds such as bald eagle, American woodcock, and grasshopper, Henslow's, and Le Conte's sparrows prefer the Indian Mounds proper during the winter.

This wilderness area is best suited for the energetic naturalist, whereas the nearby recreational area provides for a less strenuous adventure.

DIRECTIONS
From Highway 87 in Hemphill, travel east on Highway 83 for 6.7 miles. Turn south on FM 3382 for 3.7 miles then left on FST 130 to park entrance.

CONTACT INFORMATION
Site open daily with developed camping available. An annual $30.00 day-use fee is charged, but birders should see if they are in possession of a Golden Age or Golden Access Pass. Phone: 409-787-3870
For more information about the pass go to http://www.fs.fed.us/r8/texas/passes/annual_day-use_pass_brochure_2011.pdf

PRAIRIES AND PINEYWOODS - EAST

#31 Longleaf Roadside Pines Park

LOCATED AT THE JUNCTION OF TX 184 AND FM 2024, WEST OF HEMPHILL, TEXAS

KEY BIRDS
Pileated and downy woodpeckers, northern cardinal

BEST SEASON
All seasons, depending on the weather

AREA DESCRIPTION
Mature longleaf pines with a grassy understory

One of the earliest roadside parks or picnic areas in Texas, the Longleaf Pines Park was constructed by the Texas Department of Transportation in 1936. The original park benches still remain, guarded by the shade of mature longleaf pines. The grassy understory is dotted with wildflowers. A small riparian strip dissects the property, providing shrubs and taller herbaceous vegetation. While the park is relatively small, it is a good place to view birds and butterflies.

Bird species utilizing the area will vary according to the season, but resident pileated and downy woodpeckers, northern cardinals, Carolina chickadees, and tufted titmice remain year round. Look for Bachman's sparrow and painted buntings during the summer months and sedge wren, Henslow's, and grasshopper sparrows during the winter. Along the woody edges of the adjacent forest habitat look for northern bobwhite, brown thrasher, lark sparrow, eastern meadowlark, and loggerhead shrike.

DIRECTIONS
From Hemphill, go west on TX 184 for 4.7 miles to its intersection with FM 2024. The park is located on the southwest corner.

CONTACT INFORMATION:
No contact information, no camping allowed.

Northern Cardinal

PRAIRIES AND PINEYWOODS - EAST
#32 North Toledo Bend Wildlife Management Area

NORTHEAST OF BEAUMONT IN SHELBY COUNTY, ADJACENT TO TOLEDO BEND RESERVOIR

KEY BIRDS
Mallard, wood duck, gadwalls, wigeon, pintail, green- and blue-winged teals, scaup, and hooded merganser

BEST SEASON
All season

AREA DESCRIPTION
Small lakes, bottomland hardwoods, pine ridges, and old fields

The Toledo Bend Reservoir is located on the Sabine River, which is a portion of the boundary between Louisiana and Texas. The Toledo Bend Dam was completed in 1969, and the reservoir is the largest man-made body of water in Texas.

Even before you arrive at the entrance to the 3,650-acre North Toledo Bend Wildlife Management Area (WMA), you'll pass through a swamp bottomland area filled with bald cypress and black gum trees heavily buttressed in the duckweed-covered waters.

Swede Johnson Lake, a 500-acre impoundment is managed for waterfowl. The Sabine River and the northern portion of Toledo Bend Reservoir border the wildlife management area.

Bird watching is good throughout the year. During the summer look for egrets, herons, dickcissel, scissor-tailed flycatcher, blue grosbeak, as well as indigo and painted buntings. Wood stork, sedge wren, white-crowned sparrow, white-throated sparrow, Lincoln's sparrow, and waterfowl such as mallard, wood duck, gadwalls, wigeon, pintail, green- and blue-winged teals, scaup, and hooded merganser are wintertime inhabitants.

In the spring look for prothonotary warblers in the area especially around Swede Johnson Lake. Other spring species include red-eyed vireo, yellow-throated vireo, northern parula, Louisiana water-thrush, Kentucky warbler, hooded warbler, Baltimore and orchard orioles, and summer tanager.

DIRECTIONS
Driving from Center, travel east 13.4 miles on Hwy 7 to FM 2787. Go south on FM 2787 for 2.1 miles to FM 139. On FM 139 go south 2 miles to FM 2572. Go east 1.6 miles to entrance of the WMA.

PRAIRIES AND PINEYWOODS EAST

CONTACT INFORMATION

Site open daily with developed camping available. Fee charged. Ron Randle, Sabine River Authority of Texas, 1805 E Lufkin, Lufkin, TX 75901 / Phone: 936-569-8547 or 936-639-1879

Wood Duck

PRAIRIES AND PINEYWOODS - EAST
#33 Robinson's Lodge on Toledo Bend Reservoir

THIS IS A PRIVATE BUSINESS LOCATED ON THE NORTHERN SECTION OF TOLEDO BEND RESERVOIR

KEY BIRDS
Red-bellied, downy, and pileated woodpeckers, blue jay, Carolina chickadee, American kestrel

BEST SEASON
Winter, spring, and summer

AREA DESCRIPTION
Pine and hardwood forests and lake and pond-side habitat

Robinson's Lodge is located on a secluded cove of Toledo Bend Reservoir surrounded by the Sabine National Forest. The spacious lodge sleeps up to 20 people and offers a large front porch filled with rocking chairs, where one can watch birds and enjoy the peaceful surroundings.

Amenities include five acres of lakefront property, a boat ramp, and boat house. The owner is an expert fishing guide and can show you lots of wonderful places to wet a line or just enjoy the pristine beauty of east Texas.

Visitors can venture into the adjacent Sabine National Forest to discover resident pine forest species such as red-bellied, downy, and pileated woodpeckers, blue jay, Carolina chickadee, American kestrel, tufted titmouse, Carolina wren, pine warbler, and eastern bluebird.

During the warm summer months look for woodthrush, white-eyed vireo, blue grosbeak, summer tanager, hooded warbler, American redstart, indigo and painted buntings, and eastern towhee.

DIRECTIONS
From Loop 500 in Center, take Hwy 87 for 5.5 miles to FM 417 in Shelbyville. Turn left on FM 417, continue 1.3 miles to FM 2694 and bear right at the fork in the road. Follow FM 2694 for 9.5 miles to the intersection of FM 139. Turn right on FM 139 for 0.2 mile to the first left, FM 2694. Turn left and follow FM 2694 for 2.5 miles to FM 3172. Turn right and go 1.3 miles to the first left. Turn left on FR 100A and go 0.9 mile to the first gravel road on the left. Turn left and go 0.4 mile to the Robinson's Lodge mailbox; turn left and follow to the lodge.

PRAIRIES AND PINEYWOODS EAST

CONTACT INFORMATION

Site access restricted and reservations are required. The Robinsons offer a full service lodge as well as guided birding trips and a day-use area. Please call ahead for information.
Phone: **888-296-2211**
Website: www.toledobendlodge.com

American Kestrel

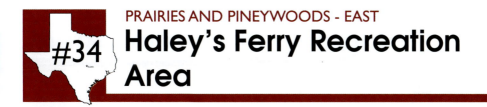

PRAIRIES AND PINEYWOODS - EAST
#34 Haley's Ferry Recreation Area

PRAIRIES AND PINEYWOODS EAST

LOCATED ADJACENT TO TOLEDO BEND RESERVOIR

KEY BIRDS
Red-cockaded woodpecker, Carolina wren, pine warbler, and eastern bluebird

BEST SEASON
All seasons

AREA DESCRIPTION
Pine forest and lakeshore

Haley's Ferry provides visitors with beautiful cove and lake views. The area is operated by the Sabine River Authority and is located within mature pine forest with a mixture of hardwoods.

A red-cockaded woodpecker cluster is located adjacent to the entrance road. The best opportunities to view these birds are at daybreak and early evenings, but please remember to minimize your disturbance.

Resident pine forest species include red-bellied, red-cockaded, and pileated woodpeckers, blue jay, Carolina chickadee, American kestrel, tufted titmouse, Carolina wren, pine warbler, and eastern bluebird. During the summer woodthrush, white-eyed vireo, blue grosbeak, summer tanager, hooded warbler, American redstart, indigo and painted buntings, and eastern towhee occur quite regularly.

Resident woodland species include blue jay, red-eyed vireo, northern parula, Acadian flycatcher, gray catbird, yellow-billed cuckoo, eastern kingbird, summer tanager, orchard oriole, yellow-throated warbler, prairie warbler, prothonotary warbler, and hooded warbler. Brightly colored neotropical songbirds also migrate through this area during the spring and fall months.

DIRECTIONS
From Center, follow Hwy 87 for 4.0 miles to Shelbyville, then go left (east) on FM 2694 for 15.0 miles to FM 3172. Turn right (south) on FM 3172 for 1.0 mile and then turn left (east) onto FS 100A for 2.0 miles to the entrance sign on the right.

CONTACT INFORMATION
This site is open for daytime use only. While you should always check on fees and possible changes, from 2000 to June 2010 they have held steady at $4 per campsite and $2 per vehicle for day use. Phone: 409-565-2273.

PRAIRIES AND PINEYWOODS - EAST
Ragtown Recreation Area

LOCATED ON TOLEDO BEND RESERVOIR

KEY BIRDS
Red-bellied, red-cockaded, and pileated woodpeckers, blue jay, Carolina chickadee, American kestrel, tufted titmouse, Carolina wren, and pine warbler

BEST SEASON
All year, weather permitting

AREA DESCRIPTION
Old pine forest with hardwood groves and lakeside habitats

Ragtown Recreation Area provides visitors with wonderful views of the lake and the surrounding Sabine National Forest. The area is operated by the Sabine River Authority and provides onsite amenities including a beautiful campground and one-mile nature trail. The trail follows the lake shoreline, then moves into a scenic mature pine forest with a sparse hardwood understory that provides excellent wildlife viewing opportunities.

Look for little and great blue herons, various egrets, yellow-crowned night and green herons, and belted kingfisher along the shoreline.

In the forest, watch for red-bellied, red-cockaded, and pileated woodpeckers, blue jay, Carolina chickadee, American kestrel, tufted titmouse, Carolina wren, and pine warbler.

Summer visitors are woodthrush, white-eyed vireo, blue grosbeak, summer tanager, hooded warbler, American redstart, indigo and painted buntings, and eastern towhee.

The area also abounds with migrating neotropical songbirds during the spring and fall months.

DIRECTIONS
From Center, follow Hwy 87 south for 11.0 miles, turn left (east) on FM 139 for 6.0 miles, bear right onto FM 3184 and follow 4.0 miles to the park entrance.

CONTACT INFORMATION
Site open daily with developed camping available. Fees are as follows: Day-use fee is $2.00 per vehicle, per day and camping is $5.00 single campsite, $8.00 double campsite per night, which includes one vehicle fee. Sabine River Authority of Texas, Rt. 1, Box 270, Burkeville, TX 75932 / Phone: 409-565-2273

PRAIRIES AND PINEYWOODS - EAST
Red Hills Lake

#36

Located on Highway 87 north of Milam, Texas

Key Birds
Carolina wren, brown-headed nuthatch, and yellow-throated, pine, Swainson's, hooded, and black-and-white warblers

Best Season
Spring, fall, and winter

Area Description
Mature pine forest

Red Hills Lake recreation area offers a picturesque 19-acre lake amidst a 17-acre mature pine forest. Visitors can drive or walk the main road or enjoy the two short hiking trails – Interpretive Trail and Tower Trail.

A walk across the grassy earthen dam offers a mid-canopy-level view into the riparian habitat below. Look for loggerhead shrike, brown thrasher, northern cardinal, northern mockingbird, lark sparrow, common grackle, eastern meadowlark, and dickcissel. During winter months, look for white-crowned, swamp, Le Conte's, fox, and grasshopper sparrows.

Hiking either of the trails or making your own trail through the pine forest, you can see species such as red-shouldered hawk, red-bellied woodpecker, downy and pileated woodpeckers, mourning dove, eastern wood-pewee, yellow-billed cuckoo, Carolina wren, and brown-headed nuthatch. Warbler species present include yellow-throated, pine, Swainson's, hooded, and black-and-white warblers. Red-eyed and white-eyed vireos, northern parula, blue jay, and American crow also reside in the area.

Directions
From the intersection of Hwy 87 and Hwy 21 in Milam, go north on Hwy 87 for 2.5 miles to the lake.

Contact Information
Site open daily with developed camping available. Operated by the Yellowpine Ranger District - U.S. Forest Service. A fee is charged. Phone: 409-787-3870.

PRAIRIES AND PINEYWOODS - EAST
Carrice Creek Bridge Area

#37

LOCATED ON THE EASTERN END OF THE CARRICE CREEK BRIDGE ON THE TOLEDO BEND RESERVOIR

KEY BIRDS
Anhinga, great egret, little blue heron, green heron, cattle egret, and red-winged blackbird

BEST SEASON
May and June

AREA DESCRIPTION
Roadside bridge near a common rookery area

This location is one where a quick stop and a casual glance will encourage you to drive on to other birding sites. However you should allow plenty of time to visit this site during May and June, because chances are very good you won't want to leave.

Located on the eastern end of the Carrice Creek Bridge over Carrice Creek on the Toledo Bend Reservoir, this rookery is alive with the sounds of nesting birds. The shallow waters support bald cypress, black willow, bays, and lotus pads. Look for birds such as anhinga, great egret, little blue heron, green heron, cattle egret, and red-winged blackbird nest and fledge their young here. The calls and cackles of these roosting birds bring the vegetation alive with sound and movement.

After the nesting season is over, the site still provides excellent bird watching opportunities. Look for ducks in the winter and the occasional bald eagle. So bring your binoculars and a camera with a long zoom lens to get a sighting or photograph of this captive audience during the nesting season.

DIRECTIONS
From the city of Milam, go east on Hwy 21 for 5.0 miles to the site. The site is located on the east end of the Carrice Creek Bridge.

CONTACT INFORMATION
This site is a day-use-only area. Phone: 409-565-2273.

PRAIRIES AND PINEYWOODS - EAST
Community Forest

#38

825 SPRING STREET
PALESTINE, TX 75801
THIS SITE IS LOCATED ACROSS FROM THE PALESTINE CIVIC CENTER

KEY BIRDS
Ruby-throated hummingbird, waterfowl, pine warbler, and tufted titmouse

BEST SEASON
Fall, as well as spring and fall migrations

AREA DESCRIPTION
Replanted pine forest, lakeside habitat

In the late 1940s, loblolly and slash pines were planted here, and are now harvested and sold to help fund recreational projects. Under special agreement, Texas Forest Service manages the forest as a "demonstration" of good forestry management practices. This 600-acre property was acquired for watershed protection of the two lakes - Upper and Lower Water Works Lakes - that served as the water supply for the City of Palestine.

Today, the forest is used primarily for recreation purposes. The Upper and Lower Water Works Lakes are teaming with fish, wildlife, and wetland vegetation and together cover 42 acres. Majestic pines line one of the entry roads along with dense underbrush in other areas. Recreation areas for picnicking encircle the lakes, and both lakes have boat ramps for fishing access. Fishing piers are located on both lakes and provide excellent access points not only for fishing but also for bird watching.

Birders are well advised to spend the required time walking the 1.7-mile trail around the 12-acre Upper Water Works Lake. Trees and shrubs along the path have been marked with interpretive signs. Bridges and walkways across low lying areas as well as a scenic overlook onto the lake are a perfect place to search for waterfowl and wading birds.

Birders should watch as well as listen for pine warblers, tufted titmice, white-eyed vireos, and the quick flying and well-defined ruby-throated hummingbird. While you are testing your ears, try to find the woodpeckers pounding on the trees for food, enlarging a hole, as well as looking for a mate during the breeding season.

DIRECTIONS
Beginning at the intersection of US 79 and US 287 in Palestine, go west on US 298/ SR 19 for 0.8 mile to Palestine Loop 256 turn south on S. Armory, go about 0.1 mile and the forest entrance is on the right; or continue 0.4 mile past the Civic Center and turn south on Upper Lake Road. There is a sign for Lakeshore Park and hiking trails.

PRAIRIES AND
PINEYWOODS EAST

Contact Information

This site is open only for day use.
Phone: 903-723-3014 or 800-659-3484.

Great Blue Heron

PRAIRIES AND PINEYWOODS - EAST

#39 Texas State Railroad State Park - Palestine Train Station

LOCATED ON PARK ROAD 70 OFF HIGHWAY 84 IN PALESTINE, TEXAS

KEY BIRDS
Crows, waterthrush, tanagers, and white-eyed vireo

BEST SEASON
March through November

AREA DESCRIPTION
Catalpa and sycamore trees, riparian corridor

The Texas State Railroad is one of the nation's largest and most unique steam train operations. Take the 50-mile Victorian-style train ride into Rusk and enjoy the beautiful scenery. The train is a fully self-contained railroad and operates on a varied schedule from March through November. The train passes through the I.D. Fairchild State Forest and provides wonderful wildlife viewing opportunities.

The raucous call of a family of crows can be heard above, while insects buzz along the trail. The woodlands offer a place of reflection and enjoyment whether bird watching or studying the abundant plant life.

The narrow creek flows over the exposed bedrock into the pool below. Listen and watch for the waterthrush that may be active around the water's edge. The enticing pond is loaded with dragonflies and aquatic plants and insects. Look along the water's edge for a large snag where red-shouldered hawks like to perch, or listen for summer tanagers and white-eyed vireos.

DIRECTIONS
Starting from the from the intersection of Loop 256 and Hwy 84 on the east side of Palestine, take Hwy 84 east 2.4 miles to the park entrance at PR 70.

CONTACT INFORMATION
Site open daily and there is $6.00 day-use fee and camping fees are from $12.00 to $25.00. Ticket for the train will be between $79.00 for seating to $325.00 for a round trip ride in the engine. Phone: 903-683-2561.

Summer Tanager

PRAIRIES AND PINEYWOODS - EAST
I.D. Fairchild State Forest

#40

NEAR THE TOWN OF RUSK, TEXAS

KEY BIRDS
Carolina wren, eastern phoebe, white- and red-eyed vireos, painted bunting, red-cockaded woodpecker

BEST SEASON
Nesting seasons, otherwise all year

AREA DESCRIPTION
Pines and mixture of upland and bottomland hardwoods

Upon entering I.D. Fairchild State Forest, you are immediately swept into a 2,740-acre wonderland teaming with birds, insects, butterflies, and other wildlife. The tall pines and mixture of upland and bottomland hardwoods offer excellent habitat for wildlife viewing.

The forest is designated as a "demonstration" forest where research areas have been installed to test various management techniques, forest genetics, and forest product utilization studies.

The endangered and spectacular red-cockaded woodpecker is a year-round resident of the forest. Early morning and late evening, especially during April through June, are the best times for viewing the birds as they are leaving and entering the roosting cavities. However, if you are in the red-cockaded woodpecker area during nesting season, please spend no more than 15 minutes in the area and cause as little disturbance as possible.

Ten miles of hiking trails meander through the forest and make their way to creeks and bottomlands, offering a variety of wildlife habitat. Don't leave your binoculars and spotting scopes in your car. This is also a great area for the photographer seeking some special images.

Hike or drive the numerous forest roads to see and hear the plethora of avian inhabitants. The forest is home to several species of woodpeckers, yellow-breasted chats, summer tanagers, indigo buntings, cedar waxwings, Carolina wrens, eastern phoebes, white and red-eyed vireos, painted buntings, eastern bluebirds, pine warblers, northern cardinals, and more.

An old bridge is located on one of the forest roads and provides a relaxing environment along a creek within the bottomland hardwood forest. Notice the gradual change in plant communities as you descend from the higher elevation upland areas into this riparian area.

DIRECTIONS

From the city of Rusk, take Hwy 84 west. The main body of the forest is 13.7 miles from Hwy 69 in Rusk, or 12.1 miles from FM 343 on the west side of town, and 3.8 miles west of Maydelle.

    Note: You will see signs on smaller, outlying tracts before you come to the main body of the forest.

CONTACT INFORMATION

Open daily with some developed camping available. Fee charged. Phone: 903-586-7545 / Website: http://txforestservice.tamu.edu

Red-breasted Nuthatch

PRAIRIES AND PINEYWOODS - EAST
Cherokee Rose B & B

#41

LOCATED A HALF-MILE WEST OF THE TEXAS STATE RAILROAD STATE PARK

KEY BIRDS
Ruby-throated hummingbird, owls, eastern kingbird, painted bunting, red-eyed vireo, pileated woodpecker

BEST SEASON
All seasons

AREA DESCRIPTION
Pineywoods and bottomland hardwoods

This charming bed and breakfast is nestled in the heart of pineywoods and bottomland hardwoods. The B & B is a reconstructed Dog Trot House similar to the style from early Texas. The large porches and numerous chairs provide ample opportunity for relaxing and watching the nearby bird feeders.

The 11-acre property provides a great opportunity for a stroll to see the abundant wildlife. The owner is a Texas Master Naturalist who is in the process of creating a butterfly garden. The surrounding natural habitat and landscaping are wildlife attractants.

Several seed and feeders are located off the back porch. Ruby-throated hummingbirds are some of the most frequent guests to the property. They can be heard buzzing and clicking as they carouse around the feeders. After feeding, the birds will zip within feet of your head as they fly in search of the perfect perch. If the lighting is right and they've slowed enough for a good look, you could glimpse the fiery red throat of the male.

Cardinals, blue jays, red-winged blackbirds, chickadees, mourning doves, and tufted titmice are frequent visitors to the seed feeders. Eastern phoebes also nest in the eaves of the B & B. Owls, eastern kingbirds, painted buntings, red-eyed vireos, pileated woodpeckers, and red-tailed hawks are also noted visitors to the property.

Stroll along the forest edge to the gazebo and spring-fed pond, which hosts catfish, bass, bluegill, and red-eared sliders. Excellent viewing opportunities of both young and adult night herons exist as they nest in the nearby trees. Bladderwort and hosts of other emergent wetland vegetation line the pond's edges and provide excellent feeding and resting grounds for wading and shore birds.

DIRECTIONS
From Hwy 69 in Rusk, take Hwy 84 west 4.5 miles to the B & B. From downtown on the square, take Hwy 84 west 3.2 miles to the B & B.

CONTACT INFORMATION
Site access is restricted. Room rates here begin at $85.00 a night. Phone: 903-683-1985 / Website: www.thecherokeerose.net

PRAIRIES AND PINEYWOODS - EAST

#42 Texas State Railroad Park - Rusk Train Station

LOCATED BETWEEN THE CITIES OF PALESTINE AND RUSK, THE RAILROAD IS ADJACENT TO US HIGHWAY 84

KEY BIRDS
Eastern bluebird

BEST SEASON
All year, especially summer and fall

AREA DESCRIPTION
Pine forests and hardwood groves

It is a great sign when eastern bluebirds welcome you to the park. The area is highlighted by a gorgeous 15-acre lake providing wetland habitats with bald cypress trees jutting out from the water surface along the northern end of the lake. Birders may hear the calls of barn swallows and the ever-noisy red-winged blackbird.

The parking area near the lake is lined with a variety of trees. As you enter the nature trail, a forested wetland appears. Observe the dark watermarks along the bases of the trees, a historical indicator of the natural ecological processes of this system.

A bird blind is located along the trail on a first-come basis and offers several viewing windows to view birds such as woodpeckers, chickadees, tufted titmice, pine warblers, Carolina wrens, and more. Birders should remember to look and listen for eastern phoebe and painted bunting in the tree branches.

The trail terminates at the campground near the restrooms and a playground. An additional trail traverses the southern side of the lake between the railroad tracks and the waters. Take the southeast side of the lake and travel to the station in Palestine. The 50-mile round trip steam-engine excursion takes about four hours.

DIRECTIONS
From the square in Rusk, take Hwy 84 west 2.7 miles to the park entrance. From the intersection of Hwy 69 and 84 West, go 4.0 miles to the station.

CONTACT INFORMATION
The Texas State Railroad Historical Park is no longer a part of the Texas State Park System and is operated by Heritage Railways. Railroad fees start at $10.00. Please all ahead. Texas State Railroad State Park, P O Box 39, Rusk TX 75785 / Phone: 903-683-5126, or campers call 512-389-8900.

PRAIRIES AND PINEYWOODS - EAST
Nichol's Green Park

#43

JACKSONVILLE, TEXAS

KEY BIRDS
Bluebirds, mockingbirds, and scissor-tailed flycatcher

BEST SEASON
All seasons

AREA DESCRIPTION
There are lots of trees and brush with some steep slopes

This is an excellent park for birders, and has a one-mile paved trail that provides access to some of the most beautiful sections of the park. The park trail winds down into riparian woodlands along a creek. The steep slopes and ample vegetation are home for many species of birds. There are several benches along the trail, so birders can stop for a brief rest or to watch a bird longer.

Cascading waterfalls flow down the native geologic formations of the area into a large reflecting pool below. The ferns and other understory plants seem to thrive in the cool, dark spaces of the forest. Watch for bathing or drinking birds at this location.

The trail passes through some open fields where bees may be observed busily pollinating the large clusters of McCartney rose shrubs. Birders should watch for sparrows, bluebirds, mockingbirds, and other edge or field-dwelling birds. In the summer, scissor-tailed flycatchers may be observed nesting in the trees near the open areas.

An interesting wetland area with a large observation platform is also located along the trail. Aquatic and emergent vegetation line the wetland edges, dominated by wax myrtle.

DIRECTIONS
At the intersection of US 79 and US 69 in Jacksonville, go south on US 69 for approximately 1.3 miles to Beaumont Street. Turn east on Beaumont Street, then right on Andrew Street; Nichol's Green Park is about 0.2 mile on the right.

CONTACT INFORMATION
This is a city park and users should limit their visits to daylight hours only. For further information phone: 903-586-5977.

PRAIRIES AND PINEYWOODS - EAST
Rose Rudman Park

#44

TYLER, TEXAS

KEY BIRDS
Pileated woodpecker, migrant songbirds, flocks of waterfowl, and several species of hawk

BEST SEASON
Winter and summer

AREA DESCRIPTION
Riparian hardwoods and creek side habitats

Visitors can take a leisurely stroll along the trail leading to the creek. Riparian hardwoods along the creek provide habitat for pileated woodpeckers, the largest North American woodpecker. Other resident species include northern cardinal, barred owl, red-headed woodpecker, American crow, American robin, wood thrush, blue jay, cardinals, eastern kingbird, eastern phoebe, bluebirds, and pine warblers.

During the winter expect to find a diversity of sparrows, including white-crowned, Harris, Savannah, song, and the more uncommon Le Conte's. Spring and fall bring migrant songbirds, flocks of waterfowl, and several species of hawks. The colorful American kestrel, the smallest falcon in North America, can be found perched on utility wires during winter months.

DIRECTIONS
At the intersection of US 69 (Broadway Street) and South Loop 323 in Tyler, turn east on Loop 323 for 0.3 mile to Donny Brook Drive, adjacent to Robert E. Lee High School. Turn right (south) on Donny Brook Drive and follow south to Shiloh Road. The park runs along Donny Brook to Shiloh in Tyler.

CONTACT INFORMATION
Open for day use. Phone: 903-531-1370.

Red-tailed Hawk

PRAIRIES AND PINEYWOODS EAST

PRAIRIES AND PINEYWOODS - EAST
Camp Tyler

#45

LOCATED FIVE MILES SOUTHEAST OF TYLER, TEXAS

KEY BIRDS
Lazuli bunting, crested caracara, peregrine falcon, roseate spoonbill, cinnamon teal, Smith's longspur, and white-winged dove

BEST SEASON
All seasons

AREA DESCRIPTION
Piney woods, scattered hardwoods, and lakeside habitat

Camp Tyler is located five miles southeast of Tyler, Texas and is one of the United States' oldest and most well-known outdoor education facilities.

In 1949, the 400-acre camp was founded by the Camp Tyler Foundation along the shores of Lake Tyler. During a typical year, Camp Tyler will provide unique outdoor experiences to thousands of youths.

Since 1949 Tyler Independent School District (TISD) has had a permanent Outdoor School at Camp Tyler. Annually, Camp Tyler has campers on the property 340 days out of the calendar year.

Located on 287 acres of variable habitat along the Lake Tyler shoreline, Camp Tyler provides excellent birding and wildlife viewing opportunities. The camp serves primarily as an educational facility serving the Tyler Independent School District and other youth groups in the east Texas area.

The site offers a diversity of habitats, including pine forest, deciduous riparian forest, shoreline, and open field/pasture. Over 220 species of birds have been recorded at this location. Common nesting species include wood duck, red-headed woodpecker, eastern bluebird, pileated woodpecker, summer tanager, blue grosbeak, yellow-breasted chat, painted bunting, and prothonotary warbler. Some of the less common species include lazuli bunting, crested caracara, peregrine falcon, roseate spoonbill, cinnamon teal, Smith's longspur, and white-winged dove. When birding throughout the grassland areas during the winter months, look for grasshopper sparrow and Henslow's sparrow. During the spring migration, over 29 species of warblers. Seven species of vireos have also been documented during spring migration.

DIRECTIONS
At the intersection of FM 848 and Spur 248 in Tyler, take FM 848 south 4.5 miles, and then turn left on McElroy Road (CR 2127). Go 0.6 mile and turn left into Camp Tyler.

Alternatively, from the intersection of Hwy 848 and 246 in Whitehouse, take 848 north 2.7 miles and turn right on McElroy Road; go 0.6 mile and turn left into Camp Tyler.

CONTACT INFORMATION

This area has restricted visitation and visitors are required to check in at the office. It would be best to call ahead.
Phone: 903-262-1225
Website: www.camptyler.org

Roseate Spoonbill

PRAIRIES AND PINEYWOODS - EAST
#46 Lake Tyler Concession Area #1

LOCATED ON LAKE TYLER

KEY BIRDS
Killdeer, great egret, little blue and great blue herons

BEST SEASON
All seasons

AREA DESCRIPTION
Lakeshore, deciduous forest, wetland, and open grassland

This site offers birders a view of multiple habitats within a very small area. Habitats include lakeshore, deciduous forest, wetland, and open grassland.

Watch for killdeer, great egret, little blue and great blue herons along the shoreline. In the winter, expect to see diving ducks, snow geese, or perhaps a bald eagle or Ross's goose. A variety of sparrows and flycatchers frequent the more open habitats. In the summer, look for painted buntings singing in the tall branches claiming a territory. Listen for the lonely call of the barred owl at dawn and dusk. Summer nesters may include Carolina chickadee, Carolina wren, tufted titmouse, American crow, northern cardinal, northern mockingbird, and red-headed woodpecker. Migrant bird species are most abundant during May and October.

DIRECTIONS
From the intersection of US 69 and South Loop 323 in Tyler, go south on US 69 for 6.9 miles to FM 346. Turn left and follow FM 346 east in Whitehouse about 2.7 miles to Concession Road. Turn left and follow Concession Road to the dam parking lot.

CONTACT INFORMATION
Site open for day use only.
Phone: 903-939-1538.

Killdeer

PRAIRIES AND PINEYWOODS - EAST
#47 Texas Freshwater Fisheries Center

FOUR MILES EAST OF ATHENS AND 75 MILES SOUTHEAST OF DALLAS

KEY BIRDS
Red-winged blackbird, northern cardinal, great egret, Carolina wren, common grackle, American crow, sedge wren

BEST SEASON
All seasons

AREA DESCRIPTION
East Texas pine habitat with man-made ponds

The Freshwater Fisheries Center is an innovative aquatic nature center and hatchery complex operated by the Texas Parks and Wildlife Department. This can be a great site for enjoying the afternoon, being close up and personal with several species of birds, and enjoying interesting static displays inside the center.

It is worth mentioning that the Texas Freshwater Fishing Hall of Fame is located in the center and, unlike many states, Texas has inducted two women into their ranks – Sugar Ferris and Kathy Majors.

Visitors can see the broad range of life that lives in the rivers and reservoirs of Texas in the 23,000-square-foot visitor center. Some of the features are 300,000 gallons of aquariums, a fishing museum, and a gift shop.

Observation blinds and kiosks throughout the property provide plenty of opportunities to observe and learn about birds, aquatic plants, and animals.

Due to the diversity of habitats, visitors can see a variety of birds, including red-winged blackbirds, northern cardinal, great egret, Carolina wren, common grackle, American crow, sedge wren, red-headed woodpecker, painted bunting, dickcissel, and lark sparrow. The diversity increases even more during spring migration.

DIRECTIONS
From the intersection of US 175 and SR 19 in Athens, go east on US 175 for 0.8 mile. Continue east on Crestway Drive for 0.5 mile. Bear right (northeast) on SR 31/ E. Tyler Street for 0.3 mile to FM 2495. Turn right on FM 2495 and follow it 4.4 miles to the Freshwater Fisheries Center on the right.

CONTACT INFORMATION
Site open for day use only. Regular admission is $5.50 for adults, $4.50 for seniors 65 and older, and $3.50 for children ages 4 through 12. Phone: 903-676-2277.

PRAIRIES AND
PINEYWOODS EAST

Boat-tailed Grackle

PRAIRIES AND PINEYWOODS - EAST
Purtis Creek State Park

#48

LOCATED ON **FM 316** NEAR **ATHENS, TEXAS**

KEY BIRDS
Eastern bluebird, painted bunting, northern cardinal, eastern wood-pewee, common grackle, mourning dove, Carolina chickadee, and tufted titmouse

BEST SEASON
All year, but especially migration months, April - May and September - October

AREA DESCRIPTION
Deciduous woodlands, open prairie, a large lake, and creek side habitat

This 1,582-acre state park offers deciduous woodlands, open prairie, and a large lake. Good fishing and shady campsites are the major attractions at Purtis Creek. The park's unique 355-acre lake offers plenty of shoreline and creek side habitats for birders.

Birders will enjoy a 1.3-mile hiking trail leading to primitive campsites, and along the northern shoreline, and into deciduous woodland. Resident woodland birds include eastern bluebird, painted bunting, northern cardinal, eastern wood-pewee, common grackle, mourning dove, Carolina chickadee, and tufted titmouse.

The extensive shoreline, coves, and snags attract a variety of water birds. Common species include double-crested cormorant, belted kingfisher, great egret, black-crowned night heron, little blue heron, white-faced ibis, eastern kingbird, and great blue heron. Watch for bald eagles during the winter months and a wide variety of dabbling and diving ducks.

Open prairie areas support red-shouldered hawk, American kestrel, and various sparrows, including the more elusive grasshopper and Bachman's sparrows. During migration months – April & May and September & October – the park is even more alive with visiting shorebirds, hawks, flycatchers, warblers, tanagers, and orioles as they drop in for food and rest.

DIRECTIONS
From the intersection of US Hwy 175 and North Loop 317 in Athens travel north on Hwy 175 for 9.0 miles to FM 316 and turn right (north) for 3.5 miles to the park entrance located on the left.

CONTACT INFORMATION
Developed camping available. Headquarters: 14225 FM 316, Eustace TX 75124
Phone: 903-425-2332
Website: http://www.tpwd.state.tx.us/spdest/findadest/parks/purtis_creek/

PRAIRIES AND
PINEYWOODS EAST

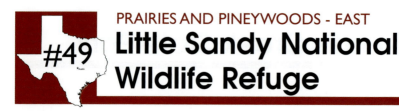

PRAIRIES AND PINEYWOODS - EAST

Little Sandy National Wildlife Refuge

#49

LOCATED ON U.S. HIGHWAY 80 BETWEEN HAWKINS, TEXAS AND MINEOLA, TEXAS

KEY BIRDS
Shorebirds, and barred, great horned, and eastern screech owls, and red-tailed and red-shouldered hawks

BEST SEASON
All seasons

AREA DESCRIPTION
Old growth bottomland forests within the Sabine River floodplain

Probably the last substantial block of old growth bottomland hardwood forest in Texas, this site offers a rare opportunity for nature enthusiasts. Visitors to the site will experience the rich diversity of life that characterizes old growth bottomland forests, and perhaps gain a greater appreciation for why this habitat is a high conservation priority in Texas.

Located within the Sabine River floodplain, this bottomland forest has been managed by the Little Sandy Hunting and Fishing Club since 1902, and was included in the National Wildlife Refuge system in 1986. A variety of wetland habitats comprise the 3,802-acre site. Two shallow lakes constructed early in the 20th century provide birders with sightings of many species of wading and shore birds. Several oxbow lakes have shrub swamps that are associated with them and provide diverse birding habitat. Because of the high quality and varied habitats, a large variety of birds can be viewed on the site during all seasons. Waterfowl, wading birds, and forest birds are especially notable. Watch for barred, great horned, and eastern screech owls, as well as red-tailed and red-shouldered hawks. Nesting birds include prothonotary warbler and northern parula. Cattle egrets nest in a rookery on one of the lakes. A visit to Little Sandy is a unique and memorable experience for anyone interested in birds and quality habitats.

DIRECTIONS
From the intersection of US 69 and US 80 East in Mineola, go east on US 80 approximately 12.6 miles. The NWR is bounded on the south by the Sabine River, on the north essentially by Hwy 80, and on the east and west by adjacent private property.

CONTACT INFORMATION
This site has limited access approval and is restricted during the fall hunting seasons. Call ahead Phone: 580-584-6211 or 903-769-2268 / Fax: 580 584-2034.

Reddish Egret and Snowy Egret

PRAIRIES AND PINEYWOODS - EAST
Tyler State Park

#50

**789 PARK ROAD 16
TYLER, TX 75706-9141**

KEY BIRDS
Chuck-will's-widow, blue-gray gnatcatcher, indigo bunting, white-breasted nuthatch, and pine warbler. During winter months, look for yellow-bellied sapsucker, brown creeper, eastern towhee, gold-crowned and ruby-crowned kinglet, cedar waxwing

BEST SEASON
All seasons

AREA DESCRIPTION
Steep terrain is found around the 65-acre lake among the pines and scattered hardwoods

The Civilian Conservation Corps constructed the 994-acre state park in 1934. Tyler State Park offers a 2.5-mile hiking trail, a 0.75-mile interpretive nature trail, a 13-mile mountain bike trail, birding, and some great wildlife viewing. The trails take visitors through varied habitats that support a wide array of birds and other wildlife. For the more adventurous, the park has a challenging mountain bike trail system that follows steep terrain around the 65-acre lake.

Pay close attention to the lake's shoreline for regulars such as wood duck and great blue heron as well as visiting gadwall, American wigeon, redhead duck, and spotted sandpiper.

During the summer months, some of the resident birds are the red-shouldered hawk, black and turkey vultures, eastern screech owl, yellow-billed cuckoo, wood thrush, red-eyed vireo, summer tanager, painted bunting, Louisiana waterthrush, red-bellied woodpecker, northern flicker, Chuck-will's-widow, blue-gray gnatcatcher, indigo bunting, white-breasted nuthatch, and pine warbler. During winter months, look for yellow-bellied sapsucker, brown creeper, eastern towhee, gold-crowned and ruby-crowned kinglets, cedar waxwing, yellow-rumped warbler, pine siskin, American goldfinch, and white-throated, Lincoln's, and song sparrows.

DIRECTIONS
From I-20 East in Tyler, take Exit 562 for FM 14. Go north on FM 14 for 2.0 miles to the park entrance, located at the intersection with PR 16.

CONTACT INFORMATION:
Site open daily with developed camping available. There are fees for day use as well as camping. Phone: 903-597-5338.

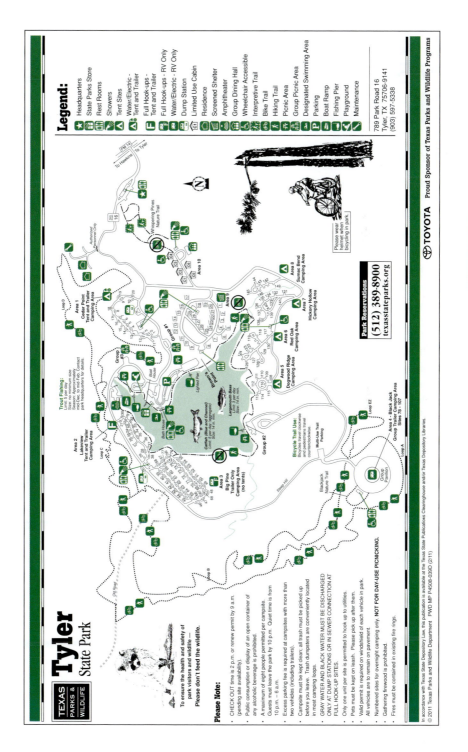

TEXAS
PARKS &
WILDLIFE

Tyler
State Park

To ensure the health and safety of
park visitors and wildlife —
Please don't feed the wildlife.

Please Note:

- CHECK OUT time is 2 p.m. or renew permit by 9 a.m. (pending site availability).
- Public consumption or display of an open container of any alcoholic beverage is prohibited.
- A maximum of eight people permitted per campsite. Guests must leave the park by 10 p.m. Quiet time is from 10 p.m. – 6 a.m.
- Excess parking fee is required at campsites with more than two vehicles (including trailers).
- Campsite must be kept clean; all trash must be picked up before you leave. Trash dumpsters are conveniently located in most camping loops.
- GRAY WATER AND BLACK WATER MUST BE DISCHARGED ONLY AT DUMP STATIONS OR IN SEWER CONNECTION AT FULL HOOK-UP SITES.
- Only one unit per site is permitted to hook up to utilities.
- Pets must be kept on leash. Please pick up after them.
- Valid permit is required on windshield of each vehicle in park. All vehicles are to remain on pavement.
- Numbered sites for overnight camping only. NOT FOR DAY-USE PICNICKING.
- Gathering firewood is prohibited.
- Fires must be contained in existing fire rings.

Legend:

- Headquarters
- State Parks Store
- Rest Rooms
- Showers
- Tent Sites
- Water/Electric - Tent and Trailer
- Full Hook-ups - Tent and Trailer
- Full Hook-ups - RV Only
- Water/Electric - RV Only
- Dump Station
- Limited Use Cabin
- Residence
- Screened Shelter
- Amphitheater
- Group Dining Hall
- Wheelchair Accessible
- Interpretive Trail
- Bike Trail
- Hiking Trail
- Picnic Area
- Group Picnic Area
- Designated Swimming Area
- Parking
- Boat Ramp
- Fishing Pier
- Playground
- Maintenance

789 Park Road 16
Tyler, TX 75706-9141
(903) 597-5338

Park Reservations
(512) 389-8900
texasstateparks.org

Please wear
helmet when
bicycling in park.

Trout Fishing:
Limit 5 per day
Size: no minimum size
Season: Approximately
mid-Dec. to mid-Feb. Contact
park headquarters for details.

Largemouth Bass
Limit: 3 per day
Size: 14 in. min.

Catfish (Blue and Channel)
Limit: per day (aggregate)
Size: 14 in. min.

Bicycle Trail Use:
Bicycles travel clockwise
and pedestrians travel
counterclockwise.

Area 2
Lakeview
Tent and Trailer
Camping Area

Area 3
Big Pine
Trailer Only
Camping Area
(no tents)

Area 1
Cedar Point
Tent and Trailer
Camping Area

Area 5
Dogwood Ridge
Camping Area

Area 6
Red Oak
Camping Area

Area 7
Hickory Hollow
Camping Area

Area 8
Sumac Bend
Camping Area

Area 9

Area 10

Area 4 - Black Jack
Group Trailer Camping Area
Sites 78 - 107

Group Pavilion

Multi-Use Trail
Parking

Loop EZ

Loop A

Loop B

Loop C

Loop D

Group #2

Group #3

Blackjack
Nature Trail

Steep Hill

Old Ring

Whispering Pines
Nature Trail

Boat House

Bath House

Lighted Pier

Authorized
Personnel Only

Boat House

To Hawkins   To Tyler

FM 14

PR
16

N

TOYOTA   Proud Sponsor of Texas Parks and Wildlife Programs

**PRAIRIES AND
PINEYWOODS EAST**

PRAIRIES AND PINEYWOODS - EAST
Sabine Bottom Wildlife Management Area

#51

NORTHEAST OF LINDALE, TEXAS

KEY BIRDS
Eastern screech owl, red-tailed and red-shouldered hawks, Carolina chickadee, tufted titmouse, northern cardinal, Carolina wren, and red-bellied and downy woodpeckers

BEST SEASON
All seasons, depending on the weather and time of year. This area is hunted.

AREA DESCRIPTION
Mostly bottomland hardwood habitat containing large stands of hardwoods such as oak, elm, and ash, and a diverse mixture of understory vegetation

Covering over 5,727-acres, this wildlife management area features important bottomland as well as hardwood habitat. There are many roads, trails, and parking areas that are available for visitor use. An information kiosk with a map of the area is located at the entrance. Visitors can enjoy 24 miles of trails accessible by bicycle or on foot. Mature oak, elm, ash, and other hardwood trees cover much of the WMA. Since it is located within the Sabine River floodplain, habitats include a variety of wetlands and oxbow lakes. Birders will see several species that include neotropical migratory songbirds, wood ducks, mallards, snowy egrets, and barred owls.

Watch for great blue heron, great egret, little blue heron, black-crowned night heron, and belted kingfisher along the shorelines of the oxbow lakes and the Sabine River. In the forest, watch for great horned and eastern screech owls, red-tailed and red-shouldered hawks, Carolina chickadee, tufted titmouse, northern cardinal, Carolina wren, and red-bellied and downy woodpeckers. During the nesting season, look for prothonotary warbler and northern parula. Swallow-tailed kites can be observed during migration.

Birders are advised to bring their own drinking water. There are no restroom facilities. Camping is available at Tyler State Park (call 903-597-5338), subject to park entrance and camping fees. Insect repellant is recommended for mosquitoes, and watch for poisonous snakes. Poison ivy is present and, during very wet conditions, rubber boots may be needed.

DIRECTIONS
From the intersection of US 69 and FM 16 East in Lindale, take FR 16 east 0.6 mile to FM 2710. Turn left on FM 2710 and go 5.0 miles north to the four-way stop at CR 4106. Go straight (north) on CR 4106 for 1.5 miles to the wildlife management area entrance.

CONTACT INFORMATION

The area is open year round, except closed for Special Permit hunts. Site access is restricted. Call ahead, and a $48.00 Public Lands Permit is needed for entry. Shaun Crook, 21187 CR 4106, Lindale, TX 75771 Phone: 903-881-8233.

Eastern Screech Owl

PRAIRIES AND PINEYWOODS - EAST

#52 Mineola Preserve on the Sabine River

LOCATED ON WOOD COUNTY ROAD 2724 – MINEOLA, TEXAS

KEY BIRDS
Blue grosbeak, summer tanager, eastern kingbird, eastern wood-pewee, Carolina wren, blue-gray gnatcatcher, northern parula, prothonotary warbler, wood stork, and white eyed, yellow-throated, and red-eyed vireos

BEST SEASON
Spring, fall, and winter

AREA DESCRIPTION
Pine uplands, open grasslands, bottomland hardwood forest

The Mineola Preserve on the Sabine River promises to be a premiere natural outdoor educational area, once site plans are fully developed. Covering 2,921 acres, the preserve includes various habitat types including pine uplands, open grasslands, bottomland hardwood forest, and pine woodlands. The diversity of habitats provides for a variety of wildlife, including over 150 bird species.

Future plans for the preserve include an elevated trail through bottomland hardwood habitat with viewing blinds at various points. There was no information at the time of this writing as to completion dates.

During the summer, look for painted and indigo buntings, blue grosbeak, summer tanager, eastern kingbird, eastern wood-peewee, Carolina wren, blue-gray gnatcatcher, white eyed, yellow-throated, and red-eyed vireo, northern parula, prothonotary warbler, and wood stork. Scope the areas of open water for a variety of wading birds and the open fields for northern bobwhite, greater roadrunner, eastern phoebe, and eastern bluebird. This is an excellent site is for migrating songbirds during spring and fall.

DIRECTIONS
From the intersection of Hwy 69 and FM 37 in Mineola, go south on US 69 for about 2.5 miles and turn left (east) on Wood County Road 2720 for less than 0.1 mile and then turn right (east) on Wood County Road 2724. The preserve is located to the right (south) as you drive one mile to the old railroad bed gate. The site is bordered on the south by the Sabine River, on the west by US 69, on the north by Wood County Road 2740, and on the east by a fence between the adjacent private property.

CONTACT INFORMATION
This site has a restricted access. Please call ahead for entry information. Phone: 903-569-6183.

Northern Pintail

PRAIRIES AND PINEYWOODS - EAST
Grand Saline Salt Marsh

#53

NEAR GRAND SALINE, TEXAS

KEY BIRDS
Snowy, piping, and semi-palmated plovers, spotted, least, and western sandpipers, and various waterfowl

BEST SEASON
Fall and winter

AREA DESCRIPTION
The site is restricted to roadside viewing only and the approaches to the Saline Creek bridges

The unique underground salt dome formation located close to the surface provides the basis for this inland salt marsh and unique habitat. The site has extensive mud flats with braided streams and an expansive salt marsh, especially prominent on the east side of the highway. Look for red-winged blackbird, killdeer, green heron, scissor-tailed flycatcher, great blue heron, belted kingfisher, and great egret in the summer. Recent surveys have indicated that this site is also an important pre-migration staging area for certain species of birds.

The highway travels through the salt prairie for 0.6 mile. Viewing may be done from a vehicle on the widened highway shoulders. What makes this site unique is its brackish water that attracts many bird species typically found farther south along the Texas coast.

During the winter months Virginia rail, snowy, piping, and semipalmated plovers, spotted, least, and western sandpipers, and various dabbling duck species are all known to visit the marsh.

The site provides an unusual opportunity to view an inland salt marsh and the diversity of wildlife it supports. Take in this area slowly, watching both the marsh and the branches of the overhanging trees.

DIRECTIONS
From the intersection of US 80 and FM 857 near the eastern city limits of Grand Saline, go south on FM 857 for 0.1 mile, crossing over the railroad tracks. At this point FM 857 enters the northern edge of the salt prairie. The salt marsh is to the east with dry salt prairie to the west.

CONTACT INFORMATION
Road and bridge side viewing during daylight only. A turn-around space is available 0.2 mile past the bridges at Van Zandt CR 1701 to the left (east) or vehicles may be parked at CR 1701 and then walk. For information call 903-962-5631.

PRAIRIES AND PINEYWOODS - EAST

#54 Tawakoni Wildlife Management Area

Pawnee Inlet, Caddo Creek, and Duck Cove Units

LOCATED NEAR THE TOWN OF LONE OAK, TEXAS

KEY BIRDS
Red-tailed and Cooper's hawks, Smith's and Lapland longspurs, pileated and downy woodpeckers, and yellow-billed cuckoo

BEST SEASON
All seasons

AREA DESCRIPTION
Highly diversified habitat of post-oak savannah, old-field, tallgrass prairie, and bottomland hardwood

The Pawnee Unit includes 1,381 acres of highly diversified habitat of post oak savannah, old field, tallgrass prairie, and bottomland hardwood associated with the Cowleech Fork of the Sabine River. The diversity of habitats provides for excellent wildlife viewing.

Throughout the bottomland and the hardwood habitats, watch for eastern kingbird, little blue heron, and barred and great horned owls. The old field and prairie areas support red-tailed and Cooper's hawks, Smith's and Lapland longspurs, and various sparrow species during the fall.

Situated along Caddo Creek before it flows into Lake Tawakoni, the Caddo Creek Unit conserves diminishing bottomland hardwood habitat. Open grassland habitat occurs along the southern end of the area.

Indigo and painted buntings, yellow-billed cuckoo, red-eyed vireo, and black-and-white warbler are found in wooded areas. During the winter, look for Smith's longspur, and vesper, Savannah, and Le Conte's sparrows in the open grasslands.

The Duck Cove Unit includes 792 acres of highly diversified habitats, which include post oak savannah, field, tallgrass prairie, and bottomland hardwoods.

Following the Lake Tawakoni shoreline, look for green and great blue herons, snowy egret, white pelican, and belted kingfisher. In the woodlands, look for orchard oriole, barred and great horned owls, yellow-billed cuckoo, eastern kingbird, and various woodpecker species. The grasslands support the stocky, broad-winged red-tailed hawk, the smaller Cooper's hawk, as well as American kestrel, eastern meadowlark, and northern bobwhite.

PRAIRIES AND PINEYWOODS EAST

DIRECTIONS

Pawnee Inlet Unit

At the intersection of US 69 North and FM 513 in Lone Oak, go left (southwest) on FM 513 for 0.5 mile. Continue west on FM 1571 for approximately 3.0 miles to the entrance.

Caddo Creek Unit

From the intersection of SR 276 and SR 34 in Quinlan go north on SR 34 approximately 2.0 miles. The site is located on the west, beginning at the south side of Caddo Creek Bridge. Access and parking are available on the old roadbed.

Duck Cove Unit

From the intersection of SR 276 and SR 34 in Quinlan, travel south on SR 34 for 0.5 mile to SR 276. Turn left (east) and go 1.1 miles to FM 751. Turn right (south) onto FM 751 and follow it south 6.9 miles to CR 3827. Turn right (west) on CR 3827 and follow it 1.3 miles to entrance.

CONTACT INFORMATION

Birders can check the Tawakoni WMA website for a list of commonly observed birds. A Public Lands Pass is needed for all state WMS. Shaun Crook, 21187 CR4106, Lindale, TX 75771 / Phone: 903-881-8233.

Harris's Hawk

PRAIRIES AND PINEYWOODS - EAST
#55 Sweeney Environmental Center

LOCATED ON FM 2101 NORTH OF QUINLAN, TEXAS

KEY BIRDS
White ibis, Bewick's wren, Smith's longspur, American avocet, and bald eagle

BEST SEASON
All seasons

AREA DESCRIPTION
Lakeshore, post-oak woodland, riparian woodland, and grassland

This location and birding area is operated by a partnership between Boles Independent School District, Texas A&M University in Commerce, and the Sabine River Authority. The Sweeney Environmental Education Center is dedicated to educating students about the natural world.

The habitats on this 350-acre site attract a diversity of birds, including white ibis, Bewick's wren, Smith's longspur, American avocet, and bald eagle. Specific to the shoreline are the white pelican, roseate spoonbill, tricolored heron, great egret, and great blue heron. Birders will find a walk into the woodland areas productive for prothonotary warbler, indigo bunting, Carolina wren, tufted titmouse, and several species of woodpeckers.

Future plans include greater access for the general public as they continue to grow as an outdoor education center.

DIRECTIONS
From the intersection of SR 276 and SR 34 in Quinlan, go north on SR 34 for 2.9 miles to FM 2101. Turn right (east) onto FM 2101 and follow 0.75 mile to the entrance.

CONTACT INFORMATION
Access to this site is currently by appointment only at 903-883-4464.

Northern Shoveler

PRAIRIES AND PINEYWOODS - EAST
Lake Tawakoni State Park

10822 FM 2475
WILLS POINT, TX 75169

KEY BIRDS
Belted kingfishers, northern shoveler, pintail, American wigeon, bufflehead, summer tanager, northern oriole, painted bunting, and eastern bluebird

BEST SEASON
Spring, summer, fall

AREA DESCRIPTION
Prairie, post oak woodland, and lakeshore

In comparison to some other Texas State Parks this park is a youngster, becoming a state park only in 2002. This 376-acre state park offers a variety of activities and amenities, including 5.5 miles of trails for birding. Habitats include tallgrass prairie, post oak woodland, and lakeshore.

Watch for birds such as summer tanager, northern oriole, painted bunting, and eastern bluebird along the nature trail. Eastern bluebirds have made good use of the 20 nest boxes erected within the park, and their offspring are plentiful. Watch the skies carefully for bald eagle, osprey, crested caracara, and Cooper's and sharp-shinned hawks. Along the lake's shoreline, look for feeding belted kingfishers and ducks such as northern shoveler, pintail, American wigeon, and bufflehead. The park also conducts guided night hikes for birders. Listen for the sounds of barred owl, great horned owl, and Chuck-will's-widow. The night sounds will also be filled with the rowdy calls of bellowing bullfrogs.

Migrating songbirds such as blackburnian and black-and-white warblers are plentiful during spring migration, because the wood-warblers are more often heard than seen during this time.

DIRECTIONS
From the intersection of US 80 and FM 47 in Willis Point, go north on FM 47 for 5.7 miles to FM 2475. Turn left (west) on FM 2475 and follow it north 4.0 miles to the park entrance.

CONTACT INFORMATION
Developed camping available. Normal state entry and camping fees apply.
Phone: 903-560-7123
Website: http://www.tpwd.state.tx.us/spdest/findadest/parks/lake_tawakoni/

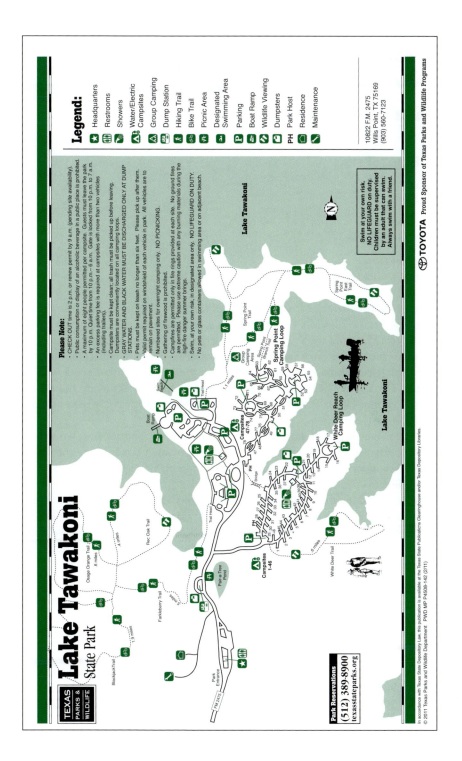

Lake Tawakoni
State Park

TEXAS
PARKS &
WILDLIFE

Park Reservations
(512) 389-8900
texasstateparks.org

Please Note:

- CHECK OUT time is 2 p.m. or renew permit by 9 a.m. (pending site availability).
- Public consumption or display of an alcoholic beverage in a public place is prohibited.
- A maximum of eight people permitted per campsite. Guests must leave the park by 10 p.m. Quiet time from 10 p.m. – 6 a.m. Gate is locked from 10 p.m. to 7 a.m.
- An excess parking fee is required at campsites with more than two vehicles (including trailers).
- Campsite must be kept clean; all trash must be picked up before leaving.
- Dumpsters are conveniently located on all camping loops.
- GRAY WATER AND BLACK WATER MUST BE DISCHARGED ONLY AT DUMP STATIONS.
- Pets must be kept on leash no longer than six feet. Please pick up after them.
- Valid permit required on windshield of each vehicle in park. All vehicles are to remain on pavement.
- Numbered sites for overnight camping only. NO PICNICKING.
- Gathering of firewood is prohibited.
- Campfires are permitted only in fire rings provided at each site. No ground fires are permitted. Please use extreme caution with any burning materials during the high-fire danger summer brings.
- Swim, at your own risk, in designated area only. NO LIFEGUARD ON DUTY.
- No pets or glass containers allowed in swimming area or on adjacent beach.

Swim at your own risk.
NO LIFEGUARD on duty.
Children must be supervised
by an adult that can swim.
Always swim with a friend.

Lake Tawakoni

Lake Tawakoni

Legend:

★ Headquarters		🚻 Parking	
🚻 Restrooms		🚤 Boat Ramp	
🚿 Showers		👁 Wildlife Viewing	
⚡ Water/Electric Campsites		🗑 Dumpsters	
⛺ Group Camping		PH Park Host	
♻ Dump Station		🏠 Residence	
🥾 Hiking Trail		✏ Maintenance	
🚲 Bike Trail			
🍴 Picnic Area			
🏊 Designated Swimming Area			

10822 F.M. 2475
Wills Point, TX 75169
(903) 560-7123

N

Osage Orange Trail   .6 miles
.4 miles
Rec Oak Trail
Blackjack Trail
Farkleberry Trail   .5 miles
1.9 miles
Pin-a-Tree Pond

Swim Beach
Trail Head
Boat Ramp
Trail Head
1.1 miles

Campsites 47-78

Group Camping Area

Spring Point Camping Loop

Spring Point Trail

Spring Point Branch Trail

Spring Point East Trail

PH
Bridge
Trail Head
.6 miles

Campsites 1-46

Park Entrance
FM 2475

White Deer Reach Camping Loop

White Deer Trail

🚘 **TOYOTA** Proud Sponsor of Texas Parks and Wildlife Programs

In accordance with Texas State Depository Law, this publication is available at the Texas State Publications Clearinghouse and/or Texas Depository Libraries.
© 2011 Texas Parks and Wildlife Department   PWD MP P4508-142 (2/11)

PRAIRIES AND
PINEYWOODS EAST

PRAIRIES AND PINEYWOODS - EAST
Wills Point Bluebird Trails

#57

PRAIRIES AND PINEYWOODS EAST

WILLS POINT, TEXAS

KEY BIRDS
Eastern bluebird

BEST SEASON
Spring, fall, and summer

AREA DESCRIPTION
Piney woods and old hardwood trees

Wills Point, a railroad town, earned the title of Bluebird Capital of Texas in 1995, three years after the local wilderness society started a campaign to bring the small bird home. The city of Wills Point and the Wills Point Wilderness Society are proud of their bluebirds.

The eastern bluebird once proliferated in the area, but its numbers declined due to the use of pesticides, some daunting winters, and the removal of old trees with natural nest cavities. The society began placing nest boxes on fence posts along the main roads into town. In no time, Wills Point had more eastern bluebirds than any other place in the state.

Follow the Bluebird Trail along major roads extending from downtown Wills Point. Eastern bluebirds use the hundreds of volunteer-maintained boxes along the fence lines to nest and rear their young each year, producing one of the highest densities of eastern bluebirds in Texas.

While driving along the trail, also watch for hawks as well as dickcissel, scissor-tailed flycatcher, painted bunting, and American kestrel along fence lines and utility lines. If you haven't stopped at Tawakoni State Park do so and look for barred owl, Louisiana waterthrush, red-bellied and downy woodpeckers, red-eyed vireo, and eastern wood-pewee along the wooded boardwalk trail.

DIRECTIONS
From Willis Point, go west on FM 751 for 0.9 mile to the Wilderness Trail entrance on the right. The Bluebird Trail spokes for miles from downtown Wills Point on every major roadway including FM 47, US Hwy 80, FM 2475, FM 751, Fm 2965, Hwy 64 and FM 3502.

CONTACT INFORMATION
Wills Point Wilderness Society, 469- 474-6123 / The Wills Point Chamber of Commerce, 903-873-3111, or on the web at www.willspoint.org / Lake Tawakoni State Park, 903-560-7123, or on their website www.tpwd.state.tx.us/laketawakoni / Let's not leave out the Texas Bluebird Society: www.texasbluebirdsociety.org

PRAIRIES AND PINEYWOODS - EAST
#58 Grace Creek Nature Area

LONGVIEW, TEXAS

KEY BIRDS
American robin, cedar waxwing, yellow-rumped warbler, and ruby-crowned kinglet

BEST SEASON
All seasons

AREA DESCRIPTION
Creek banks and city park grassy areas with large trees

Grace Creek and the nature area is a strip of green winding its way through central Longview, and provides some valuable wildlife habitat right in the middle of town.

During the winter months, birders should look for flocks of songbirds, including yellow-rumped warblers and ruby-crowned kinglets, while flocks of American robins and cedar waxwings strip the yaupon shrubs bare. During the summer, barn swallows nest under the many bridges crossing the creek and scissor-tailed flycatchers patrol the more open areas. In the spring, watch for nesting songbirds and an occasional raptor.

Residents during most of the year are northern cardinals, blue jays, and Carolina wrens. Watch for raptors such as the red-shouldered hawk hunting the woodland edges of open grass.

DIRECTIONS
From I-20 take Exit 596 onto US 259. Go north on US 259 for 3.7 miles to US 80 in Longview. Turn left (west) on US 80 for 2.5 miles to the nature area along Grace Creek, just after Spur 63. The nature area bisects Longview on US 80 about four blocks from downtown and crosses many neighborhood streets as well as Marshall Avenue, Cotton Street, and TX 31.

CONTACT INFORMATION
This site open only during daylight hours. For additional information call 903-237-1291.

American Robin

PRAIRIES AND PINEYWOODS - EAST

#59 Lake Gilmer Park & Kelsey Creek Sanctuary

LOCATED AT FM 852, 4 MILES WEST OF DOWNTOWN GILMER

KEY BIRDS
Summer tanager, red-bellied woodpecker, yellow-breasted chat, as well as herons and egrets

BEST SEASON
All seasons, with best times during migrations

AREA DESCRIPTION
Creek bank, along with wooded, grass, and brushy fields

This site was developed by the city of Gilmer. Plans include trails and wildlife viewing areas. Wetlands, open grasslands, and riparian areas provide habitat for a diversity of birds and other wildlife.

The Kelsey Creek Sanctuary, Inc. is a non-profit organization, and was formed and later became the city of Gilmer's Kelsey Creek Advisory Board.

Watch the trees along the creek carefully for prothonotory warbler, indigo bunting, summer tanager, and red-bellied woodpecker. The nearby brushy fields attract yellow-breasted chats, red-winged blackbirds, and dickcissels. Black vultures roost on the dam while the adjoining wetlands provide habitat for a variety of herons, egrets, and other wading and shore birds.

DIRECTIONS
I-20 take Exit 571A onto US 271, go north on US 271 for 12.7 miles to the intersection of US 80 and US 271 North in Gladewater. Drive north on US 271 for 14.4 miles into Gilmer. Turn left (west) on E. Redbud Street and follow it 0.3 mile to Cherokee Trace. Turn right (north) on Cherokee Trace and follow 2.5 miles to Lake Gilmer Dam. This property is downstream of the dam and west of Lake Gilmer. Lake Gilmer Park and Kelsey Creek Sanctuary Nature Trails are now open at Lake Gilmer located on Armadillo Road, just off Cherokee Trace.

CONTACT INFORMATION
This site is only open for daytime usage. For additional information Lake Ranger Danny Lancaster may be contacted at 903-843-8206, ext. 206 or 903-843-8209 / Webite: www.gilmer-tx.com

PRAIRIES AND PINEYWOODS - EAST
Caddo Lake Wildlife Management Area

#60

UNCERTAIN, TEXAS

KEY BIRDS
Great blue and little blue herons, common loon, horned and eared grebes, bald eagle, double-crested cormorant, and osprey

BEST SEASON
All seasons

AREA DESCRIPTION
Natural lake area with pine and hardwood forest

Birders will enjoy a slow trip through the pristine cypress swamps of 8,005-acre Caddo Lake Wildlife Management located in Marion and Harrison Counties, as they explore the backwater areas of this part of Caddo Lake.

It should be noted here that Caddo Lake is the only natural lake in Texas. All other lakes and reservoirs are man made.

Caddo Lake has been designated by the Ramsar Convention as "a wetland of international importance, especially as waterfowl habitat". The WMA contains permanently flooded bald cypress swamp and seasonally flooded bottomland hardwoods. Islands in the lake make up most of the landmass. An on-the-water trip is highly recommended to fully appreciate everything this WMA has to offer.

Summer birders can find green, great blue, and little blue herons, common loon, horned and eared grebes, bald eagle, double-crested cormorant. Osprey prefer the area during the cooler winter months, although some have been seen in residence all year. Ducks are known to winter here and include mallard, wood duck, gadwall, American wigeon, pintail, green- and blue-winged teal, scaup, northern shoveler, hooded merganser, common goldeneye, redhead, and bufflehead. Other aquatic species observed include Virginia rail, common snipe, Bonaparte's gull, ring-billed gull, and Forster's tern.

This is the place to take a canoe (or rent one) and spend some time enjoying the primordial beauty of nature as you course your way through the cypress trees of Caddo Lake Wildlife Management Area. Several heron rookeries are accessible in the backwater of Goat Island and Clinton Lake.

Caddo Lake has boat lanes marked by numbered posts, which will guide visiting boaters through the many coves and backwaters on the lake.

DIRECTIONS
From the intersection of US 59 North and SR 43 in Marshall, go right (northeast) on SR 43 for 27.0 miles. Several access points to the WMA are available along CR 805 (MC 3416), Grenning Road (MC 3402) off of Johnson Road from Hwy 43, city of Uncertain and CR 3502.

CONTACT INFORMATION
Users of the WMA are required to possess the Public Lands Permit from TPW. For more information, contact: Vanessa Adams, P.O. Box 226
Karnack, TX 75661 / Phone: 903-679-9817 or 903-927-2633.

Mallard

PRAIRIES AND PINEYWOODS - EAST
Caddo Lake State Park

#61

245 PARK RD 2
KARNACK, TX 75661

KEY BIRDS
Wood stork, pied-billed grebe, anhinga, green heron, yellow-crowned night heron, great blue heron, and little blue herons, snowy and great egrets

BEST SEASON
All seasons

AREA DESCRIPTION
Bald cypress swamp, mature upland pine forest and open grassy areas

Caddo Lake State Park gets its name from Caddo Lake, a sprawling maze of bayous and sloughs covering 26,810 acres of cypress swamp. The average depth of the lake is eight to ten feet, with deeper water in the bayou averaging 20 feet. Caddo Lake was the only natural lake in Texas until it was artificially dammed in the early 1900s. A new dam replaced the old one in 1971. Caddo Indian legend attributes the formation of the lake to a giant flood. Scientists believe the lake formed when floodwaters, blocked by massive logjams on the Red River, backed up into the Cypress Bayou watershed, forming the lake.

The park contains a diverse array of habitats including bald cypress swamp, mature upland pine forest, and open grassy areas. Naturalists can enjoy stately cypress trees, American lotus, and lily pads.

While birding along the pier in sawmill pond, watch for belted kingfisher, wood stork, pied-billed grebe, anhinga, green, yellow-crowned night, great blue, and little blue herons, snowy and great egrets, wood duck, and red-winged blackbird. Throughout the woodlands adjacent to the pond you may see several species including red-shouldered hawk, barred owl, Louisiana waterthrush, eastern kingbird, white-eyed, red-eyed and yellow-throated vireos, prothonotary, hooded, and pine warblers, American and fish crows, and various woodpecker species.

Hiking the 2.5 miles of trail winding through the pine forest, birders may see brown-headed nuthatch, northern flicker, wood thrush, American redstart, hairy woodpecker, American robin, Carolina chickadee, and tufted titmouse. In open grassy areas, watch for northern bobwhite, eastern bluebird, indigo bunting, dickcissel, greater roadrunner, eastern meadowlark, eastern phoebe, mourning dove, lark and chipping sparrows.

While in the area, be sure to stop at the high point — located at the southwest corner of Hwy 43 and FM 2198 intersection — to look for fall migrants. The Hwy 43

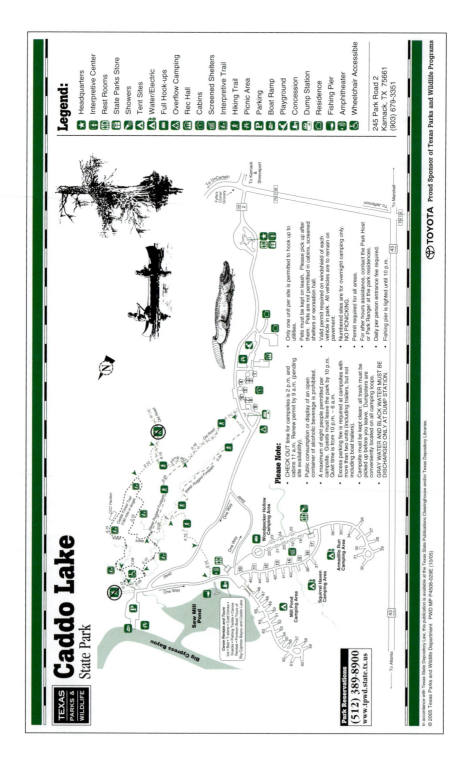

Caddo Lake
State Park

TEXAS PARKS & WILDLIFE

Park Reservations
(512) 389-8900
www.tpwd.state.tx.us

Legend:

- Headquarters
- Interpretive Center
- Rest Rooms
- State Parks Store
- Showers
- Tent Sites
- Water/Electric
- Full Hook-ups
- Overflow Camping
- Rec Hall
- Cabins
- Screened Shelters
- Interpretive Trail
- Hiking Trail
- Picnic Area
- Parking
- Boat Ramp
- Playground
- Concession
- Dump Station
- Residence
- Fishing Pier
- Amphitheater
- Wheelchair Accessible

245 Park Road 2
Karnack, TX 75661
(903) 679-3351

Please Note:

- CHECK OUT time for campsites is 2 p.m. and cabins 11 a.m. Renew permit by 9 a.m. (pending site availability).
- Public consumption or display of an open container of alcoholic beverage is prohibited.
- A maximum of eight people permitted per campsite. Guests must leave the park by 10 p.m. Quiet time is from 10 p.m. – 6 a.m.
- Excess parking fee is required at campsites with more than two units (including trailers), but not including boat trailers).
- Campsite must be kept clean; all trash must be picked up before you leave. Dumpsters are conveniently located on all camping loops.
- GRAY WATER AND BLACK WATER MUST BE DISCHARGED ONLY AT DUMP STATION.
- Only one unit per site is permitted to hook up to utilities.
- Pets must be kept on leash. Please pick up after them. Pets are not permitted in cabins, screened shelters or recreation hall.
- Valid permit required on windshield of each vehicle in park. All vehicles are to remain on pavement.
- Numbered sites are for overnight camping only. NO PICNICKING.
- Permit required for all areas.
- For after hours assistance, contact the Park Host or Park Ranger at the park residences.
- Daily per person entrance fee required.
- Fishing pier is lighted until 10 p.m.

To Atlanta

To Marshall

To Jefferson

To Karnack & Shreveport

To UnCertain

Forty's Corner Grocery

Canoe Rentals and Tours
Ice • Bait • T-shirts • Cold Drinks •
Snacks • Fishing Tackle • Canoe
Rentals • Pontoon Boat Tours of
Big Cypress Bayou and Caddo Lake

Big Cypress Bayou

Saw Mill Pond

Mill Pond Camping Area

Squirrel Haven Camping Area

Armadillo Run Camping Area

Woodpecker Hollow Camping Area

One Way

Swamp

Old Road

CCC Pavilion

Steep Rugged Footpath

TOYOTA Proud Sponsor of Texas Parks and Wildlife Programs

bridge (south side) at Big Cypress Bayou is a good spot to observe brown-headed nuthatch and warblers in the adjacent willow trees.

DIRECTIONS

From the intersection of US 59 North and SR 43 in Marshall, go right (north) on SR 43 for 14.7 miles to FM 2198. Turn right (east) on FM 2198 and follow 0.5 mile to PR 2. Turn left (north) on PR 2 and follow approximately 0.25 mile to the entrance.

CONTACT INFORMATION

This site is open daily, and developed sites for camping are available. The normal state park entry and camping fees apply.

Phone: 903-679-3351

Website: http://www.tpwd.state.tx.us/spdest/findadest/parks/caddo_lake/

Yellow-rumped Warbler

PRAIRIES AND PINEYWOODS - EAST

Coleman Lake Park

#62

JUST OFF I-30 IN SULPHUR SPRINGS, TEXAS

KEY BIRDS
Waterfowl, purple martin, chimney swift, and common nighthawk

BEST SEASON
All seasons

AREA DESCRIPTION
Large reservoir, creek bed, and riparian woodland habitats

This large reservoir surrounded by walking trails provides access to creek bed and riparian woodland habitats. Scan the lake for wading birds such as great blue, green, and little blue herons, and cattle, snowy, and great egrets.

In winter the lake hosts a variety of waterfowl. An Eagle Scout Duck Habitat Project and a School District Bluebird House Project have been completed on the nature trail.

Nearing the far end of the lake the nature trail enters some woodlands that provide habitat for white-eyed vireos and yellow-billed cuckoos. Other birds to look for include purple martin, chimney swift, and the common nighthawk.

DIRECTIONS
From I-30 in Sulphur Springs, take Exit 122. The south entry is on the north access road to I-30 approximately 0.7 mile east of Hwy 19. To reach the north entry, go north on SR 19 to Main Street. Turn right on Main Street and follow 0.4 mile east to the park entrance on the right.

CONTACT
INFORMATION
This site is open for day use only and no fees are charged. Phone: 903-439-1189, or Kevin McCarty, Director at 903-439-1189, or Jody Price, Assistant Director at 903 885-7541 / Website: www.colemanpark.com

Common Nighthawk

PRAIRIES AND PINEYWOODS - EAST
Cooper Lake State Park

#63

South Sulphur, Doctors Creek Units

NORTHWEST OF SULPHUR SPRINGS, TEXAS

South Sulphur Unit: Located on the southern edge of the 19,000-acre Lake Cooper.
Doctors Creek Unit: Located on the northeast side of Cooper Lake, this cozy unit offers a variety of outdoor opportunities. Facilities consist of campsites with electric & water hook-ups, limited use cabins, and screened shelters. The park also has restrooms and 6.2 miles of shoreline. A two-mile hike/bike trail is also available.

KEY BIRDS

Vagrant gulls intermixed with the abundant ring-billed gulls, killdeer, and eastern phoebes

BEST SEASON

All seasons

AREA DESCRIPTION

Lakeshore areas and pine and hardwood trees

The lake has evolved into one of the best all-around fishing lakes in the region. The park offers great views of the water and access to the wooded shoreline. During peak fishing months, the boat ramp and camping sites may be congested. Planning ahead and advance reservations are a must during peak months.

During the winter, the lake supports a variety of waterfowl and occasionally vagrant gulls intermixed with the abundant ring-billed gull. In the summer, look for killdeer near the parking areas and eastern phoebes perched on overhanging branches. Other resident birds include red-bellied woodpecker, brown thrasher, and red-eyed vireo.

DIRECTIONS – SOUTH SULPHUR UNIT

From I-30 in Sulphur Springs, take Exit 122 on the west side of Sulphur Springs. Go north on SR 19 for 11.0 miles to FM 71. Turn left (west) on FM 71 for 4.1 miles to FM 3505. Go north for 1.4 miles on FM 3505 to the park entrance.

DIRECTIONS – DOCTORS CREEK UNIT

The park unit is located on FM 1529 south of the towns of Cooper and Commerce. Follow FM 1529 to the park gate.

CONTACT INFORMATION

Note: A fee is charged to use the Tira boat ramp.
South Sulphur Unit: 1690 FM 3505, Sulphur Springs TX 75482 / Phone: 903-945-5256
Website: http://www.tpwd.state.tx.us/spdest/findadest/parks/cooper_lake/
Doctors Creek Unit: 1664 FR 1529, South Cooper, TX 75432 / Phone: 903-395-3100

PRAIRIES AND PINEYWOODS EAST

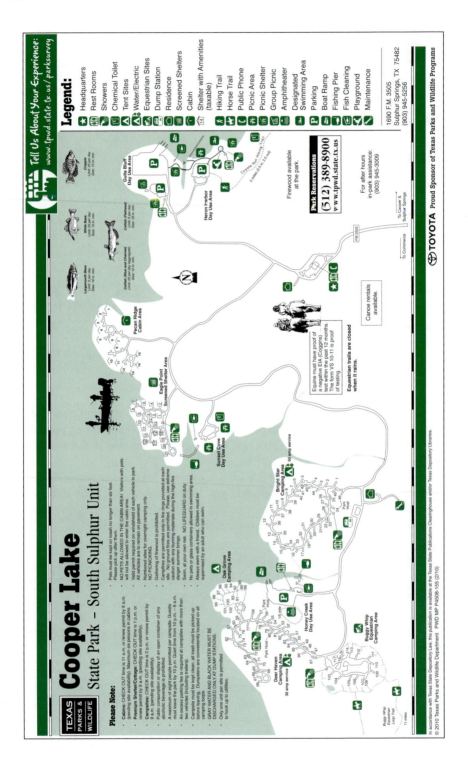

PRAIRIES AND PINEYWOODS EAST

Cooper Lake
State Park – South Sulphur Unit

TEXAS PARKS & WILDLIFE

Please Note:

- **Cabins:** CHECK OUT time is 11 a.m. or renew permit by 9 a.m. (pending site availability). Maximum six persons in cabins.
- **Premium Shelter/Cottage:** CHECK OUT time is 1 p.m. or renew permit by 9 a.m. (pending site availability).
- **Campsites:** CHECK OUT time is 2 p.m. or renew permit by 9 a.m. (pending site availability).
- Public consumption or display of an open container of any alcoholic beverage is prohibited.
- A maximum of eight people permitted per campsite. Guests must leave the park by 10 p.m. Quiet time from 10 p.m. – 6 a.m.
- An excess parking fee is required at campsites with more than two vehicles (including trailers).
- Campsite must be kept clean; all trash must be picked up before leaving. Dumpsters are conveniently located on all camping loops.
- GRAY WATER AND BLACK WATER MUST BE DISCHARGED ONLY AT DUMP STATIONS.
- Only one unit per site is permitted to hook up to utilities.

- Pets must be kept on leash no longer than six feet. Please pick up after them.
- NO PETS ALLOWED IN THE CABIN AREA. Visitors with pets will not be allowed to enter the cabin area.
- Valid permit required on windshield of each vehicle in park. All vehicles are to remain on pavement.
- Numbered sites for overnight camping only. NO PICNICKING.
- Gathering of firewood is prohibited.
- Campfires are permitted only in fire rings provided at each site. No ground fires are permitted. Please, use extreme caution with any burning materials during the high-fire danger summer times.
- Swim, at your own risk. NO LIFEGUARD on duty. Always swim with a friend. Children must be supervised by an adult who can swim.
- No pets or glass containers allowed in swimming area.

Tell Us About Your Experience:
www.tpwd.state.tx.us/parksurvey

Legend:

- Headquarters
- Rest Rooms
- Showers
- Chemical Toilet
- Tent Sites
- Water/Electric
- Equestrian Sites
- Dump Station
- Residence
- Screened Shelters
- Cabin
- Shelter with Amenities (taxable)
- Hiking Trail
- Horse Trail
- Public Phone
- Picnic Area
- Picnic Shelter
- Group Picnic
- Amphitheater
- Designated Swimming Area
- Parking
- Boat Ramp
- Fishing Pier
- Fish Cleaning
- Playground
- Maintenance

Equine must have proof of a negative EA (Coggins) test within the past 12 months. The form VS 10-11 is proof of testing.

Equestrian trails are closed when it rains.

Firewood available at the park.

Park Reservations
(512) 389-8900
www.tpwd.state.tx.us

For after hours in-park assistance:
(903) 945-3009

Canoe rentals available.

1690 F.M. 3505
Sulphur Springs, TX 75482
(903) 945-5256

TOYOTA Proud Sponsor of Texas Parks and Wildlife Programs

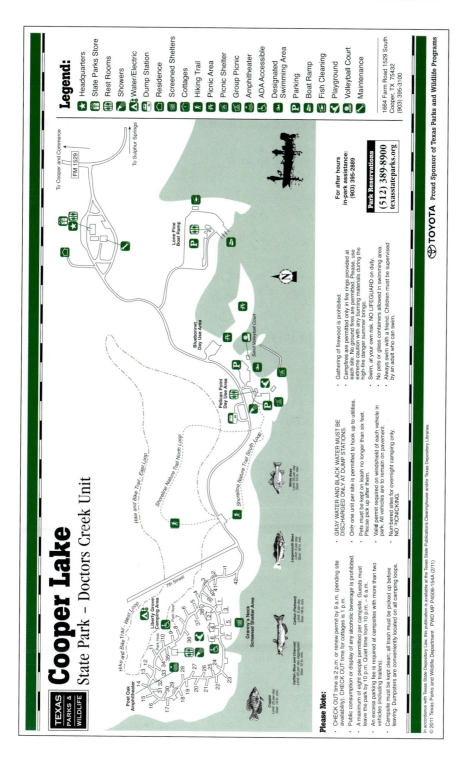

Cooper Lake
State Park – Doctors Creek Unit

Legend:

- Headquarters
- State Parks Store
- Rest Rooms
- Showers
- Water/Electric
- Dump Station
- Residence
- Screened Shelters
- Cottages
- Hiking Trail
- Picnic Area
- Picnic Shelter
- Group Picnic
- Amphitheater
- ADA Accessible
- Designated Swimming Area
- Parking
- Boat Ramp
- Fish Cleaning
- Playground
- Volleyball Court
- Maintenance

1664 Farm Road 1529 South
Cooper, TX 75432
(903) 395-3100

Park Reservations
(512) 389-8900
texasstateparks.org

For after hours
in-park assistance:
(903) 395-2889

To Cooper and Commerce

To Sulphur Springs

FM 1529

Lone Pine
Boat Ramp

Bluebonnet
Day Use Area

Sand Volleyball Court

Pelican Point
Day Use Area

Shoreline Nature Trail North Loop

Shoreline Nature Trail South Loop

Hike and Bike Trail – East Loop

Hike and Bike Trail – West Loop

7th Street

Post Oak
Amphitheater

Liberty Grove
Camping Area

Granny's Neck
Screened Shelter Area

Catfish (Blue and Channel)
Limit 25 per day
Size: 12 in. min.

Catfish (Flathead)
Limit 5 per day
Size: 18 in. min.

Largemouth Bass
Limit 5 per day
Size: 14 in. min.

White Bass
Limit 25 per day
Size: 10 in. min.

Crappie
Limit 25 per day
Size: 10 in. min.

Please Note:

- CHECK OUT time is 2 p.m. or renew permit by 9 a.m. (pending site availability). CHECK OUT time for cottages is 1 p.m.
- Public consumption or display of any alcoholic beverage is prohibited.
- A maximum of eight people permitted per campsite. Guests must leave the park by 10 p.m. Quiet time from 10 p.m. – 6 a.m.
- An excess parking fee is required at campsites with more than two vehicles (including trailers).
- Campsite must be kept clean; all trash must be picked up before leaving. Dumpsters are conveniently located on all camping loops.

- GRAY WATER AND BLACK WATER MUST BE DISCHARGED ONLY AT DUMP STATIONS.
- One one unit per site is permitted to hook up to utilities. Please pick up after them.
- Pets must be kept on leash no longer than six feet.
- Valid permit required on windshield of each vehicle in park. All vehicles are to remain on pavement.
- Numbered sites for overnight camping only. NO PICNICKING.

- Gathering of firewood is prohibited.
- Campfires are permitted only in fire rings provided at each site. No ground fires are permitted. Please, use extreme caution with any burning materials during the high-fire danger summer brings.
- Swim, at your own risk. NO LIFEGUARD on duty.
- No pets or glass containers allowed in swimming area.
- Always swim with a friend. Children must be supervised by an adult who can swim.

TOYOTA Proud Sponsor of Texas Parks and Wildlife Programs

PRAIRIES AND
PINEYWOODS EAST

PRAIRIES AND PINEYWOODS - EAST
#64 Cooper Wildlife Management Area

PRAIRIES AND PINEYWOODS EAST

NORTH OF SULPHUR SPRINGS, TEXAS

KEY BIRDS
Painted and indigo buntings, ruddy turnstone, dunlin, and interior least tern

BEST SEASON
Spring, summer, fall

AREA DESCRIPTION
Bottomland hardwood forests, mixed upland hardwoods, native prairies, flooded dead standing timber, riparian habitat, and shoreline

The Cooper WMA consists of 14,160 acres along the South Sulphur River. Located in Delta and Hopkins counties, the WMA is managed under a license agreement with the US Army Corps of Engineers. The WMA has designated hunting seasons and is open year round for fishing, hiking, biking, and wildlife viewing.

A portion of the WMA between the dam and SH 154 is a refuge, which currently allows hunting only during late winter for hogs. This access road running below the dam allows visitors to observe many species of birds early and late in the day.

An additional 12 access points on this area provide an abundance of wildlife viewing opportunities for the public.

The diversity of terrestrial habitats along with the 19,280-acre lake hosts an impressive variety of birds. Many rare sightings for northeast Texas have been documented in the vicinity of Cooper Lake. Numerous wading birds and waterfowl may be found on the lake and drainages, including resident wood ducks. Gulls, terns, and shorebirds are common, with uncommon species like the ruddy turnstone, dunlin, and interior least tern being spotted. Also, American white pelicans and wood storks congregate on the lake. Along the woodland edges, look for painted bunting and indigo bunting. Be especially watchful for black-and-white warbler and white-breasted nuthatch in the forested areas. Near and around the parking area below the dam, birders should watch for the scissor-tailed flycatcher and green heron.

The shoreline grass along the spillway access road is good habitat for eastern meadowlark and dickcissel. Lapland longspur, Smith's longspur, and many other sparrow species have been sighted during the winter months.

DIRECTIONS
From I-30 West in Sulphur Springs, take Exit 122 and go north on SR 19 for 14.3 miles to CR 4795. Turn left and travel west on CR 4795 for 0.8 mile to the Tira Boat Ramp Road. The WMA office is located on the Tira Boat Ramp Road on the left.

CONTACT INFORMATION

Open year round, but open for day use only. Howard Crenshaw, 829 CR 4795, Suphur Springs, TX 75482-0402 / Phone: 903-945-3132 /
Website: http://www.tpwd.state.tx.us/huntwild/hunt/wma/find_a_wma/list/?id=6

PRAIRIES AND PINEYWOODS EAST

Western Meadowlark

PRAIRIES AND PINEYWOODS - EAST
Gibbs Rockin' G Ranch

#65

NORTHWEST OF MT. VERNON, TEXAS

KEY BIRDS
Grasshopper sparrow, eastern meadowlark, crested caracara, and small songbirds

BEST SEASON
Winter, spring and summer

AREA DESCRIPTION
Open prairies, shady hardwoods, and dense deciduous forest in the bottomlands

This 2000-acre private ranch is home to diverse populations of wildlife. The open prairies surrounded by shady hardwoods are complemented by dense deciduous forest in the bottomlands. The ranch is dotted with numerous natural and man-made ponds, which attract all varieties of creatures. Feeding and watering Brangus cattle attracts cattle egrets many times of the year. During the mating season this nonnative species will have a light brown crest.

This private ranch is home to dozens of species of birds and other wildlife. Be on the watch for the pair of crested caracara (a.k.a. Mexican eagle)! They nest on the ranch and are often seen eating dead fish, turtles, and other carrion on the banks of one of the ranch's ponds.

The ranch offers visitors access to large open grasslands and bottomland hardwood forest along White Oak Creek. Grasslands support numerous grasshopper sparrows and eastern meadowlarks along with eastern kingbirds and dickcissels. Watch for indigo buntings and summer tanagers along the woodland edges and wild hogs and wild turkeys along the creek. Bald eagles have been known to nest near the creek. Visitors are asked to please keep a respectful distance from an eagle's nest. Winter is the best season to watch the open fields for passing flocks of geese and occasionally, longspurs.

DIRECTIONS
From Exit 146 on I-30 travel north on SR 37 for 1.4 miles to the intersection of SR 37 and US 67 in Mt. Vernon. Go west on US 67 for 4.2 miles to CR NW1018. Turn north onto Franklin CR NW1018, follow the meanderings of NW1018 for 2.8 miles to the Gibbs Ranch on the left (west). It is a large brown brick ranch house about 100 yards back from road; the entry is marked at the road.

CONTACT INFORMATION
This is a working cattle ranch, so the gates are always closed. Reservations are required, and visitors must check in at ranch headquarters prior to entry. Fees will run from $10 to $30, depending on the birder's requirements. No facilities are available, but there is some primitive camping. Phone: 903-537-2351 / Email: info@gibbsranch.org

PRAIRIES AND PINEYWOODS - EAST

#66 Dupree Park Nature Preserve

ONE BLOCK WEST OF MAIN STREET AND U.S. 37 IN MT. VERNON, TEXAS

KEY BIRDS
Painted bunting, downy woodpecker, and yellow-billed cuckoo

BEST SEASON
All seasons

AREA DESCRIPTION
Pine hardwood and creek side habitats

A 57-acre nature preserve with winding hiking trails adjacent to the historic association's 1868 home of Henry Clay Thruston, tallest soldier of the Civil War at seven feet, seven and a half inches. Opened in October of 2002, the preserve with a marked nature trail is open from dawn to dusk.

Birders using the area should listen for the songs of painted buntings. There is a two-mile trail leading through the preserve's 57 acres. The trail takes you through a maze of mesquite brush, so watch for singing field sparrows before the trail ends at the creek. During winter months, look for a variety of sparrows. Once you enter the creek bottom, listen for the quiet tapping of downy woodpeckers or the insect-like croaking of yellow-billed cuckoos.

DIRECTIONS
From Exit 146 on I-30 take SR 37 north 1.7 miles to CR NW1017. Turn left and follow CR NW1017 for 0.2 mile to the preserve on the right (Note: heading west on Mount Vernon's Main Street, cross US 37 and you are on CR NW1017).

CONTACT INFORMATION
This is a day-use site only. Locally guided nature tours are available. Phone 903-537-4760 or 903-537-2027.

PRAIRIES AND PINEYWOODS - EAST
#67 Choctaw Trails / Bluebird Trails

LOCATED BETWEEN HIGHWAY 271 AND TEXAS 37 ON HIGHWAY ON FM1896, BETWEEN MT. VERNON AND MT. PLEASANT

KEY BIRDS
Eastern kingbird, scissor-tailed flycatcher, painted bunting, and northern bobwhite

BEST SEASON
All seasons

AREA DESCRIPTION
Wooded areas with brush and creek bottom habitats

The Choctaw Trail is one of the earliest highways in Texas. Over a hundred years ago pioneers from the east traveled this road. Before European settlement, the Choctaw trail was part of a larger trading network used by Native Americans. Today, the trail passes through forest and fields, regularly crossing streams and creek beds.

Birders will find numerous species such as painted buntings and northern bobwhite in the grassy fields. Watch the roadside thickets for brown thrashers and overhead for red-shouldered and red-tailed hawks.

During the spring and summer, eastern kingbirds and scissor-tailed flycatchers line the fence rows while dickcissels call from every direction.

Winter birders will find a variety of sparrows along with northern harriers and American kestrels.

Northern Bobwhite

DIRECTIONS
From Exit 146 on I-30 take SR 37 north 1.7 miles to US 67. Go east on US 67 for 0.3 mile to CR NE2010. Turn left (east) on CR NE2010 for 4.1 miles (east 1.0 mile of FM 1896).

CONTACT INFORMATION
This site is open for day use. For more information call 903-537-2264.

PRAIRIES AND PINEYWOODS - EAST
#68 Lake Bob Sandlin State Park

LOCATED ON THE HEAVILY WOODED NORTH SHORE OF THE 9400-ACRE LAKE BOB SANDLIN, SOUTHWEST OF MT. PLEASANT, TEXAS

KEY BIRDS
Red-eyed vireo, great-crested flycatcher, and rough-winged swallow

BEST SEASON
All seasons

AREA DESCRIPTION
Wooded lake shoreline

Begin your day on the nature trail in this 640-acre state park, as it guides visitors through the woods and along the shore of the lake, providing limitless opportunities for wildlife viewing. In the open areas near the trailhead, look and listen for painted buntings. While walking in the forest areas, listen and watch for red-eyed vireos and great-crested flycatchers.

Along the shorelines you may see several species of wading birds. There are a variety of swallows that can be seen feeding, perching, and preening on the numerous dead snags. Watch for tree and rough-winged swallows among the more common purple martins and cliff swallows.

DIRECTIONS
Take I-30 East into Mount Pleasant, take Exit 160 and go left (south) on US 271/ W. Ferguson Rd. for 1.6 miles. Turn right (south) on FM 127 and follow it south 10.1 miles to FM 21. Bear left (south) on FM 21 for 0.9 mile to Lake Bob Sandlin State Park. / From I-30 West in Mount Vernon, take Exit 146. Go right on FM 37 for 0.8 mile to FM 21. Go left on FM 21 for about 10.0 miles to the park.

CONTACT INFORMATION
This park is open daily and offers developed camping. The normal state park entry and camping fees apply. Contact: 341 State Park Road, 2117 Pittsburg, TX 75686 / Phone: 903-572-5531.

Prairies and Pineywoods East

Lake Bob Sandlin
State Park

TEXAS PARKS & WILDLIFE

Please Note:

- CHECK OUT time is 2 p.m. or renew permit by 9 a.m. (pending site availability).
- Public consumption or display of an open container of alcoholic beverage is prohibited.
- A maximum of eight people permitted per campsite. Guests must leave the park by 10 p.m. Quiet time is from 10 p.m. — 6 a.m.
- Excess parking fee is required at campsites with more than two vehicles (including trailers).
- Campsite must be kept clean; all trash must be picked up before you leave. Dumpsters are conveniently located in all camping loops.
- GRAY WATER AND BLACK WATER MUST BE DISCHARGED ONLY AT DUMP STATION.
- Only one unit per site is permitted to hook up to utilities.
- Pets must be kept on leash. Please pick up after them. Pets not allowed in buildings.
- Valid permit is required on windshield of each vehicle in park. All vehicles are to remain on pavement.
- Numbered sites are for overnight camping only. NO PICNICKING.
- Gathering of firewood is prohibited.
- Campfires are permitted only in fire rings provided at each site. No ground fires are permitted. Please, use extreme caution with any burning materials during the high-fire danger summer brings.
- Swim at your own risk. NO LIFEGUARD on duty.
- No pets or glass containers allowed in swimming area.
- Always swim with a friend. Children must be supervised by an adult who can swim.

Park Reservations
(512) 389-8900
www.tpwd.state.tx.us

Texas State Parks Store
Firewood, gifts and state park maps are available at the park headquarters building.

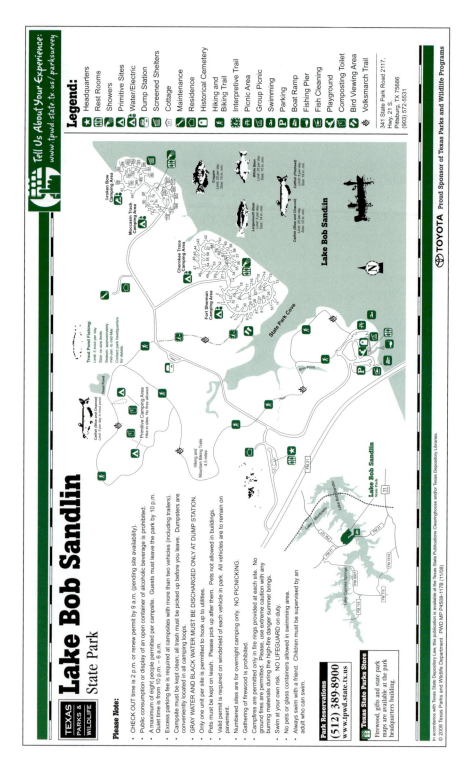

Tell Us About Your Experience:
www.tpwd.state.tx.us/parksurvey

Legend:
- Headquarters
- Rest Rooms
- Showers
- Primitive Sites
- Water/Electric
- Dump Station
- Screened Shelters
- Cottage
- Maintenance
- Residence
- Historical Cemetery
- Hiking and Biking Trail
- Interpretive Trail
- Picnic Area
- Group Picnic
- Swimming
- Parking
- Boat Ramp
- Fishing Pier
- Fish Cleaning
- Playground
- Composting Toilet
- Bird Viewing Area
- Volksmarch Trail

341 State Park Road 2117,
Hwy. 21 S.
Pittsburg, TX 75686
(903) 572-5531

TOYOTA Proud Sponsor of Texas Parks and Wildlife Programs

PRAIRIES AND PINEYWOODS - EAST
#69 Lake Cypress Springs

SOUTH OF MT. VERNON, TEXAS

KEY BIRDS
Wood duck, black-bellied whistling-duck, pine warbler, and brown-headed nuthatch

BEST SEASON
All seasons, with winter being number one

AREA DESCRIPTION
Large lake with tall trees and shoreline habitat

The best way to see Lake Cypress Springs is from the water. Boats may be rented from one of the numerous marinas around the lake.

Take the time to explore the shallow bays and watch for great egrets, great blue herons, and waterfowl such as wood ducks and black-bellied whistling-ducks.

In winter, the lake fills with ducks and attracts a sizeable flock of American white pelicans. Bald eagles also occur during the winter months and often perch on the tall pine trees flanking the lake. Pine trees along the shore provide habitat for pine warblers and brown-headed nuthatches as well as other woodland species. If a boat ride doesn't interest you, there are several access points around the shore where you can view the lake.

DIRECTIONS
From the intersection of SR 37 and US 67 in Mount Vernon, go south on SR 37 for 1.7 miles to the frontage road south of I 30. Turn left (east) and go 0.5 mile on the frontage road to FM 115. Bear right (south) onto FM 115 and follow south 13.0 miles CR 3007. Turn left onto CR 3007 and go 3.2 miles to the dam and picnic and camping areas.

CONTACT INFORMATION
Operated by the Franklin County Water District in Mount Vernon, Texas, this location is open daily, but call to check on unscheduled closers. There are six developed camping locations around the park where a fee is charged. Phone: 903-537-4536 / Website: www.fcwd.com

Black-bellied Whistling-duck

PRAIRIES AND PINEYWOODS - EAST
Bringle Lake

#70

NORTHWEST OF TEXARKANA, TEXAS

KEY BIRDS
Pileated woodpecker, great crested flycatcher, red-eyed vireo, and summer tanager

BEST SEASON
Early spring and fall

AREA DESCRIPTION
Lakeshore and pine forest

There is a lovely park — part of the Texarkana park system — along the shores of Lake Bringle that birders will enjoy. The habitat attracts woodland birds such as pileated woodpecker, great crested flycatcher, red-eyed vireo, and summer tanager. Watch for a variety of waterfowl in winter, including the bufflehead duck and the majestic white pelican. The lake's shoreline is a great location to watch for great blue and green herons.

DIRECTIONS
From I-30 in Texarkana, take Exit 220B for Richmond Road. Go left (northwest) on Richmond Road for 3.9 miles to where it merges with FM 559. Bear right (north) on FM 559 and follow it north 0.9 mile to FM 2311 in Wamba. Turn right (north) on FM 2311 for 0.6 mile to FM 2312/ Waterworks Road. Turn right (east) on FM 2312 and follow it 0.4 mile to its dead end at Brindle Lake Dam and spillway. CR 2312 runs into a city-owned road that is NOT an all-weather road. Heavy rains will make traveling this road rough, unless in a four-wheel-drive vehicle - but the road dries quickly.

CONTACT INFORMATION
There are no fees for day use, however campers must check in and pay a fee. Parks & Recreation, 3222 West 7th Street, Texarkana, TX 75501 / Phone: 903-798-3978.

PRAIRIES AND PINEYWOODS - EAST
#71 Sparks Lane

NORTH OF TEXARKANA, TEXAS

KEY BIRDS
Fish crow, Baltimore oriole, cattle egret, great blue, little blue, and green herons, and perhaps a yellow-crowned night-heron

BEST SEASON
All seasons, depending on the weather

AREA DESCRIPTION
Freshwater marsh with some flooded timber

The Texarkana area and all along Sparks Lane is an eastern birding destination, and has bragging rights on some several species not too commonly found throughout Texas. Some of these species include the fish crow and the Baltimore oriole and some visiting bald eagles. Some other species of interest are black vulture, purple martin, cliff and barn swallows, red-eyed vireo, great crested flycatcher, killdeer, and northern mockingbird.

The north side of Sparks Lane is bordered by a beautiful freshwater marsh. The marsh runs for one mile north of the road. During the summer, look for wading birds such as cattle egret, great blue, little blue, and green herons, and perhaps a yellow-crowned night-heron.

Wood ducks are year-round residents, and migratory waterfowl can be observed during winter. The marsh provides habitat for a variety of wetland species while surrounding open fields provide habitat for northern bobwhite, eastern kingbird, and dickcissel.

Watch for raptors such as red-tailed, red-shouldered, and Cooper's hawks hunting the open areas during the winter.

DIRECTIONS
From I-30 in Texarkana, take Exit 222 for Summerhill Road North. Follow Summerhill Road North 4.0 miles. Turn left (west) onto Sparks Lane. The marsh runs for 1.0 mile north of the road.

CONTACT INFORMATION
This site is only open for day use.
Phone: 903-798-3978.

Cattle Egret

PRAIRIES AND PINEYWOODS - EAST
Atlanta State Park
#72

ON LAKE WRIGHT PATMAN DAM IN CASS COUNTY, A FEW MILES SOUTHWEST OF TEXARKANA

KEY BIRDS
Bald eagle, red-eyed vireo, summer tanager, and great-crested flycatcher

BEST SEASON
Winter, spring, fall

AREA DESCRIPTION
Lakeshore and pine and hardwood trees

This beautiful 1,475-acre state park on Lake Wright Patman offers seasonal colors, variable terrain, pine forests, and great sunsets. Caddo Indians, the most culturally advanced tribe in Texas, once made this area their home. The park offers lake swimming, a nature trail, a five-mile hiking trail, boating, and fishing. Camping, picnicking, and biking are also popular activities.

Added to the numerous woodland species such as yellow-throated warbler, red-eyed vireo, summer tanager, and great crested flycatcher, there has been a resident pair of bald eagles who have nested and raised their offspring. The pair and their young have been known to frequent the park year round. Please keep your distance from nesting trees and sites.

The Wright Patman Lake's shoreline provides habitat for killdeer and other shore birds in migration as well as local scavengers such as black vulture and American and fish crows. The numerous vantage points to scan the reservoir make for excellent waterfowl watching in the winter.

DIRECTIONS
From I-30 in Texarkana, take Exit 220A for US 59 South. Follow US 59 South 21.5 miles to FM 96. Go west on FM 96 for 7.0 miles to FM 1154. Turn right (north) on FM 1154 and follow it 1.6 miles to PR 42. Follow PR 42 for 0.2 mile into Atlanta State Park.

CONTACT INFORMATION
Entrance Fees: $2 per day per person 13 and older, staying for day use only. Camping fees: Campsites with electric and water hookups are $12 per night, and campsites with electric, water, and sewer hookups are $14 per night. 927 Park Rd 42 Atlanta TX 75551 / Phone: 903-796-6476 / Website: http://www.tpwd.state.tx.us/spdest/findadest/parks/atlanta/

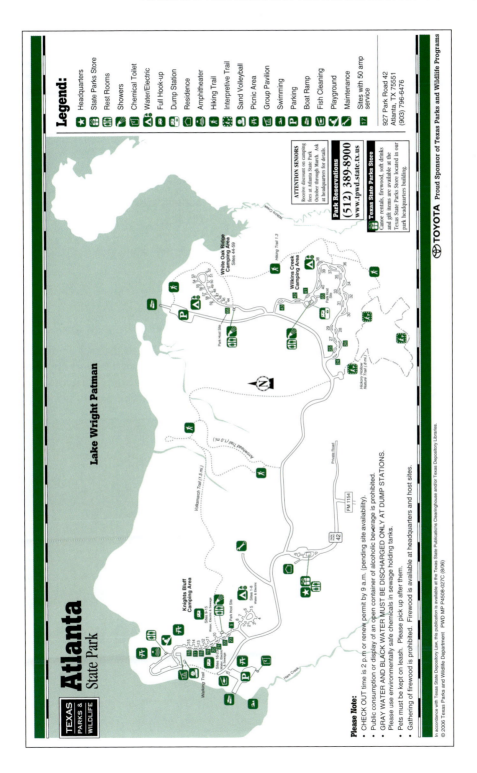

Atlanta
State Park

TEXAS
PARKS &
WILDLIFE

Lake Wright Patman

Legend:

	Headquarters		Residence
	State Parks Store		Amphitheater
	Rest Rooms		Hiking Trail
	Showers		Interpretive Trail
	Chemical Toilet		Sand Volleyball
	Water/Electric		Picnic Area
	Full Hook-up		Group Pavilion
	Dump Station		Swimming
			Parking
			Boat Ramp
			Fish Cleaning
			Playground
			Maintenance
17	Sites with 50 amp service		

ATTENTION SENIORS
Receive discount on camping fees at Atlanta State Park October through March. Ask at headquarters for details.

Park Reservations
(512) 389-8900
www.tpwd.state.tx.us

Texas State Parks Store
Canoe rentals, firewood, soft drinks and gift items are available at the Texas State Parks Store located in our park headquarters building.

927 Park Road 42
Atlanta, TX 75551
(903) 796-6476

TOYOTA   **Proud Sponsor of Texas Parks and Wildlife Programs**

White Oak Ridge
Camping Area
Sites 44-59

Wilkins Creek
Camping Area

Hiking Trail 1.3

Hickory Hollow
Nature Trail (.8 mi.)

Volksmarch Trail (1.5 mi.)

Arrowhead Trail (1.0 mi.)

Private Road

Park Host Site

Park Host Site

Knights Bluff
Camping Area

Sites 16-43
Water, Electric & Sewage

Sites 9-15
Water, Electric & Sewage

Sites 1-8
Water & Electric

Park Host Site

Walking Trail

Ham Creek

Wilkins Creek

FM 1154

PARK
ROAD
42

Please Note:
• CHECK OUT time is 2 p.m or renew permit by 9 a.m. (pending site availability).
• Public consumption or display of an open container of alcoholic beverage is prohibited.
• GRAY WATER AND BLACK WATER MUST BE DISCHARGED ONLY AT DUMP STATIONS. Please use environmentally safe chemicals in sewage holding tanks.
• Pets must be kept on leash. Please pick up after them.
• Gathering of firewood is prohibited. Firewood is available at headquarters and host sites.

In accordance with Texas State Depository Law, the publication is available at the Texas State Publications Clearinghouse and/or Depository Libraries.
© 2006 Texas Parks and Wildlife Department   PWD MP P4508-027C (8/06)

**PRAIRIES AND
PINEYWOODS EAST**

PRAIRIES AND PINEYWOODS - EAST
#73 Caddo National Grasslands

NORTHEAST OF BONHAM, TEXAS

KEY BIRDS
Summer tanager, eastern wood-pewee, painted bunting, field sparrow, yellow-billed cuckoo, and eastern phoebe

BEST SEASON
All seasons, depending on weather for winter viewing

AREA DESCRIPTION
Pine and hardwood forests with lakes and lakeside habitats

BOIS D'ARC TRAIL

A walk or ride along the Bois d'Arc Trail offers an introduction to the mosaic of habitats composing the Caddo National Grasslands. Birds seen along this trail include summer tanager, painted bunting, and field sparrow. Watch closely for eastern bluebirds in open areas. Others to watch for are the numerous Carolina chickadee and tufted titmouse flocks for neotropical migrants and the occasional nuthatch.

DIRECTIONS
From the intersection of US 82 and SR 78 in Bonham, go north on SR 78 for 0.8 mile to FM 898. Turn right (north) on FM 898 and follow it 5.9 miles to FM 1396. Go right (east) on FM 1396 for 7.2 miles to FM 2029. Turn left (northwest) for 3.8 miles to FM 409. Turn right (east) on FM 409 and travel 2.5 miles to the Bois D'arc Trailhead.

White-crowned Sparrow

Coffeemill Lake

Scan the lake in late summer for wandering terns, including the endangered interior least tern, which occasionally visits the lake from nesting habitats along the Red River. Check the campground at the north end of the lake for woodland species such as summer tanager and eastern wood-pewee. More open areas will attract insect eaters such as eastern kingbird and purple martin.

Directions

From the intersection of SR 82 and SR 78 in Bonham, go north on SR 78 for 0.8 mile to FM 898. Turn right (north) on FM 898 and follow it 5.9 miles to FM 1396. Go right (east) on FM 1396 for 7.2 miles to FM 2029. Turn left (northwest) for 3.8 miles to FM 409. Turn right (east) on FM 409 and travel 3.4 miles to Coffeemill Lake.

Lake Crockett

Lake Crockett, like Coffeemill Lake, is popular with fishermen and fish-eating wildlife. Green and great blue herons frequent the undisturbed banks and terns can appear from time to time. Watch for a variety of waterfowl during the winter months. The woodland surrounding the lake resounds in birdsong early in the day; for example, songs of northern cardinals and blue jays blend with the insect-like croaking of yellow-billed cuckoos or calls of eastern phoebes.

Directions

From the intersection of SR 82 and SR 78 in Bonham, go north on SR 78 for 0.8 mile to FM 898. Turn right (north) on FM 898 and follow it 5.9 miles to FM 1396. Go right (east) on FM 1396 for 7.2 miles to FM 2029. Turn left (northwest) for 3.8 miles to FM 409. Turn right (east) on FM 409 and travel 6.2 miles to Lake Crocket (west), continue 0.8 mile across the dam to Lake Crockett (east).

Lake Fannin

The lake provides habitat for a variety of waterfowl in winter and during migration, although wood ducks can be found year round. During the spring and summer, green herons nest in the trees along the banks while the woodlands around the lake host summer tanager, painted bunting, and blue-gray gnatcatcher, which are all easily heard and seen by birders. Patience is the key to seeing these birds.

Directions

From the intersection of FM 2029 and FM 273 in Telephone, go west on FM 273 for 6.8 miles to PR 34. Follow PR 34 for 1.8 miles to Lake Fannin.

Contact Information

This site is open daily and offers some developed camping. A fee is charged but no one was available for details. Call for information: 940-627-5475 / Website: www.fs.fed.us/r8/texas/recreation/index.shtm

Prairies and Pineywoods East

PRAIRIES AND PINEYWOODS - EAST
#74 Gambill Goose Refuge

ON GIBBONS LAKE NORTHWEST OF PARIS, TEXAS

KEY BIRDS
Waterfowl

BEST SEASON
Winter migration

AREA DESCRIPTION
Lakeshore and wetlands areas

Many years ago on the banks of Gibbons Lake, a man named John Gambill started feeding migratory geese on his land. The practice eventually attracted several thousand geese annually. When John Gambill died in 1961, his 600 acres became a permanent refuge for waterfowl, and is today managed by the city of Paris.

Although spectacular in winter, the lake hosts a variety of wildlife year round. Visitors driving along the western shore in summer could see downy and red-bellied woodpeckers, along with lark sparrows and dickcissels. The lake also attracts a diversity of swallows, with barn swallows and purple martins being most numerous. There is a healthy resident population of Canada geese that, at times, are joined by summering snow, blue, or white-fronted geese. The geese are commonly fed and the easy food source attracts dozens of sizeable western chicken turtles, red-eared sliders, and a good-sized gathering of several species of fish.

DIRECTIONS
From the intersection of US 82 and US 271 in north Paris, go west on US 82 for 1.3 miles to FM 79. Bear right (west) on FM 79 and travel 3.3 miles to FM 2820. Turn left on FM 2820 and follow it west 2.0 miles to the refuge road on the right. Turn right and go 0.6 mile to the lakeshore access road on the right.

CONTACT INFORMATION
This site is only open during the daylight hours. For additional information and feeding times call 903-784-9299.

Canada Geese

PRAIRIES AND PINEYWOODS - EAST
Lennox Woods Preserve

#75

NORTH OF CLARKSVILLE, TEXAS

KEY BIRDS
Brown-headed and white-breasted nuthatches, tufted titmouse, pine warbler, red-headed woodpecker

BEST SEASON
All seasons, but spring rates #1

AREA DESCRIPTION
Old-growth woodland of fully mature, virgin timber found in the state, mixed evergreen-deciduous forest of the shortleaf pine-oak series dominated by shortleaf pine, white oak, loblolly pine, southern red oak, red maple, and various hickories

Lennox Woods Preserve is located along State Highway 37 in Red River County, about 10 miles north of Clarksville.

The Martha Lennox Memorial Nature Trail takes birders through a variety of habitats from upland short leaf pine oak forest to bottomland hardwoods. A walk along the trails beneath the magnificence of old growth timber is a rare privilege provided at this preserve.

These mature forests provide habitat for a variety of woodpeckers. Red-headed woodpeckers may be seen in more open areas, while pileated woodpeckers are more common within the forest. During the spring, these trees welcome numerous wood warblers, with northern parulas and pine warblers singing from the treetops and hooded and Kentucky warblers chipping from dense brush along the streams. Late summer will produce flocks of Carolina chickadees, tufted titmice, and black-and-white warblers. These mixed flocks often host brown-headed and white-breasted nuthatches year round and the occasional red-breasted nuthatch in winter. While you are there, ask about an interpretive brochure and bird list.

DIRECTIONS
From the intersection of US 82 and SR 37 in Clarksville, drive north on SR 37 for 10.1 miles to FM 2118. Turn left (west) on FM 2118 and go 1.5 miles. Turn left onto CR 2227 a gravel road at the Mt. Pleasant Missionary Baptist Church sign. The entrance to the preserve is 1.4 miles from FM 2118.

CONTACT INFORMATION
Site open for day use only and is operated by the Texas Nature Conservancy. Please call: 903-568-4139 / Websites: www.nature.org/texas /nature.org/wherewework/ northamerica/states/texas/preserves/

PRAIRIES AND PINEYWOODS - EAST
Terrapin Hill

#76

NEAR CLARKSVILLE ON CR 4220

KEY BIRDS
Painted and indigo buntings, ruby-throated hummingbird, waterfowl, and wading birds

BEST SEASON
All seasons

AREA DESCRIPTION
Pine and hardwood forests with many wet areas

Birders will find numerous birdhouses and feeders throughout the gardens of this property that attract birds such as painted and indigo bunting, ruby-throated hummingbird, and several species of woodpecker.

Watch the tall pines to the rear of the house buzz with pine warblers, and a pair of prothonotary warblers regularly nest on the porch. Behind the house, a series of trails allow visitors to explore mixed hardwood forest.

There are also additional trails across from the main house that lead downhill to the lake, where belted kingfishers and great blue and green herons can be seen stalking

prey in the shallows. Watch for a variety of waterfowl during the winter. Winter has brought more than 100 goldfinches to visit the property, while summer visitors should search the woods for yellow-billed cuckoos during the day and listen for the songs of whip-poor-wills during the early evenings.

DIRECTIONS
From the intersection of US 82 and SR 37 in Clarksville, go east on US 82 for 9.0 miles to FM 44. Turn right (south) on FM 44 and follow it 5.6 miles to CR 4230. Go right on CR 4230 and drive 1.4 miles to CR 4220. Turn left on CR 4220 and drive up hill to Terrapin Hill on the right after approximately 100 yards.

CONTACT INFORMATION
Site open for day use. For more information call 903-697-3619.

Northern Waterthrush

Canada Geese

PRAIRIES AND PINEYWOODS - EAST
#77 Daingerfield State Park

SOUTHEAST OF DAINGERFIELD, TEXAS

KEY BIRDS
Acadian flycatcher, eastern kingbird, brown thrasher, blue-gray gnatcatcher, wood thrush, and broad-winged hawk

BEST SEASON
All seasons

AREA DESCRIPTION
Pine forests surrounding a lake

This 551-acre state park includes the 80-acre Lake Daingerfield. Surrounded by pine forests, a trail takes birders into the trees for slow walks observe the many species attracted here.

During fall and spring migrations there have been over 172 species of birds observed in the park. The fall migration of broad-winged hawks is a spectacular annual event. During the last two weeks in September over 3,700 broad-winged hawks have been counted in a single day.

Other species observed during this time include sharp-shinned and Cooper's hawks, osprey, American kestrel, Mississippi kite, fleet merlin, peregrine falcon, wood stork, anhinga, double-crested cormorant, and American white pelican.

During the spring and summer expect to see red-bellied, pileated, and downy woodpeckers, great crested and Acadian flycatchers, eastern kingbird, brown thrasher, blue-gray gnatcatcher, wood thrush, summer tanager, and several species of vireos and warblers. The open areas of the park support killdeer, indigo bunting, eastern meadowlark, field and chipping sparrows, mourning dove, eastern bluebird, and eastern phoebe.

DIRECTIONS
From Daingerfield take SH 11/49 east for 3.0 miles to PR 17 and the park entrance.

CONTACT INFORMATION
In 2010, the park underwent major renovation to its facilities and campgrounds. Fees apply for entry and camping. There are also cabins that can be rented. Phone: 903-645-2921. See the appendix for information on Texas State Parks and Wildlife Management Areas.

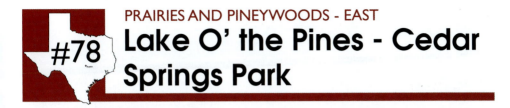

PRAIRIES AND PINEYWOODS - EAST

#78 Lake O' the Pines - Cedar Springs Park

SOUTH SHORE OF LAKE, SOUTHEAST OF DAINGERFIELD, TEXAS

KEY BIRDS
Osprey, cormorant, belted kingfisher

BEST SEASON
All seasons

AREA DESCRIPTION
Lakeside areas with flooded timber and rotted stumps

Cedar Springs Park provides an excellent vantage to scan the lake just south of the SR 155 bridge, with its numerous exposed snags, pilings, and other convenient perches for osprey and cormorants in winter and during migrations, and belted kingfisher year round.

The water's edge is perfect for great blue heron and great egret, but almost anything could turn up in late summer when juvenile birds start wandering away from the coast. Check the tall pines and dense thickets of the park for neotropical migrants such as the white-eyed vireo, often heard scolding from the brush.

DIRECTIONS
From the intersection of US 259 and SR 155 south of Lone Star, follow SR 155 east 0.6 mile to Upshur County Landing Road on the right. Turn right (south) and go 1.3 miles to Cedar Springs Park.

CONTACT INFORMATION
Boaters must pay a fee to use the ramp. The park is open all year and operated by US Army Corps of Engineers.
Phone 903-665-2336 or 903-665-3911
Website: http://155.84.70.101/lakeopines/

PRAIRIES AND
PINEYWOODS EAST

Osprey

Prairies & Pineywoods West

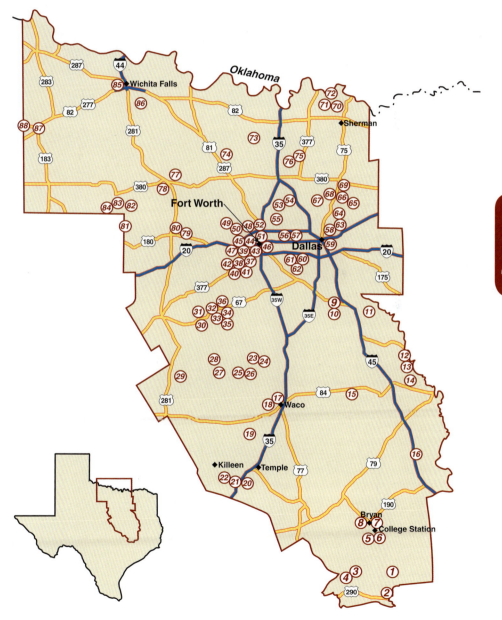

PRAIRIES & PINEYWOODS WEST LOCATIONS

#1- Washington-On-The-Brazos State Historic Park
#2- Chappell Hill / Brazos River Valley Trail
#3- Somerville Lake
#4- Lake Somerville State Park Complex
#5- Lick Creek Park
#6- D.A. "Andy" Anderson Arboretum
#7- Brazos Valley Museum of Natural History
#8- Lake Bryan
#9- Bluebonnet Park
#10- Buffalo Creek Wetland
#11- Reed Wildlife Ranch
#12- Richland Creek Wildlife Management Area
#13- Gus Engeling Wildlife Management Area
#14- Fairfield Lake State Park
#15- Fort Parker State Park
#16- Fort Boggy State Park
#17- Cameron Park
#18- Lake Waco Wetlands
#19- Mother Neff State Park
#20- Miller Springs Natural Area
#21- Stillhouse Hollow Lake - Chalk Ridge Falls Park
#22- Stillhouse Hollow Lake - Dana Peak Park
#23- Lake Whitney
#24- Lake Whitney State Park
#25- Clifton City Park
#26- Dahl Park
#27- Norse Historic District
#28- Meridian State Park
#29- Huggins Mesa Vista Ranch
#30- Fossil Rim Wildlife Center
#31- Dinosaur Valley State Park
#32- Glen Rose Bird Sanctuary
#33- Paluxy Heritage Park
#34- Country Woods Inn
#35- Cedars on the Brazos
#36- Somervell County Park
#37- Benbrook Lake - Holiday Park
#38- Benbrook Lake Natural Area - Trinity Flats
#39- Wheaton: Pyramid Road
#40- Winscott Plover Road
#41- Benbrook Lake - Mustang Park and Mustang Point Campground
#42- Benbrook Lake Natural Area - Richardson Area
#43- Fort Worth Oakmont Park
#44- Fort Worth Forest Park
#45- Fort Worth Botanic Gardens

#46- Tanglewood
#47- Foster Park
#48- Fort Worth Nature Center & Refuge
#49- Camp Joy and Wildwood Park
#50- Old State Fish Hatchery, Lake Worth
#51- Tarrant County Junior College
#52- Cement Creek Lake
#53- Walnut Grove Park/Lake Grapevine
#54- Bob Jones Park
#55- Colleyville Nature Center
#56- Village Creek Drying Beds
#57- River Legacy Parks
#58- The Dallas Arboretum and Botanical Garden
#59- Leonhardt Lagoon / Dallas Museum of Natural History
#60- Cedar Ridge Preserve
#61- Cedar Hill State Park
#62- Audubon Center at Dogwood Canyon/Cedar Mountain Preserve
#63- Woodland Basin Nature Area
#64- Rowlett Creek Greenbelt
#65- Lake Lavon Trinity Trail
#66- Spring Creek Park Preserve and Spring Creek Forest Preserve
#67- Arbor Hills Nature Preserve
#68- Connemara Conservancy
#69- Heard Natural Science Museum and Wildlife Sanctuary
#70- Eisenhower State Park
#71- Hagerman National Wildlife Refuge
#72- Cross Timbers Hiking Trail
#73- Miss Kitty's Bird & Bath
#74- LBJ National Grasslands
#75- Ray Roberts Lake State Park / Isle du Bois Unit
#76- Greenbelt Corridor at Ray Roberts Lake State Park
#77- Lost Creek Reservoir State Trailway
#78- Fort Richardson State Park and Historic Site
#79- Clark Gardens
#80- Lake Mineral Wells State Park and Trailway
#81- Possum Kingdom State Park
#82- Wildcatter Ranch and Resort
#83- Hockaday Ranch B & B
#84- Backside
#85- Lucy Park
#86- Lake Arrowhead State Park
#87- City of Seymour - City Park
#88- Ranger Creek Ranch

PRAIRIES AND PINEYWOODS – WEST

PRAIRIES AND PINEYWOODS - WEST

#1 Washington-On-The-Brazos State Historic Park

EAST OF BRENHAM, OFF OF HWY 105 EAST

KEY BIRDS
Spotted towhee, fox and Harris's sparrows, common goldeneye, grebes, cormorants, and pond ducks

BEST SEASON
All seasons

AREA DESCRIPTION
Hackberry thicket, and a mixture of open grassland and prairie areas

Known as the "Birthplace of Texas," this 293-acre park was founded in 1916 to commemorate Texas' independence from Mexico. Here, Texas delegates met in a general convention in 1836 to declare Texas' independence from Mexico, as well as draft the constitution and create the first government of Texas. The park includes the town of Washington (once the capital of the nation of Texas), a visitor's center, Barrington Living History Farm, the Star of the Republic Museum, scenic overlooks of the Brazos River, a picnic area, and a well-maintained nature trail.

The nature trail extends through several habitats offering a diverse bird watching experience. Follow the trail by the beaver pond, a hackberry thicket, and a mixture of open grassland/prairie areas looping to a scenic overlook of the Brazos River. The shaded picnic area in the open understory of pecan trees offers a great opportunity to watch overhead for birds attracted to the Brazos River.

The winter months will attract multiple species of sparrows that can be observed along the nature trail, including spotted towhee as well as fox and Harris's sparrows.

Bewick's wrens are present in the woodland areas. Some of the less frequent species are pyrrhuloxia, American bittern, and bald eagle. The beaver pond draws aquatic species such as wood duck, lesser scaup, northern pintail, American wigeon, common goldeneye, grebes, cormorants, and other pond ducks. Resident species that will nest and raise their young include Mississippi kite, dickcissel, and several species of buntings, vireos, and flycatchers. The popular pileated woodpecker can be seen year round.

During migration, birds observed along the Brazos River include vireos, warblers, tanagers, and orioles, with blue grosbeak observed at the Barrington Farm area of the site. Watch for neotropical migrants, including warblers, in the picnic areas along the nature trail that parallels the Brazos River.

DIRECTIONS

From Brenham, take Hwy 105 East for 14.0 miles, turn right on FM 1155 and follow to the park entrance. From Navasota, take Hwy 105 West for 8 miles, and turn left on FM 1155 to park entrance.

CONTACT INFORMATION

This is a day-use area only. Box 305, Washington, TX 77880-0305 / Call for information: 936-878-2214 / Website: www.brenhamtexas.com

PRAIRIES AND PINEYWOODS WEST

Spotted Towhee

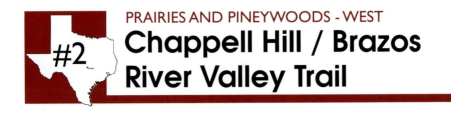

PRAIRIES AND PINEYWOODS - WEST

Chappell Hill / Brazos River Valley Trail

JUST INSIDE AND ALONG THE OUTSKIRTS OF THE TOWN OF CHAPPELL HILL, TEXAS

KEY BIRDS
Indigo and painted buntings, blue grosbeak, dickcissel, blue-gray gnatcatcher, red-eyed vireo, summer tanager, Wilson's phalarope, and black tern

BEST SEASON
All seasons

AREA DESCRIPTION
Riverside habitat and large trees along the roads

Spring and fall migrations release a river of neotropical birds through this area. The land adjacent to FM 2447 and Brazos River Road includes cropland, fallow fields, and improved pastures. The trees along the highway right-of-way provide habitat for a diversity of birds. Because FM 2447 and Brazos River Road are lightly traveled, the right-of-way enables safe viewing from the shoulders. Two creek crossings along FM 2447 provide for viewing of resident indigo and painted buntings, blue grosbeak, dickcissel, blue-gray gnatcatcher, red-eyed vireo, and summer tanager during the nesting season. Rarities such as black-bellied plover, Wilson's phalarope, and black tern have been seen during fall migration.

The winter season's birders may see raptors, meadowlarks, and sparrows, with rare sightings of white-tailed kite and Say's phoebe. During the summer nesting, residents include orchard oriole, lark sparrow, red-winged blackbird, northern parula, buntings, grosbeaks, and dickcissel. Watch the trees closely for nesting Mississippi kite in and around the historic downtown Chappell Hill, and wild turkey in the rural areas.

This has been called one of the better sites offering year-round bird watching opportunities along quiet country roads.

DIRECTIONS
This site includes multiple roadway right-of-ways beginning at the intersection of Hwy 290 and FM 1155 in Chappell Hill. From the Hwy 290 and FM 1155 intersection, travel north 0.5 mile through historic downtown Chappell Hill to the FM 1155 and FM 2447 intersection. Turn right (east) on FM 2447. Red Gully Creek bridge is 3.3 miles and New Years Creek bridge is 4.6 miles down FM 2447.

Brazos River Road is gravel and is located after 5.6 miles and doglegs to the right. Where the Brazos River Road again elbows to the right is the end of the site on this road.

The end of the pavement on FM 2447 is 7.0 miles and represents the end of the site on FM2447.

CONTACT INFORMATION

There is no contact information. Please observe safe parking and walking along these roadsides. Website: www.brenhamtexas.com

Killdeer

PRAIRIES AND PINEYWOODS - WEST
Lake Somerville

#3

NEAR THE TOWN OF SOMERVILLE, TEXAS

KEY BIRDS
Greater and lesser yellowlegs, pectoral, spotted, least, Baird's, and white-rumped sandpipers, killdeer, ring-billed gull

BEST SEASON
All seasons

AREA DESCRIPTION
A small section of native tallgrass prairie, and lakeside habitat

Nestled on the southeastern edge of Lake Somerville, Overlook Park offers access to the dam and nearby inlets as well as 70 acres of woodland habitat. Amenities include a picnic area, marina, and campground.

Visitors to Overlook Park are immediately drawn to the lakeshore which, depending on the season, can support muddy banks that provide habitat for migrating shore birds. Glass the numerous snags that line the banks for perching double-crested cormorant and the occasional osprey or wintering bald eagle. The shores also hold great blue and green herons, great and snowy egrets, and a variety of migrant shore birds including greater and lesser yellowlegs, as well as pectoral, spotted, least, Baird's, and white-rumped sandpipers and killdeer.

The steady stream of Forster's tern patrolling the open waters of Lake Somerville are joined by ring-billed gull in winter and Franklin's gull during migration. The areas of open water are also a great place to search for swallows. Barn and cliff swallows can be found skimming the surface for tiny prey and taking the occasional sip of water. Watch for both species nesting on structures near the dam.

The small patches of post oaks scattered through the park support breeding painted bunting and Inca dove while the white-eyed vireo can be heard calling in late spring and early summer. The more open areas of parkland provide habitat for eastern bluebird and scissor-tailed flycatcher. Watch especially close for red-bellied woodpecker and belted kingfisher perched on branches and utility poles.

A popular addition to Yegua Creek Park is taking a quiet hike along the interpretive nature trail. This easy trail takes the visitor through lakeside habitats found on the southern shores of Lake Somerville and includes a small section of native tallgrass prairie. Many of the trees and shrubs along the trail are identified, providing a good opportunity to learn about the native plants of the area. The song of many species of songbird can be heard in spring months. Watch for migrant white-eyed vireo, along with resident tufted titmouse and Carolina wren.

Rocky Creek Park offers extensive access to the southern shores of Lake Somerville and features several great areas for wildlife viewing. Visitors can walk through the park on a well-mowed trail that runs through woods and fields, providing opportunities to see white-eyed vireo, painted bunting, and migrant songbirds. The park runs along a peninsula jutting out into the lake. Look on the western side of the peninsula and the open waters for Forster's tern and, at times, Franklin's gull and migrant shore birds.

The eastern side of the peninsula is shallower and muddier with a large heron and egret rookery on the far bank. Hundreds of cattle egret with lesser numbers of little blue heron and double-crested cormorant gather to nest and hatch their young. Black or river vultures are also common here.

Follow the peninsula all the way to the point and look for scissor-tailed flycatcher and eastern kingbird in the treetops. During the winter, this is a great place to glass for waterfowl and bald eagles. Birders have seen osprey here year round.

DIRECTIONS

Overlook Park

From Brenham, go north on SR 36 for 9.0 miles to FM 1948. Go left (southwest) on FM 1948 for 0.1 mile. Turn right (northwest) onto LBJ Drive and follow it 0.6 mile to Overlook Park.

Yegua Creek Park

From Brenham, go north on SR 36 for 9.0 miles to FM 1948. Go left (southwest) on FM 1948 for 2.7 miles to Yegua Creek Park. Turn right and go 1.0 mile to the gate.

Rocky Creek Park

From Brenham, go north on SR 36 for 9.0 miles to FM 1948. Go left (southwest) on FM 1948 for 5.0 miles to Rock Creek Park. Turn right and follow the road 0.3 mile to the gate.

CONTACT INFORMATION

Site open daily. Developed camping available. Fee charged. Phone: 959-596-1622 / http://swf67.swf-wc.usace.army.mil/somerville

PRAIRIES AND PINEYWOODS - WEST
Lake Somerville State Park Complex

#4

LOCATED ON LAKE SOMERVILLE

KEY BIRDS
Painted bunting, Carolina wren, white-eyed vireo, scissor-tailed flycatcher, snowy and great egrets, and American white pelican

BEST SEASON
All seasons

AREA DESCRIPTION
Post oak savannah, lake, creek, pond, prairie, riparian and upland forest

In the post oak savannah vegetation region, Lake Somerville State Park includes a diversity of habitats, including lake, creek, pond, prairie, and riparian and upland forest.

These habitats are linked by 16 miles of multi-use nature trails, including a 1.8-mile accessible trail and the 13-mile trail named the Somerville Railway, connecting to the Birch Creek Unit.

The Somerville Trailway passes through dense stands of yaupon, post oak, hickory, blackjack oak, and water oak forests, past scenic overlooks and water crossings. The trail has one of the best spring wildflower displays in the Texas State Park System.

Nails Creek is located on the south shore of Lake Somerville along a major tributary to the Brazos River. Both the Nails Creek

PRAIRIES AND PINEYWOODS WEST

Great Egret

Unit and the Birch Creek Unit to the north offer a multitude of recreational opportunities such as birding, camping, picnicking, boating, fishing, hiking, biking, and backpacking.

In spring and summer, the peaceful cove lined with mixed oak and elm riparian forest hosts painted bunting, Carolina wren, white-eyed vireo, and scissor-tailed flycatcher. Birders will enjoy watching snowy and great egrets as they hunt along the shorelines. American white pelicans, with their nine-foot wingspan, commonly fish and rest in the deeper waters of the lake during the winter, spring, and fall.

Flag Pond, located approximately four miles from the Nails Creek Unit and nine miles from the Birch Creek Unit along the Somerville Trailway, provides wildlife viewing opportunities in conjunction with a system of interpretive trails, nature study, outdoor classrooms, and wildlife photography. The Flag Pond Nature Theater provides an excellent wildlife-viewing platform.

Located on the north shore of Lake Somerville and connected to the Nails Creek Unit on the south shore by the 13-mile Somerville Trailway, the Birch Creek Unit provides wonderful opportunities for outdoor enthusiasts. The wide grass-covered banks and many lake access points make it ideal for swimming, fishing, viewing the large flocks of wintering waterfowl, or quiet contemplation from one of the many secluded coves. In addition to the 13-mile Trailway, several miles of nature trails wind through the prairie and forest, linking many natural areas of interest to the campsites. Total trail mileage (including the railway) is 19 miles with 13 for backpacking and equestrian use and the entire 19 for day hiking, mountain biking, birding, and nature study.

Roadrunners can often be seen along the forest and field edges while driving through the park. During the late spring and early summer watch for families of Carolina wren, chickadees, and white-eyed vireo foraging together with their hungry fledglings. Also listen for the call of the yellow-billed cuckoo.

Over 20 species of waterfowl, some in large numbers, spend their winter on Lake Somerville, often accompanied by bald eagle and osprey. Green-winged teal, ring-necked duck, bufflehead, hooded merganser, mallard, and northern pintail are common. Great and snowy egrets, green and little blue herons, and the occasional wood stork also feed in the shallows of the lake edge. Whatever the time of year, the Birch Creek Unit is sure to reward the visitor with quality, close-up encounters with the natural world.

DIRECTIONS

Nails Creek Unit

From the intersection of US 290 and FM 180, about 6.5 miles east of Giddings, go left (northeast) on FM 180 for 13.1 miles until the road ends into the park.

Birch Creek Unit

From the intersection of SR 36 and FM 60, about 3.7 miles northwest of Somerville, go left (southwest) on FM 60 for 7.1 miles. Turn left (south) on PR 57 and follow 4.2 miles to the Birch Creek Unit of Lake Somerville State Park.

CONTACT INFORMATION

Site open daily. State Park entry, day-use, and camping fees apply. Phone: 979-535-7763.

PRAIRIES AND PINEYWOODS WEST

PRAIRIES AND PINEYWOODS - WEST
Lick Creek Park

#5

COLLEGE STATION, TEXAS

KEY BIRDS
American woodcock, northern parula, Kentucky and Swainson's warblers, white-eyed and yellow-throated vireos, and summer tanager

BEST SEASON
All seasons, with spring at the top of the list

AREA DESCRIPTION
City landscaped park with wooded, open, and grassy areas

This is a premier nature preserve and birding site, established in College Station as part of land negotiations to create a city industrial park. The site has a variety of plant and animal species indigenous to this area. The 515-acre park currently offers several miles of trails and provides an excellent opportunity for birders.

Depending on the time of year, a visit to Lick Creek Park can reveal a variety of different birds. Birders visiting or passing through would be well advised not to skip this location.

Listen for the "peents" and "whirrs" of displaying American woodcock in late winter or warbles of painted bunting in early summer. Northern cardinals are probably the most common bird heard throughout the year. There is also a diversity of warblers and vireos that can be seen during their migrations.

Year-round dwellers and nesting species can include northern parula, Kentucky and Swainson's warblers, white-eyed and yellow-throated vireos, and summer tanager. The winter months are alive with shrub birds such as savannah, vesper, field, white-throated, and Henslow's sparrows have been known to stop here. There are approximately 3.5 miles of improved trails that are available to birders.

DIRECTIONS
From the intersection of University Drive and SR 6 in College Station, go southeast on SR 6 for 6.4 miles to the Greens Prairie Road Exit. Turn left (northeast) on Greens Prairie Road for 1.8 miles to Rock Prairie Road. Turn right on Rock Prairie Road and go 1.4 miles to the park entrance and parking area on the right.

CONTACT INFORMATION
Lick Creek Park is a day-use-only park. There is no entrance fee but visitors are asked to please police their trash. For additional information call **979-764-3486** / Website: www. cstx.gov

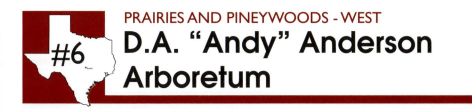

PRAIRIES AND PINEYWOODS - WEST
D.A. "Andy" Anderson Arboretum

#6

1900 ANDERSON STREET
COLLEGE STATION, TEXAS 77840

KEY BIRDS
Green heron, yellow-billed cuckoo, killdeer, nightjars, and migrating warblers and vireos

BEST SEASON
All seasons depending on the weather

AREA DESCRIPTION
Wooded and open grassy areas

Originally named the Brazos County Arboretum, it was founded in 1976 as part of the USA Bicentennial celebration. It was renamed in 1986, in honor of D.A. Anderson, a former mayor of College Station. The Texas Parks and Wildlife Department has provided partial funding for this park. The 26.5-acre Bee Creek Park is also located here.

Located on 17 wooded acres bounded by the cemetery, Bee Creek, and Business 6, the Arboretum contains a shelter and an interpretive trail system. It is an area that is to be used as a place where trees and shrubs are cultivated for educational and scientific purposes.

The D. A. "Andy" Anderson Arboretum provides access to a variety of habitats right in downtown College Station. This natural area is part of Bee Creek Park and is connected to other city parks with an extensive pedestrian and bicycle trail system. Walking the numerous trails through the forest will eventually lead to the banks of Bee Creek and several wooded ponds.

These areas have a diversity of birds throughout the year. In summer green heron and yellow-billed cuckoo can be heard calling from above the ponds, while painted bunting are spotted along the edges of woodlands, water sources, and feeding stations. During the winter look for species such as curve-billed and brown thrashers and hermit thrush flying in and out of the sometimes-thick underbrush. Watch for roosting nightjars during their migrations, along with migrating warblers and vireos. Killdeer can often be seen on the neighboring baseball field and purple martin and chimney swift cruise overhead.

DIRECTIONS
From the intersection of University Drive and Texas Avenue/ SR 6 Business in College Station, go southeast on Texas Avenue/ SR 6 Business for 2.1 miles to Southwest Parkway. Turn right (southwest) on Southwest Parkway for 0.3 mile to Anderson Street. Turn left on Anderson Street and travel to the parking lot in Bee Creek Park at the end of the road.

PRAIRIES AND
PINEYWOODS WEST

CONTACT INFORMATION
No fees are charged for day use.
For other information call 979-764-3486
Website: www.cstx.gov

Little Green Heron

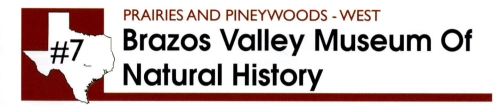

PRAIRIES AND PINEYWOODS - WEST
Brazos Valley Museum Of Natural History

#7

3232 BRIARCREST DRIVE
BRYAN, TX 77802

KEY BIRDS
White-eyed, red-eyed, yellow-throated, and blue-headed vireos, red-bellied and downy woodpeckers, and three species of swallow

BEST SEASON
All seasons, with spring and fall usually better than the rest

AREA DESCRIPTION
Wooded area with trails behind the museum proper

The museum's current mission is to preserve and protect natural and cultural history, to stimulate its understanding, and to encourage responsible stewardship of all natural and cultural resources. The museum now has the Marion C. Pugh Bird Collection of about 1,100 specimens, whole mounts, study skins, skeletons, and eggs collected in Texas between 1876 and 1940.

The Brazos Valley Nature Museum offers several excellent exhibits dedicated to the cultural and natural history of the region. Visitors can also enjoy an interpretive nature trail that traverses the woods behind the museum. Birders should watch for white-eyed, red-eyed, yellow-throated, and blue-headed vireos during spring, with both white-eyed and yellow-throated species staying to nest and raise their young. The winter months are the time to watch for white-throated and Lincoln's sparrows along with resident Carolina wren and red-bellied and downy woodpeckers.

The bridge near the museum on the eastern corner of the property is a good place to test your identification skills for the three species of swallow – barn, cliff, and cave swallows.

DIRECTIONS
From the intersection of University Drive and SR 6 in College Station, go north on SR 6 for 1.7 miles to the Briarcrest Drive Exit. Turn right (northeast) on Briarcrest Drive/ FM 1179 and follow it northeast 0.3 mile to the museum on the right.

CONTACT INFORMATION
Hours of operation are 10am to 5pm Tuesday through Saturday. Fees are $5.00 for adults, with children (4-17), senior citizens, Friends of the Museum, and university students at $4.00. Children three and under are free with a paying adult. For more information call 979-776-2195 / Website: http://www.brazosvalleymuseum.org

PRAIRIES AND PINEYWOODS WEST

PRAIRIES AND PINEYWOODS - WEST
Lake Bryan

#8

8200 SANDY POINT ROAD
BRYAN, TX 77807

KEY BIRDS
Rare birds, like the tundra swan and Hudsonian godwit

BEST SEASON
Winter

AREA DESCRIPTION
The area is very open and somewhat bare, with the lake providing most of the useable habitat

A visitor who shall remain nameless when asked about Lake Bryan had this to say: "This is the saddest lake I've ever seen in my life. If I could give this place zero stars for the lake, and three stars for the running/walking path, I'd do that, but seriously...the saddest lake in the world overrides even the paths."

Not a super good review. However, some interesting birds have been seen in and around the lake. The lake is at its best during the winter when waterfowl and white pelican are present in large numbers.

During summer, check the pilings for roosting Forster's tern and watch the shallows for stalking great blue heron and great egret. During migration the shoreline can attract a variety of shore birds such as least, pectoral, white-rumped, and Baird's sandpipers. Look for blue-gray gnatcatcher and yellow-billed cuckoo in the surrounding woodlands and marsh and sedge wren in the lakeside reeds.

Over the years, a number of rarities have been seen on the lake, including tundra swan and Hudsonian godwit.

DIRECTIONS
From the intersection of University Drive/ FM 60 and Texas Avenue/ Business SR 6 in College Station, drive west on University Drive/ FM 60 for 2.6 miles to FM 2818. Turn right onto FM 2818 and travel north 6.8 miles to FM 1687. Turn left onto FM 1687 and go 3.3 miles to the entrance to the lake on the right.

CONTACT INFORMATION
The park on the lake is open year round. There are no reservations taken and the site is on a first-come, first-served basis. Fees range from $5.00 for a day pass to $10.00 per vehicle for camping. For more information call 979-361-0861 / Website: www.lakebryan. com

PRAIRIES AND PINEYWOODS WEST

Tundra Swan

PRAIRIES AND PINEYWOODS - WEST
Bluebonnet Park

#9

002 E. ENNIS AVENUE
ENNIS, TEXAS 75119

KEY BIRDS
White-eyed vireo, downy woodpecker, northern cardinal, tufted titmouse, loggerhead shrike, and scissor-tailed flycatcher

BEST SEASON
All seasons, depending on the weather

AREA DESCRIPTION
Very open with some wooded areas along the jogging path

This 47-acre park was opened in May, 1996. The facility includes 10 acres of dedicated recreational open space, a two-acre fishing lake, and a .07-mile jogging path.

Bluebonnet Park is the latest addition to Ennis's growing family of community parks. The park offers a large pond and a nature trail, as well as a picnic area and baseball diamonds. Pay attention to the open lawns near the main parking area, where loggerhead shrike and scissor-tailed flycatcher may be concentrated around the large pond. On a hike along the nature trail, birders may see white-eyed vireo and downy woodpecker along with northern cardinal and tufted titmouse. Watch for migrants in the trees during spring and fall, especially after a north wind and rain.

DIRECTIONS
From I-45/ US 287 in Ennis, take Exit 251 and continue north on the frontage road to US 287 Business/ E. Ennis Ave. Turn left on US 287 Business and follow west 2.3 miles to Ennis Parkway. Turn left (south) onto Ennis Parkway and travel 0.4 mile to Joe Barton Parkway, crossing over US 287. Turn left on Joe Barton Parkway and travel 0.2 mile to Bluebonnet Park; turn right into the park.

Scissor-tailed Flycatcher

CONTACT INFORMATION
Phone: 972-878-4748 or 972-875-1234, ext. 2248
Website: www.visitennis.org

PRAIRIES AND PINEYWOODS - WEST
Buffalo Creek Wetland

#10

LOCATED IN THE BLACKLAND PRAIRIE REGION OF TEXAS NEAR ENNIS

KEY BIRDS
Wood duck, great blue heron, great egret, dickcissel, and many species of waterfowl

BEST SEASON
All seasons

AREA DESCRIPTION
Blackland prairie and flooded timber

Three different types of wetland are present in the Buffalo Creek Wetland complex. Heron Lake, a portion of which will be continuously flooded, will contain a mixture of moist soil as well as submerged plants. An island was constructed in Heron Lake to provide protection for waterfowl from predators. Beaver Slough is a green tree reservoir or wooded wetland, which should attract a variety of riparian wildlife, including the wood duck.

Buffalo Creek Wetland is the ideal place for an early morning stroll or a late afternoon bike ride. The series of ponds at the center of the park hold numerous species of wildlife. Great blue heron and great egret are seen in the shallows fishing for frogs and crayfish. During the spring and nesting season, red-winged blackbirds loudly proclaim their territory. The winter wetlands attract waterfowl, including blue-winged and green-winged teal. Shore birds tend to drop in for short visits throughout the spring and fall. The trail into the woods allows a slow walk to search for woodland species such as downy and red-bellied woodpeckers. Watch the trees and larger branches for nighttime species such as the barred owl, that will sometimes call when a birder enters its area. The areas of open grassland adjacent to the dam are where to find dickcissel and numerous sparrows in the winter.

DIRECTIONS
From I-45/ US 287 in Ennis, take Exit 246 and continue north on the frontage road to US 287 Business. Turn left (south) and follow 3.4 miles to Ensign Road. Turn left (south) onto Ensign Road and follow 1.4 miles to Observation Drive. Turn right on Observation Drive and travel 1.1 miles to Bardwell Dam Road. Turn left on Bardwell Dam Road and travel 1.3 miles to the Buffalo Creek Wetland on the right.

CONTACT INFORMATION
For more information, contact Park Ranger Joanne Murphy at 972-875-5711 or 972-875-1234 / Website: www.swf-c.usace.army.mil/bardwell/

PRAIRIES AND
PINEYWOODS WEST

PRAIRIES AND PINEYWOODS - WEST
Reed Wildlife Ranch

#11

LOCATED ON THE TRINITY RIVER OUTSIDE CORSICANA, TEXAS

KEY BIRDS
Black and turkey vultures, crested caracara

BEST SEASON
Spring, winter, and fall

AREA DESCRIPTION
Grassland and oak savanna

The Reed family has lived along the Trinity River for generations, and over the years has gained a wonderful appreciation for the land. Cabins stand where Plains Indians once camped, providing sweeping views of the river and the woods and prairies that follow its meanderings.

There are approximately 900 acres of river, wetlands, flooded timbers, lakes, ponds, and slough areas making up habitat for a whole host of wildlife. Birds seen here include several species of duck and other migratory waterfowl.

Areas supporting edge habitat located between open grassland and oak savanna are good places to see indigo and painted buntings, while lark sparrow are more common in the open fields. Black and turkey vultures cruise the skies in search of carrion and are joined at times by crested caracara, an uncommon resident this far north and east. The many ponds scattered throughout the property attract wading birds such as herons and egrets in summer and large flocks of waterfowl in the winter.

DIRECTIONS
Take Exit 231 off I-45 in Corsicana and go east on SR 31 for 12.7 miles to FM 636 in Kerens. Turn left onto FM 636 and go 1.8 miles to NE 2160, turn right and travel 1.4 miles to NE 3070. At NE 3070 turn left and go 0.7 mile to NE 3090, turn right onto NE 3090 and continue 2.0 miles to the entrance gate at the end of Sandy Lane.

CONTACT INFORMATION
This is a hunting ranch, so a call is required (903-872-6836) for current fees and open dates. The web site, although lengthy, offers little access information.
Website: www.reedfamilyranch.com

Crested Caracara

PRAIRIES AND PINEYWOODS WEST

PRAIRIES AND PINEYWOODS - WEST
Richland Creek Wildlife Management Area

#12

NORTH OF FAIRFIELD, TEXAS

KEY BIRDS
Scissor-tailed flycatcher, herons, egrets, dickcissel, painted bunting

BEST SEASON
During spring and fall migrations

AREA DESCRIPTION
Located in an ecotone separating the post oak savannah and blackland prairie ecological regions

This Texas WMA lies almost entirely within the Trinity River floodplain and is subject to periodic and prolonged flooding. The area supports a wide array of bottomland- and wetland-dependent wildlife and vegetation communities.

Bottomland hardwood forest characterized by cedar elm, sugarberry, and green ash dominate the area. Honey locust, boxelder, and black willow are also common. Pockets of bur oak, shumard oak, overcup oak, water oak, willow oak, and native pecan also occur. These forests serve as nesting and brood rearing habitat for many species of neotropical birds.

Numerous marshes and sloughs throughout the area provide habitat for migrating and wintering waterfowl, wading birds, and shore birds, as well as diverse aquatic life.

The north unit of the management area has numerous open fields and natural and man-made wetlands. Birds such as dickcissel, painted bunting, scissor-tailed flycatcher, herons, and egrets are often seen here. During the spring and fall, migratory shore birds are very common. Watch for many species of waterfowl in the winter and wood storks during the late summer.

The north unit is the site for a cooperative agreement between TPW and Tarrant Regional Water District, where 2,000 acres of shallow water impoundments are being constructed. Over 250 species of birds have been verified on the management area, the majority of which have been in conjunction with wetlands on the north unit.

The south unit is characterized by bottomland hardwood forest with massive bald cypress. The large trees along the entry road host northern parula as well as prothonotary warbler. Scope the large pond near the entrance for snowy egret and little blue heron, and along the power lines for red-tailed hawk.

PRAIRIES AND PINEYWOODS WEST

DIRECTIONS

North Unit

From I-45 in Corsicana, take Exit 229 for US 287. Go south on US 287 for 24.2 miles to the designated entry point on the left.

South Unit

From I-45 in Corsicana, take Exit 229 for US 287. Go south on US 287 for 24.1 miles to FM 488 (directly behind Richland Chambers Dam). Turn right (south) on FM 488 and travel 2.4 miles to the designated entry point on the left.

CONTACT INFORMATION

Use of this area requires purchase of an APHP or LPUP, with required daily registration. Please note that the entire area is closed to the general public during special, permitted hunts. For information, contact Matthew Symmank, 1670 FM 488, Streetman, TX 75859 / Phone: 903-389-7080 / Website: http://www.tpwd.state.tx.us/huntwild/hunt/wma/find_a_wma/list/?id=23

PRAIRIES AND
PINEYWOODS WEST

PRAIRIES AND PINEYWOODS - WEST
Gus Engeling Wildlife Management Area

NORTHWEST OF PALESTINE, TEXAS

KEY BIRDS
Pileated woodpecker, prothonotary warbler, parula warbler, purple gallinule

BEST SEASON
All seasons, depending on weather

AREA DESCRIPTION
Wetlands, bogs, and hardwood bottomland floodplain

The area is comprised of 2,000 acres of hardwood bottomland floodplain and almost 500 acres of natural watercourse, 350 acres of wetlands, and nearly 300 acres of sphagnum moss bogs.

The area has rolling sandy hills dominated by post oak uplands, bottomland hardwood forests, natural springs, pitcher plant bogs, sloughs, marshes, and relict pine communities.

Oak trees mostly water and willow oak are the dominant trees in the bottomlands. Depending on rainfall and weather conditions, spring displays of flowering dogwood and wildflowers can be spectacular.

The Gus Engeling WMA has a rich variety of wildlife. Currently, 36 mammals, 140 birds, 55 reptiles and amphibians, 53 fishes, and 975 plant species have been documented. Birders will find their days filled watching the many species of bird such as wood duck, purple gallinule, pileated woodpecker, and prothonotary warbler in bottomland forests; and watching the tallest trees for parula warbler.

A self-guided auto tour takes a visitor through ten stops which address wildlife and habitat management techniques. In addition, the Beaver Pond Nature Trail and Dogwood Nature Trail offer visitors the chance to personally experience the lush green mysteries of East Texas.

Birders should also keep a watchful eye to the ground, because all four varieties of venomous snakes occur in this area.

No permit is required for the driving tour and nature trails, but a more extensive use of the area requires purchase of an Annual Public Hunting Permit or Limited Public Use Permit and daily on-site registration. These permits are available at all license sale locations in Texas or by calling 1-800-895-4248.

DIRECTIONS
From the intersection of US 287 West and SH 19 in Palestine, go west on US 287 for 16.2 miles.

PRAIRIES AND
PINEYWOODS WEST

CONTACT INFORMATION

Permits are not for sale at the WMA. Please note that the entire area is closed to the general public during special, permitted hunts. For more information about the area, contact Jeffrey Gunnels, 16149 North US Hwy 287, Tennessee Colony, TX 75861 / Phone: 903-928-2251 / Website: http://www.tpwd.state.tx.us/huntwild/hunt/wma/find_a_wma/list/?id=10

PRAIRIES AND PINEYWOODS WEST

Purple Gallinule

PRAIRIES AND PINEYWOODS - WEST
Fairfield Lake State Park

NORTHEAST OF FAIRFIELD, TEXAS

KEY BIRDS
Forster's tern, prothonotary warbler, and barred owl

BEST SEASON
Fall, winter, and spring

AREA DESCRIPTION
Lakeshore habitat and woodlands

Fairfield Lake is well renowned for its winter population of bald eagle and osprey, but it hosts many more species as well. The deep woods and flooded forest around the lake host numerous prothonotary warblers in spring and summer and in the late afternoon the woods reverberate with the deep hoots of the barred owl.

In the two-mile nature trail takes visitors to the edges of the lake where families of wood ducks paddle through the reeds and red-winged blackbirds call loudly and constantly.

During the summer months, Forster's terns can be seen perched on the navigation buoys and flying in search of fish.

Lucky birders will see the occasional visiting Franklin's gulls and white pelican. A 15-mile trail provides hiking and mountain bike access from one end of the park to the other. Much of the trail is adjacent to the 2400-acre Fairfield Lake. While entering and leaving the park, be sure to check the hummingbird feeder at the entrance for the ruby-throated hummingbird.

DIRECTIONS
The park is six miles northeast of Fairfield off FM 2570 on FM 3285 adjacent to Fairfield Lake. It is 90 miles south of the Dallas/ Fort Worth area, 150 miles north of the Houston area, and 60 miles east of Waco. The park is located just a few miles from Interstate 45, northeast of the city of Fairfield, Texas.

CONTACT INFORMATION
The standard Texas park day use and camping fees apply. Call for additional information: Phone 903-389-4514 / 123 State Park Rd 64, Fairfield TX 75840.

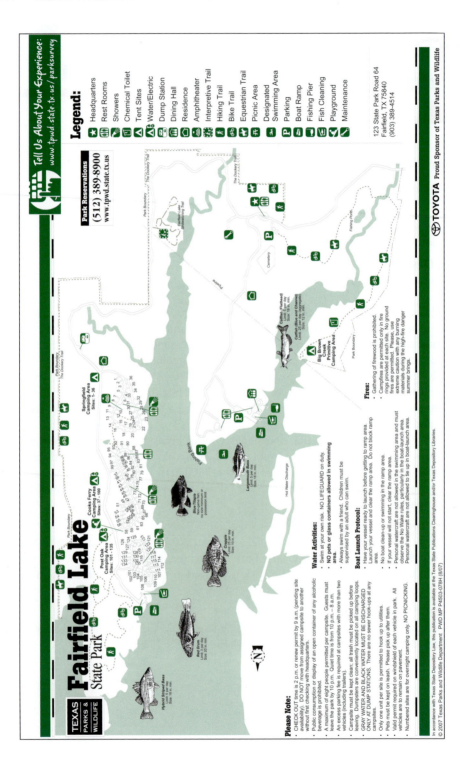

In accordance with Texas State Depository Law, this publication is available at the Texas State Publications Clearinghouse and/or Texas Depository Libraries.
© 2007 Texas Parks and Wildlife Department   PWD MP P4503-078H (8/07)

PRAIRIES AND PINEYWOODS - WEST
Fort Parker State Park

#15

194 PARK ROAD 28
MEXIA, TX 76667

KEY BIRDS
Pelicans, double-crested and a few neotropic cormorants, waterfowl

BEST SEASON
All seasons

AREA DESCRIPTION
Lakeshore and woodlands habitat

Fort Parker State Park includes 1458.8 acres – 758.8 land acres and a 700-acre lake – between Mexia and Groesbeck, in Limestone County.

The park was named for Fort Parker, a nearby historic settlement established in 1833, and the site of the well-known Comanche Indian raid in May 1836, during which Cynthia Ann Parker was captured. During captivity, Cynthia Ann became the mother of the last great Comanche chief, Quanah Parker, whose stronghold was within the depths of the Palo Duro Canyon.

Fort Parker State Park encircles a small reservoir on the Navasota River. The lake and the surrounding woodland provide excellent opportunities for wildlife viewing. In winter, the lake attracts the white pelican as well as double-crested and, on occasion, a few neotropic cormorants. Waterfowl can be seen in the winter months and wood duck are present year round. Woodlands along the Navasota River upstream from the reservoir ring with the cries of red-bellied, redheaded, downy, and hairy woodpeckers. While watching these birds, be aware that this is great habitat for the eastern screech owl, great horned and barred owls. Great blue or green herons are also commonly seen in this same area.

The Friends of Fort Parker, an outstanding park-support organization, operates boat tours of Lake Fort Parker. Weekend tours are Saturday at 10am and 2pm and Sunday at 2pm.

Contact the park for lake level/conditions and a current schedule. Wildflower tours (on a trailer with bench seating) are available March through July, Monday through Friday by reservation.

DIRECTIONS
At the intersection of Hwy 84 and 14 in Mexia, go south 6.6 miles on Hwy 14 to PR 28. Turn right and the park headquarters will be on your right.

PRAIRIES AND
PINEYWOODS WEST

PRAIRIES AND PINEYWOODS WEST

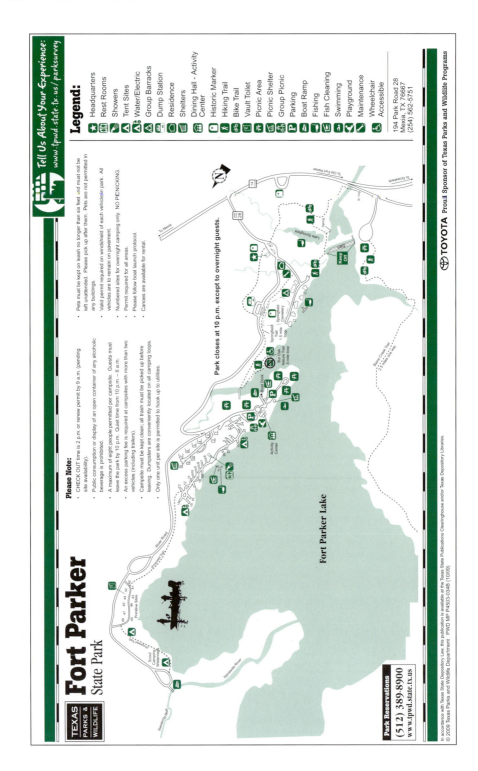

TEXAS PARKS & WILDLIFE

Fort Parker
State Park

Park Reservations
(512) 389-8900
www.tpwd.state.tx.us

Please Note:

- CHECK OUT time is 2 p.m. or renew permit by 9 a.m. (pending site availability).
- Public consumption or display of an open container of any alcoholic beverage is prohibited.
- A maximum of eight people permitted per campsite. Guests must leave the park by 10 p.m. Quiet time from 10 p.m. – 6 a.m.
- An excess parking fee is required at campsites with more than two vehicles (including trailers).
- Campsite must be kept clean; all trash must be picked up before leaving. Dumpsters are conveniently located on all camping loops.
- Only one unit per site is permitted to hook up to utilities.

- Pets must be kept on leash no longer than six feet and must not be left unattended. Please pick up after them. Pets are not permitted in any buildings.
- Valid permit required on windshield of each vehicle in park. All vehicles are to remain on pavement.
- Numbered sites for overnight camping only. NO PICNICKING.
- Permit required for all areas.
- Please follow boat launch protocol.
- Canoes are available for rental.

Park closes at 10 p.m. except to overnight guests.

Tell Us About Your Experience:
www.tpwd.state.tx.us/parksurvey

Legend:

Headquarters	
Rest Rooms	
Showers	
Tent Sites	
Water/Electric	
Group Barracks	
Dump Station	
Residence	
Shelters	
Dining Hall - Activity Center	
Historic Marker	
Hiking Trail	
Bike Trail	
Vault Toilet	
Picnic Area	
Picnic Shelter	
Group Picnic	
Parking	
Boat Ramp	
Fishing	
Fish Cleaning	
Swimming	
Playground	
Maintenance	
Wheelchair Accessible	

194 Park Road 28
Mexia, TX 76667
(254) 562-5751

TOYOTA Proud Sponsor of Texas Parks and Wildlife Programs

Fort Parker Lake

To Old Fort Parker
To Groesbeck
To Mexia

CONTACT INFORMATION

The park is open all year. The standard Texas parks day use and camping fees apply. For additional information.
Phone: 254-562-5751
Website: http://www.tpwd.state.tx.us/spdest/findadest/parks/fort_parker/

PRAIRIES AND
PINEYWOODS WEST

Brown Thrasher

PRAIRIES AND PINEYWOODS - WEST
Fort Boggy State Park

#16

4994 HWY. 75 SOUTH
CENTERVILLE, TX 75833

KEY BIRDS
Brown thrasher, blue-gray gnatcatcher, summer tanager, and black-and-white warbler

BEST SEASON
All seasons

AREA DESCRIPTION
Wooded, rolling hills, bottomland meadows, and wetlands

The 1,847-acre park is located along Boggy Creek, which flows east into the Trinity River.

The abundant wildlife includes white-tailed deer, raccoon, squirrel, fox, and beaver. Resident birds such as brown thrasher, blue-gray gnatcatcher, summer tanager, and black-and-white warbler can be seen during spring and early summer.

Other interesting birds include the barred owl and red-shouldered hawk. A large portion of the park is subject to flooding during wet periods, providing excellent habitat for waterfowl and other varieties of aquatic wildlife.

DIRECTIONS
From I-45 in Centerville, Exit 164 and go east 0.4 mile on Hwy 7; then south on Hwy 75 for 4.9 miles to the park on the right. Or, from I-45 in Leona take Exit 156 and go east on Hwy 977 for 0.7 mile, then go north on Hwy 75 for 2.3 miles to the park on the left.

CONTACT INFORMATION
The standard Texas park day use and camping fees apply. For additional information, Phone 903-344-1116 / Website: http://www.tpwd.state.tx.us/spdest/findadest/parks/fort_boggy/

PRAIRIES AND PINEYWOODS WEST

PRAIRIES AND PINEYWOODS - WEST
Cameron Park

#17

WACO, TEXAS

KEY BIRDS
Eastern wood pewee, veery, Swainson's, and gray-cheeked-thrushes, northern, Baltimore, and Bullock's orioles, rose-breasted grosbeak

BEST SEASON
All seasons

AREA DESCRIPTION
River front habitat with cliffs and hardwood timber

Cameron Park encompasses 416 acres along both sides of the Brazos River in downtown Waco. It is nationally renowned as one of the largest city parks in the country, as well as having some of the best mountain biking trails in Texas. As a boy, I would hike and climb the cliffs with my cousins. It also happens to be a great spot to watch wildlife.

Cameron Park features scenic overlooks, wildlife, and 20-plus miles of nationally recognized trails that weave through the natural landscape. The park runs along towering limestone bluffs and overlooks the confluence of the Brazos and Bosque rivers.

Near the rivers, watch for great blue and green herons during the summer months and a variety of waterfowl in winter. Riverside brush should be watched for common yellowthroat and the larger trees for red-bellied woodpecker. The cliffs along the river are good places to watch for black-chinned and ruby-throated hummingbirds, tufted and black-crested titmice, and several species of swallow.

Other species include northern flicker, yellow bellied sapsucker, brown creeper, blue-gray gnatcatcher, Carolina wren, yellow-breasted chat, eastern screech owl, barred owl, great horned owl, black-chinned hummingbird, and ladder-backed woodpecker.

This park is large enough that even during high activity months there will be plenty of quiet areas to walk and watch for birds. However, birders are advised that on weekends the park will be best for birding before one in the afternoon – before the families and semi-controlled children are turned loose on the area. Food and other amenities are only blocks away.

DIRECTIONS
From I-35 in Waco, take Exit 335-B/ University Parks Drive and go northwest on University Parks Drive for 1.4 miles to the park.

PRAIRIES AND
PINEYWOODS WEST

CONTACT INFORMATION

As are most city parks, Cameron Park is only open during daylight hours and there are no fees charged to enter the park.

For additional park information phone: 254-750-8080

Website: www.waco-texas.com

PRAIRIES AND PINEYWOODS - WEST
Lake Waco Wetlands

#18

WACO, TEXAS

KEY BIRDS
Migratory shore birds, great blue heron, great egret, snowy egret, cattle egret, dickcissel, hawks, and vultures

BEST SEASON
All seasons

AREA DESCRIPTION
Wetlands, river, and lake habitat

Operated by the City of Waco Water Utility Services, the Lake Waco Wetlands area provides a great place to go bird watching.

The Lake Waco Wetlands cover 180 acres along the North Bosque River. The ecosystem is now thriving, but these wetlands are man-made. It was created to mitigate habitat loss when the level of Lake Waco was raised by seven feet.

PRAIRIES AND
PINEYWOODS WEST

Snowy Egret

Visitors can stop in the 6,000-square-foot Research and Education Center that offers informational materials and observation decks. Trails branch out from the center. An ADA trail allows visitors to travel through a wooded area to a platform overlooking the wetlands.

Explore the area via a 2.5-mile gravel path that leads visitors around and through the wetlands.

As for the wetlands itself, the Lake Waco Wetlands offer a diverse array of plant and animal life, including marshes and groves of hardwoods, and birds such as the great blue heron and great egret.

In spring and fall, the wetlands attract numerous migratory shorebirds, and winter brings in the waterfowl.

Summertime is marked by dozens of singing dickcissel, competing for perching space with the red-winged blackbird. During the early summer the wetlands are filled with the purple blooms of pickerelweed and the white blooms of duck potato. The trees in the marsh are filled with great and snowy egrets, while the neighboring bottomlands host wrens and woodpeckers. A little higher elevation in the drier oak scrub near the road is worth checking for painted bunting, while red-shouldered and red-tailed hawks along with vultures may be seen overhead.

Directions

From I-35 in Waco, take Exit 330 at Hwy 6 and Loop 340. Drive 10.8 miles northwest on Hwy 6 to FM 185. Turn right (east) on FM 185. After 0.5 mile, turn left on Eichelberger Crossing. The wetlands are 1.6 miles down on the right. Directional signs will be posted.

Contact Information

The Lake Waco Wetlands is open Monday-Friday 8am - 4pm, and on alternating Saturdays from 8am - noon.
For more information call 254-848-9654
Website: www.waco-texas.com

PRAIRIES AND PINEYWOODS - WEST
Mother Neff State Park

#19

NEAR TEMPLE, TEXAS ON ST 236

KEY BIRDS
Mourning dove, white-winged dove, collared dove, eastern phoebe, great crested flycatcher, and painted bunting

BEST SEASON
Spring and fall

AREA DESCRIPTION
Heavily wooded

Mother Neff State Park is the first official state park in Texas and is named for Mrs. Isabella Eleanor (Mother) Neff, who donated six acres of land along the Leon River in 1916.

These six acres became the first Texas State Park site. Her son was Texas Governor Pat M. Neff, who served as Governor from 1921 to 1925. After the death of his mother in 1921, Governor Neff created the Mother Neff Memorial Park, which later became the nucleus of the Texas State Park System. An excavation in 1935 led to the discovery of three Indian graves and many artifacts. During prehistoric times, this area was occupied by several groups of Native Americans, including some groups probably related to the Tonkawas.

Heavily wooded, the park is ideal for birding, camping, hiking, picnicking, and fishing. Watch the picnic area for red-bellied woodpecker, eastern phoebe, and great crested flycatcher. In the drier habitats, listen for the painted bunting singing from mesquite trees and watch mourning, white-winged, and the invasive collared doves flying overhead.

DIRECTIONS
In Temple, take Exit 299 from I-35 onto SR 36. Turn north and go 2.1 miles to its intersection with SR 53. Turn northwest and continue 14.2 miles on SR 36 to SR 236. Turn right (north) on SR 236 and follow it 5.2 miles to the park entrance on the left.

CONTACT INFORMATION
The standard Texas park day use and camping fees apply. Because of flood damage, Mother Neff State Park had limited camping available. As of this writing, restrooms with showers have been restored.
Call for additional information Phone 254-853-2389
Website: http://beta-www.tpwd.state.tx.us/state-parks/parks/find-a-park/mother-neff-state-park

PRAIRIES AND PINEYWOODS WEST

PRAIRIES AND
PINEYWOODS WEST

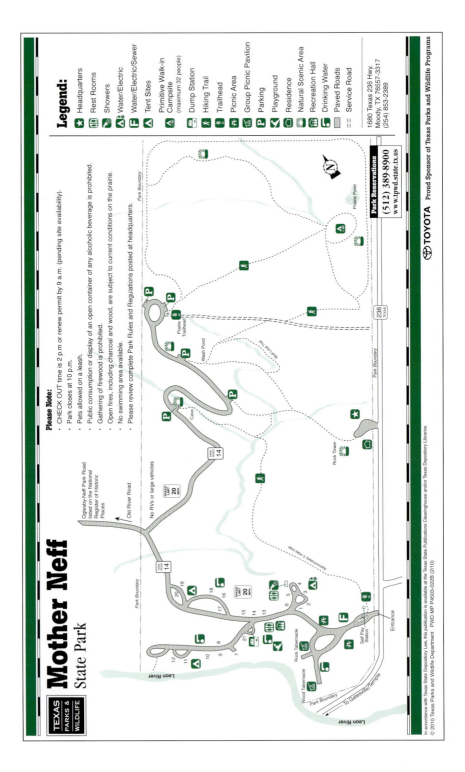

Mother Neff
State Park

TEXAS
PARKS &
WILDLIFE

Please Note:

- CHECK OUT time is 2 p.m. or renew permit by 9 a.m. (pending site availability).
- Park closes at 10 p.m.
- Pets allowed on a leash.
- Public consumption or display of an open container of any alcoholic beverage is prohibited.
- Gathering of firewood is prohibited.
- Open fires, including charcoal and wood, are subject to current conditions on the prairie.
- No swimming area available.
- Please review complete Park Rules and Regulations posted at headquarters.

Legend:

- Headquarters
- Rest Rooms
- Showers
- Water/Electric
- Water/Electric/Sewer
- Tent Sites
- Primitive Walk-in Campsite (maximum 32 people)
- Dump Station
- Hiking Trail
- Trailhead
- Picnic Area
- Group Picnic Pavilion
- Parking
- Playground
- Residence
- Natural Scenic Area
- Recreation Hall
- Drinking Water
- Paved Roads
- Service Road

1680 Texas 236 Hwy.
Moody, TX 76557-3317
(254) 853-2389

Park Reservations
(512) 389-8900
www.tpwd.state.tx.us

TOYOTA   Proud Sponsor of Texas Parks and Wildlife Programs

White-winged Dove

PRAIRIES AND PINEYWOODS - WEST
Miller Springs Natural Area

#20

NEAR TEMPLE, TEXAS

KEY BIRDS
Nashville and yellow-rumped warblers, lark sparrow

BEST SEASON
All seasons of fair weather

AREA DESCRIPTION
Located on the eastern edge of the Edwards Plateau, it has rocky grasslands and ash juniper woodlands

Miller Springs Nature Center is a 260-acre scenic natural area located between the Leon River and 40-foot high bluffs, immediately east of the Lake Belton Dam. The natural preserve is open to the public on a self-guided basis at no charge, each day of the year, from dawn to dusk.

It is an undeveloped area administered by the Miller Springs Alliance, Inc., a non-profit, 501(c)(3) corporation whose purpose is to promote conservation and management of natural and cultural resources and to provide an educational and recreational nature area for "children" of all ages.

The Miller Springs Natural Area sits right on the eastern edge of the Edward's Plateau. Rocky grasslands and ash juniper woodlands support a mixture of eastern and western species.

When hiking and birding along the escarpment, watch for flycatchers such as western kingbird and great crested flycatcher. Some birders will spot the occasional lark sparrow perched on the numerous snags. Chipping sparrows can be found among the junipers as can various migrant passerines in spring and fall. These include black-and-white, Nashville, and yellow-rumped warblers, as well as white-eyed and red-eyed vireos.

DIRECTIONS
From I-35 in Temple, take Exit 293A and go north on SR 317 for 2.6 miles to FM 439. Turn left (west) on FM 439 for 2.2 miles to FM 2271. Turn right and follow FM 2271 for 1.0 mile to the nature center on the right.

CONTACT INFORMATION
This natural area is only open during daylight hours. Phone: 254-939-2461 / Website: http://bellnetweb.brc.tamus.edu

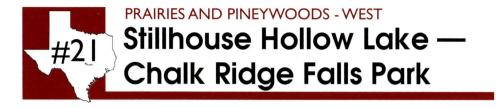

PRAIRIES AND PINEYWOODS - WEST
#21 Stillhouse Hollow Lake — Chalk Ridge Falls Park

Southwest of Belton, Texas

Key Birds
Cardinals, yellow-billed cuckoo, red-eyed vireo, and migrating yellow warbler

Best Season
Spring and summer

Area Description
Tall bottomland forest

Stillhouse Hollow Lake is an extremely clear and deep reservoir with a reported maximum depth of 107 feet and a surface area of 6,429 acres. The main lake area is dominated by a steep rocky shoreline with limited amounts of standing timber. Stillhouse Hollow Lake is located near the Fort Hood Army Base, which has several points of interest for the military buff.

Thanks to some useful information from other birders, it has been made known to us that this park occasionally closes following dam discharges due to heavy rains. These can take place weeks after heavy rains. The official website does not always post these closings, so it may be a good idea to call ahead before making the trip out there.

Following the Lampasas River from the Stillhouse Hollow Dam, travelers soon enter a tall bottomland forest. Throughout this forest, a series of boardwalks and bridges cross the creeks flowing to the river. Birders will see several impressive waterfalls along the way. Photographers may need to spend some time around the falls and watch the water's edge for several species of small water birds. Watch for yellow-billed cuckoo, red-eyed vireo, and migrating yellow warbler.

Directions
From I-35 take Exit 293B for US 190 in Belton. Go west on US 190 for 2.0 miles to FM 1670 Exit. Travel along the frontage road 2.4 miles to FM 1670. Turn left (south) on FM 1670 and go 2.1 miles to the entrance to the park on the left. Follow the road down the hill for 0.6 mile to the parking area.

Contact Information
The last available information was that there were no fees involved, unless you are camping or in your RV. Call for more information: 254-939-1829.

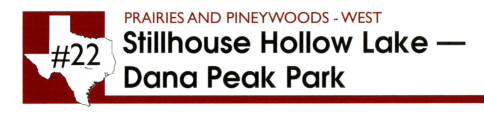

PRAIRIES AND PINEYWOODS - WEST
#22 Stillhouse Hollow Lake — Dana Peak Park

SOUTHWEST OF BELTON, TEXAS

KEY BIRDS
Endangered black-capped vireo, black-chinned hummingbird, Bewick's wren

BEST SEASON
Spring and summer

AREA DESCRIPTION
Typical Edward's Plateau vegetation, with numerous clumps of low-growing oak trees

Dana Peak Park features typical Edward's Plateau vegetation, with numerous clumps of low-growing oak that, on occasion, will host a pair of endangered black-capped vireos. Greater roadrunners are abundant on these dry rocky hillsides, and the sound of Bewick's wren can be heard buzzing everywhere. black-chinned hummingbirds zip back and forth throughout the park. The lake offers the possibility for migrant and vagrant waterfowl and shore birds. Of particular interest is the sandy swimming beach, which can host white-rumped and Baird's sandpipers as well as other peeps among the more regular killdeer.

DIRECTIONS
From I-35 take Exit 293B for US 190 in Belton. Go west on US 190 for 7.1 miles to Nolanville Road. Turn left onto Nolanville Road and go 1.0 mile to FM 2410. Turn right on FM 2410 and go 2.2 miles to Comanche Gap Road. Turn left and follow Comanche Gap Road 2.3 miles to the entrance to the park.

Bewick's Wren

CONTACT INFORMATION
The site is open for day use only. Fee charged. The last available information was there were no fees involved, unless you are camping or in your RV. Call for more information: 254-939-1829.

PRAIRIES AND PINEYWOODS - WEST
Lake Whitney

#23

ABOUT 30 MILES NORTHWEST OF WACO AND ABOUT 15 SOUTHWEST OF HILLSBORO

KEY BIRDS
Bald eagle, American white pelican, roadrunners, owls, blue heron, and swallows

BEST SEASON
All seasons

AREA DESCRIPTION
Lakeshore, lake, and wooded habitats

Lake Whitney is located on the Brazos River. Brazos de Dios means "in the arms of God." It is a large lake with 225 miles of shoreline and 37 square miles of coverage. The lake is 45 river miles long and is up to four miles wide at the widest point.

Bird and wildlife watchers delight in the area's 300 migratory and non-migratory bird species, and a local wildlife population that features more than 50 different species of mammals, including the white-tailed deer, foxes, and wild turkeys.

Among the birds that visitors have observed are bald eagle, American white pelican, roadrunners, owls, and blue heron. Swallows arrive each spring to make their nests high up on the limestone cliffs surrounding the lake.

Each January, for over 20 years, the annual Mid-Winter Bald Eagle Count is held on Lake Whitney — on a single day, as many as seven bald eagles have been spotted.

The birds come to Lake Whitney for the winter, and the severity of the winter up north helps to determine how many of the birds will migrate here.

Nesting pairs will stay on the lake year round. Migratory birds can be seen from early fall until springtime, but January is the best time to spot them. They tend to nest and perch high up in dead trees, so look up to see them.

In past years, eagles have been spotted near the Cedron Creek / Katy Bridge area, in Lake Whitney State Park, in Lofers Bend Park, and in the White Bluff area.

Depending on the time of year, you'll find painted bunting and scissor-tailed flycatcher. Birders have reported more than 194 bird species that have been seen around the lake.

Bird Island, toward the south end of the lake across from the state park, is a local hang-out for hundreds of birds. Because it is free from predators, many birds head there each evening to sleep. Depending on the time of year, you can watch hundreds of white cattle egret returning to the island around dusk.

DIRECTIONS
Take TX Hwy 22 southwest out of Hillsboro, Texas. Go through Whitney to the lake.

CONTACT INFORMATION
For additional information call: 254-694-2540
Website: http://lakewhitneychamber.com
Email: bluewater@lakewhitneychamber.com

Bald Eagle

PRAIRIES AND PINEYWOODS - WEST
Lake Whitney State Park

#24

LOCATED ALONG THE EASTERN SHORES OF LAKE WHITNEY, SOUTHWEST OF HILLSBORO, TEXAS

KEY BIRDS
Bald eagle, wild turkeys, Forster's tern, scissor-tailed flycatcher

BEST SEASON
All seasons

AREA DESCRIPTION
Open, disturbed tallgrass prairie remnants with scattered groves of live oak and a small area of post oak/blackjack oak woodland

Lake Whitney State Park is located in the Grand Prairie subregion of the Blackland Prairie natural region. It hosts year-round birding and is a great way to explore the area's wildlife. Various hawks and the elegant scissor-tailed flycatcher feed, and at times nest, in and near the open areas. Watch for Forster's tern flying over the lake in search of dinner, while spotted sandpiper and red-eared slider frequent the muddy banks.

The park's nature trail will get birders to more secluded areas of the park, where great blue heron hunt in the shallows. As the trail passes through several dense oak thickets, watch for white-eyed vireo and yellow-billed cuckoo.

DIRECTIONS
From I-35 North in Hillsboro, take Exit 364B. Go northwest onto US 77/ US 81 for 2.9 miles to SH 22/ W. Elm St. From I-35 South take Exit 370. Go southwest onto US 77/ US 81 to SH 22/ W. Elm Street. Turn west on SH 22 and follow 11.7 miles to the town of Whitney. Turn right (west) on E. Polk Avenue for 0.5 mile to S. Colorado Street. Turn left (south) on S. Colorado Street and follow 0.4 mile to FM 1244. Turn right (west) and go 2.2 miles to the park.

CONTACT INFORMATION
The standard Texas park day use and camping fees apply. Information and prices are subject to change. Please call the park or park information for the latest updates. To contact this park, call 254-694-3793 or 800-792-1112.

PRAIRIES AND
PINEYWOODS WEST

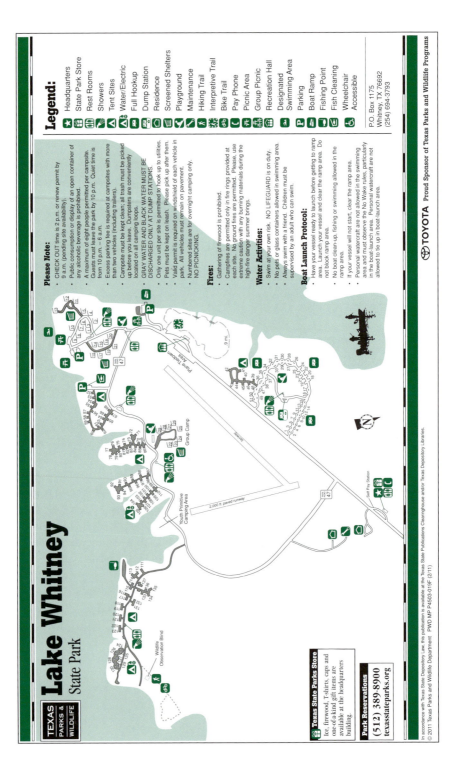

Lake Whitney
State Park

TEXAS
PARKS &
WILDLIFE

Texas State Parks Store

Ice, firewood, T-shirts, caps and one-of-a-kind gift items are available at the headquarters building.

Park Reservations
(512) 389-8900
texasstateparks.org

Wildlife Observation Blind

Group Camp

Youth Primitive Camping Area

Surf Pay Station

2,000 ft. paved runway

Plane Tiedown Area

9 ml.

Marina

Please Note:

- CHECK OUT time is 2 p.m. or renew permit by 9 a.m. (pending site availability).
- Public consumption or display of an open container of any alcoholic beverage is prohibited.
- A maximum of eight people permitted per campsite. Guests must leave the park by 10 p.m. Quiet time is from 10 p.m. — 6 a.m.
- Excess parking fee is required at campsites with more than two vehicles (including trailers).
- Campsite must be kept clean, all trash must be picked up before you leave. Dumpsters are conveniently located on all camping loops.
- GRAY WATER AND BLACK WATER MUST BE DISCHARGED ONLY AT DUMP STATIONS.
- Only one unit per site is permitted to hook up to utilities.
- Pets must be kept on leash. Please pick up after them.
- Valid permit is required on windshield of each vehicle in park. All vehicles must remain on pavement.
- Numbered sites are for overnight camping only. NO PICNICKING.

Fires:

- Gathering of firewood is prohibited.
- Campfires are permitted only in fire rings provided at each site. No ground fires are permitted. Please, use extreme caution with any burning materials during the high-fire danger summer brings.

Water Activities:

- Swim at your own risk. NO LIFEGUARD is on duty.
- No pets or glass containers allowed in swimming area.
- Always swim with a friend. Children must be supervised by an adult who can swim.

Boat Launch Protocol:

- Have your vessel ready to launch before getting to ramp area. Launch your vessel and clear the ramp area. Do not block ramp area.
- No boat clean-up, fishing or swimming allowed in the ramp area.
- If your vessel will not start, clear the ramp area.
- Personal watercraft are not allowed in the swimming area and must observe the No Wake rules, particularly in the boat-launch area. Personal watercraft are not allowed to tie up in boat-launch area.

Legend:

- Headquarters
- State Park Store
- Rest Rooms
- Showers
- Tent Sites
- Water/Electric
- Full Hookup
- Dump Station
- Residence
- Screened Shelters
- Playground
- Maintenance
- Hiking Trail
- Interpretive Trail
- Bike Trail
- Pay Phone
- Picnic Area
- Group Picnic
- Recreation Hall
- Designated Swimming Area
- Parking
- Boat Ramp
- Fishing Point
- Fish Cleaning
- Wheelchair Accessible

P.O. Box 1175
Whitney, TX 76692
(254) 694-3793

⊕ TOYOTA   Proud Sponsor of Texas Parks and Wildlife Programs

PRAIRIES AND PINEYWOODS - WEST
Clifton City Park

#25

The city of Clifton, southwest of Whitney Lake

Key Birds
Great-crested flycatcher, red-bellied woodpecker, orchard oriole

Best Season
All seasons

Area Description
A riparian corridor with tall oaks and pecan trees and some dense thickets

Clifton City Park stretches out along the Bosque River granting access to a beautiful riparian corridor. The tall oaks and pecans that line the river are home to the great-crested flycatcher and the red-bellied woodpecker.

Looking quietly in the dense thickets, birders will find black-crested titmouse and white-eyed vireo. This is an area of Texas where the migration season may provide many surprises, from colorful warblers to those "hard to identify" flycatchers.

Wading birds such as great blue and green herons and snowy egret can be seen flying and hunting small fish Keep an eye on the shallow puddles, especially on hot days for bathing cardinal, orchard oriole, and dickcissel.

Directions
From the intersection of Hwy 6 and FM 219 in Clifton, turn east on FM 219 for 0.4 mile to FM 219/ Park Road. Turn left into the city park.

Contact Information
Phone: 800-344-3720 or 254-675-8337 / Website: www.cliftontexas.org

Baltimore Oriole

PRAIRIES AND PINEYWOODS WEST

PRAIRIES AND PINEYWOODS - WEST
Dahl Park

#26

LOCATED OFF 3RD STREET AND AVENUE K IN CLIFTON, TEXAS

KEY BIRDS
Yellow and Wilson's warblers, common yellowthroat, blue jay, northern mockingbird, and chimney swift

BEST SEASON
All seasons

AREA DESCRIPTION
Woodland edges and stream habitat

Dahl Park is inside Clifton and is the perfect stopover to view a surprising number of bird species in a very small area.

The park includes woodland edges and stream habitat. The little creek that passes through the rear of the park attracts numerous species looking for a drink and a refreshing bath, especially during the hot summer months.

Neotropical migrants such as yellow and Wilson's warblers and common yellowthroat share the creek with the more familiar residents. Also, mourning dove, common grackle, northern cardinal, blue jay, northern mockingbird, and chimney swift can be found along the creek.

DIRECTIONS
From the intersection of Hwy 6 and FM 219 in Clifton, go west on FM 219 for 0.2 mile to Avenue K. Turn right (north) on Avenue K and follow it to its dead end at the park entrance.

CONTACT INFORMATION
This is a day-use-only location.
Phone: 800-344-3720
Website: www.cliftontexas.org

Northern Mockingbird

PRAIRIES AND PINEYWOODS - WEST
#27 Norse Historic District

CLIFTON, TEXAS

KEY BIRDS
Lark sparrow, scissor-tailed flycatcher, western kingbird

BEST SEASON
All seasons, depending on the weather

AREA DESCRIPTION
Some woods and city vistas – open areas with low trees

Taking a slow drive through the Norse District will take you through some of the oldest Norwegian settlements in North America.

Drive slowly as you pass through various fields, ranging from open grassland to thick cedar groves. Watch for lark sparrow, scissor-tailed flycatcher, and western kingbird along the fence rows.

Particularly good places to stop are at two churches. Our Savior's Lutheran Church is on the right after 4.1 miles and the Rock Church is on the right after 10.5 miles. Red-tailed hawks are seen soaring on the air currents in search of prey or perching on a roadside pole.

DIRECTIONS
From the intersection of SR 6 and FM 219 in Clifton take FM 219 east for 3.4 miles to CR 4145 and veer right. The next 10.5 miles on CR 4145 is a very scenic drive, and areas are available to stop and view nature at its best.

CONTACT INFORMATION
For additional information call: 800-344-3720 / Website: www.cliftontexas.org

PRAIRIES AND PINEYWOODS WEST

Western Kingbird

PRAIRIES AND PINEYWOODS - WEST
Meridian State Park

#28

173 PARK ROAD #7
MERIDIAN, TX 76665

KEY BIRDS
Golden-cheeked warbler, greater roadrunner

BEST SEASON
All seasons, depending on weather

AREA DESCRIPTION
Lakeside habitat plus a hiking trail with large hardwoods, open areas, limestone outcroppings, and aquatic vegetation

Hidden away in the wooded hills northwest of Waco in Bosque County, this 505-acre park is a haven for nature lovers and birders. Bird watching is excellent and there is a good chance of seeing the rare golden-cheeked warbler.

The park's 72-acre lake offers fishing in addition to swimming and no-wake boating. A hiking trail encircling Lake Meridian features limestone outcroppings with fossils, a scenic overlook, and aquatic vegetation. Meridian State Park provides a habitat mosaic centered on Lake Meridian, with several roads providing lakeside access.

While scanning the lake and its shore for great blue heron and wood duck, watch the trees for white-eyed vireo and yellow-billed cuckoo. The lakeside trail habitat is mostly ashe juniper/oak woodland and is home to a small population of golden-cheeked warblers. This beautiful endangered songbird is highly sought by birders, and several pair nest along the trail. Other birds to look for along the trail include greater roadrunner, black-chinned hummingbird, and blue-gray gnatcatcher.

DIRECTIONS
Take State Highway 174 from Cleburne, State Highway 144 from Glen Rose or State Highway 6 from Waco. Join State Highway 22 and proceed southwest to the park. Take State Highway 22 from Hillsboro or Hamilton. The park is located about 3 miles southwest of Meridian off State Highway 22.

CONTACT INFORMATION
The standard Texas park day-use and camping fees apply. Information and prices are subject to change. Please call the park or park information (1-800-792-1112) for the latest updates. Phone: 254-435-2536/ Website: http://www.tpwd.state.tx.us/spdest/findadest/parks/meridian/

Legend:

- ★ Headquarters
- State Parks Store
- Restrooms
- Showers
- Tent Sites
- Water/Electric
- R.V. RV Water/Elec./Sewer
- Sponsored Youth Camp
- Dump Station
- 10 Screened Shelters
- Hiking Trail
- Picnic Area
- Dining Hall
- P Parking
- Maintenance
- Residence
- Designated Swimming Area
- Boat Ramp
- Wheelchair Accessible

TEXAS PARKS & WILDLIFE

Meridian
State Park

Please Note:

- CHECK OUT time is 2 p.m. for all sites. Renew permit by 9 a.m. subject to availability.
- Public consumption or display of an alcoholic beverage is prohibited. All areas within this park are "public".
- Numbered sites are for overnight camping only. NO PICNICKING
- Park and drive on paved surfaces only.
- Quiet hours are enforced from 10 p.m. to 6 a.m. or at anytime a disturbance is created.
- Excess parking fee is required at campsites with more than two vehicles including trailers. All excess vehicles will be relocated to the overflow parking area.
- A maximum of eight people at any numbered campsite or shelter. All day-use visitors MUST leave the park prior to 10 p.m.
- No person shall use electrical speakers or radios at a volume which emits beyond their immediate campsite.
- No pets allowed in any park facility. Pets must not be left unattended or cause a disturbance.
- Gathering firewood prohibited.
- Swim at your own risk. NO LIFEGUARD on duty.

Golden-cheeked Warbler

Sponsored Youth Camping Area

To Meridian

Lime Springs Trail - 4 miles

Little Forest Junior Trail - .7 miles

One Way

Bosque Hiking Trail - 2.5 miles

NO WAKE LAKE

Lake Meridian

To Cranfills Gap & Hamilton

Water Only Camping Sites

Shinnery Ridge Trail - 1.64 miles

Paved Section

Primitive Camping Area

CCC Refectory

Park Reservations
(512) 389-8900
texasstateparks.org

Texas State Parks Store
Ice, firewood and one-of-a-kind gift items are available at the Texas State Parks Store in our park headquarters building.

173 Park Road 7
Meridian, TX 76665
(254) 435-2536

TOYOTA Proud Sponsor of Texas Parks and Wildlife Programs

PRAIRIES AND PINEYWOODS WEST

Ladder-backed Woodpecker

PRAIRIES AND PINEYWOODS - WEST
Huggins Mesa Vista Ranch

#29

LOCATED ON CR 214, 5.2 MILES FROM FM 219

KEY BIRDS
Dickcissel, lark sparrow, scissor-tailed flycatcher, and various woodpeckers

BEST SEASON
Summer, spring, fall

AREA DESCRIPTION
Large mesas of oaks and junipers, rolling native prairie

The Huggins Mesa Vista Ranch itself is situated on rolling native prairie interspersed with wooded areas. Several ponds dot the landscape. Open, grassy areas provide habitat for dickcissel, lark sparrow, and scissor-tailed flycatcher while various woodpeckers frequent the dead trees near the ponds. Great horned owls can sometimes be observed. While on the ranch, listen for the two-note whistle of the northern bobwhite, or the raucous chuckling of a wild turkey. This is a working ranch so please call ahead for permission.

DIRECTIONS
From Hico travel south 8.5 miles on Hwy 281 to FM 219, turn east onto FM 219. Go east 5.2 miles to CR 214; turn south on CR 214 and follow 0.2 mile to the house on right.

CONTACT INFORMATION
This location has restricted access, so please call before you go. Call: 254-796-1905.

PRAIRIES AND PINEYWOODS WEST

PRAIRIES AND PINEYWOODS - WEST
Fossil Rim Wildlife Center

#30

2155 COUNTY ROAD 2008
GLEN ROSE, TEXAS 76043

KEY BIRDS
Golden-cheeked warbler, black-capped vireo, Attwater's prairie chicken, wild turkey

BEST SEASON
All seasons

AREA DESCRIPTION
Rolling hills, grassland prairie, some wooded areas

Located about five miles from the town of Glen Rose, Fossil Rim Wildlife Center is best experienced from its nine-mile driving loop that passes through five large pastures, where rare and exotic wildlife roam in a natural setting. Although best known for such exotics as gemsbok, cheetah, white rhino, and Arabian oryx, Fossil Rim has many native Texas species to see as well.

While driving through the park, watch for resident flocks of wild turkey. There are also roadrunners along the roadway or perhaps a great horned owl. The area around the café and gift shop is of special wildlife-watching interest, since it hosts several breeding pairs of the endangered golden-cheeked warbler. The center is also actively working to improve habitat for the black-capped vireo, another of Texas's rare species.

The wildlife center is globally renowned for its captive breeding of some of the world's rarest animals. Although the center supports breeding programs for numerous African species, they also have a very successful restoration and breeding program for the Attwater's prairie chicken, an endangered species native to Texas coastal prairies. Visitors wishing to see the prairie chickens should take the Behind-the-Scenes Tour. Other activities within the park include guided mountain biking tours, two different lodges for overnight accommodations, and regularly scheduled education programs for children of all ages.

DIRECTIONS
From the intersection of US 67 and FM 56 in Glen Rose, take US 67 west 3.7 miles. Turn left (south) onto CR 2008 at the Fossil Rim sign. Go 1.2 miles to the stonework entrance to the Scenic Wildlife Drive on the right.

CONTACT INFORMATION:
This site is reportedly a non-profit facility, but their prices range from reasonable to expensive. However, if the birds are there it is well worth the price. Some prices may be found on the Center's web site.
Please call ahead for additional information at: 254-897-2960
Website: www.fossilrim.org

Rio Grande Turkey

PRAIRIES AND PINEYWOODS - WEST
Dinosaur Valley State Park

#31

NORTHWEST OF GLEN ROSE, TEXAS

KEY BIRDS
Black vulture, golden-cheeked warbler, black-capped vireo, great crested flycatcher, and blue-gray gnatcatcher

BEST SEASON
Weather permitting, all seasons

AREA DESCRIPTION
River and riverside habitats mixed with trees and open brush

Although best known for its prehistoric residents, this state park is an excellent way to see some of north Texas' more current avian residents.

Most visitors are immediately drawn to the Paluxy River and its famous dinosaur footprints. However, additional exploration throughout the park via the hike and bike trails can be very rewarding. The river is an excellent place to search for several species of birds. The ridges overlooking the river ring with the calls of the great crested flycatcher and blue-gray gnatcatcher. Watch the skies for soaring black vultures that are occasionally joined by one of the resident red-tailed hawks.

In the open brush land above the river, painted buntings abound and eastern bluebirds are scattered throughout the larger meadows. The park also hosts habitat for the endangered golden-cheeked warbler and black-capped vireo.

DIRECTIONS
From the intersection of US 67 and FM 205 in Glen Rose, go west on FM 205 for 2.7 miles to PR 59. Turn right on PR 59 and follow 0.6 mile to the park headquarters.

CONTACT INFORMATION
The standard Texas park day-use and camping fees apply. Information and prices are subject to change. Call the park at 254-897-4588 or park information (1-800-792-1112) for the latest updates.

Black Vulture

PRAIRIES AND PINEYWOODS - WEST
Glen Rose Bird Sanctuary

#32

107 SW BANARD STREET
GLEN ROSE, TEXAS

KEY BIRDS
Carolina wren, American robin, red-bellied woodpecker, eastern phoebe, cedar waxwing, and yellow-rumped warbler

BEST SEASON
All seasons, as you are a short walk away from a cup of coffee

AREA DESCRIPTION
This vacant lot on SW Barnard Street in Historic Glen Rose, Texas lies between two-century-old buildings

Located in the Town Square, Glen Rose Bird Sanctuary serves as an important example of what can be achieved for wildlife in an urban setting with some hard work and dedication. The Texas Commission on Environmental Quality has even produced a 30-minute video for PBS titled "Taking Care of Texas" that prominently features the sanctuary and its volunteer efforts to keep the Paluxy River clean.

Located in downtown Glen Rose on a seasonal stream, the park is augmented by several bird feeders, making it an attractive residence or stopover for any migrant in the vicinity.

In summer, nesting species include Carolina wren, American robin, red-bellied woodpecker, and eastern phoebe. During the winter months, species to look out for include cedar waxwing, yellow-rumped warbler, and American goldfinch.

Depending on the correct weather conditions during migration, almost anything could turn up, from wood warblers to eastern wood pewees to flycatchers. This site is small but well laid out and well worth a birder's time, whether it's for an hour or for the day and whatever the time of year, the bird sanctuary is always worth a look.

DIRECTIONS
From the intersection of FM 56 and US 67 in Glen Rose, go east on FM 56/ Hereford Street for 0.3 mile to Barnard Street. Turn left and go 0.1 mile to the Glen Rose Bird Sanctuary on the right. The sanctuary is located just off the downtown square in Glen Rose. Park anywhere around the courthouse and walk to the corner of Barnard Street and Elm Street, and go 1/4 block west on Barnard Street.

CONTACT INFORMATION
Volunteer Information Coordinator, Rod Hale - 1375 CR 313, Glen Rose, Texas 75043 / Phone: 254 - 897 – 3484 / Website: http://www.glenrosearea.com/pages/birds.html

PRAIRIES AND
PINEYWOODS WEST

PRAIRIES AND PINEYWOODS - WEST
#33 Paluxy Heritage Park

CORNER OF E. ELM STREET AND MATTHEWS STREET
GLEN ROSE, TEXAS

KEY BIRDS
Red-bellied and downy woodpeckers, mourning dove, scissor-tailed flycatcher, western kingbird, great blue and green herons

BEST SEASON
Depending on the weather, all seasons

AREA DESCRIPTION
City landscapes and river frontage habitats

Glen Rose's Heritage Park includes several celebrated buildings from the earliest days of European settlement in the region. Situated among the historic houses are native oaks, which support red-bellied and downy woodpeckers, as well as mourning dove. The scissor-tailed flycatcher and western kingbird prefer the roadside habitat, while great blue and green herons can be found along the river. During the summer months, nesting cliff swallows frequent the park's Elm Street Bridge.

A great feature here is that you really have two parks available to bird watchers. From Heritage Park, a path takes you to Big Rocks Park. There's a nice walkway that was recently constructed. This path runs along the Paluxy River and there's a dock and an overlook along the way. This walkway terminates at the dam just before Big Rocks Park. You can walk across the dam and be in Big Rocks in no time. This is probably about a quarter-mile walk.

DIRECTIONS
From the intersection of US 67 and FM 56/ Hereford Street in Glen Rose, go east on FM 56 for 0.3 mile to Barnard Street. Turn left and go 0.1 mile to Elm St./ SR 144; turn right and go south across the Paluxy Bridge. Continue one block and turn left into the park just across the Paluxy River from Downtown Square.

CONTACT INFORMATION
The parks are open only during daylight hours. No fees are charged to bird these parks.
Phone: 254-897-9737
Website: http://trtdg.com/2010/05/12/paluxy-heritage-park-in-glen-rose-texas/

PRAIRIES AND PINEYWOODS - WEST
Country Woods Inn

#34

4208 GRAND AVENUE
GLEN ROSE, TEXAS 76043

KEY BIRDS
Wild turkey, black-crested titmouse, yellow-billed cuckoo, great-crested flycatcher

BEST SEASON
Spring and fall

AREA DESCRIPTION
Riverside meadows and dense woodlands

Country Woods Inn is located along the Paluxy River, just downstream from the Heritage Park. This delightful B & B offers a diversity of 13 different accommodations, ranging from glorious country houses to a fully furnished boxcar. These guest quarters are spread out across 40 acres of riverside meadows and dense woodlands, providing a variety of bird watching opportunities. Birds such as the wild turkey, black-crested titmouse, and yellow-billed cuckoo can be heard and observed. Several trails lead from the open meadow into the woodland along the river. This is the best area to watch for the great-crested flycatcher.

DIRECTIONS
In the square around the Court House in downtown Glen Rose, take Elm St./ SR 144 south 0.2 mile and look for the Citgo Gas Station at the road fork and stay left. After one block turn left on Grand Avenue and follow it north 0.4 mile to its end. Upon reaching the inn's entrance, continue and you will see signs at each cabin. The main house is at the end of the lane.

CONTACT INFORMATION
If the gate is locked, call for the gate code: 817-279-3002.
For information, call 888-849-6637
Website: http://www.countrywoodsinn.com
Email: countrywoodsinn@yahoo.com

PRAIRIES AND
PINEYWOODS WEST

Black-crested Titmouse

PRAIRIES AND PINEYWOODS - WEST
Cedars On The Brazos

#35

2920 COUNTY ROAD 413
GLEN ROSE, TEXAS 76043

KEY BIRDS
Great-horned owl, whip-poor-will, wild turkey, black-chinned hummingbird

BEST SEASON
All seasons

AREA DESCRIPTION
River frontage and overlook with some wooded and low brush areas

Another B & B for birders, the Cedars on the Brazos shatters all preconceived notions about log cabins and cedar trees. This three-room bed and breakfast sits on a tranquil bend of the Brazos River, providing access to peace, quiet, and some astounding wildlife.

Located atop a bluff overlooking the river, it sits among 110 beautiful, heavily wooded acres. It is the perfect place for a birding trip as well as to just relax. This location is also a bird watcher's paradise! Listen to the evening sounds of the great horned owl and whip-poor-will, just to mention a few.

Many species can be found a short distance from the B & B, with nine-banded armadillos wandering the creek beds, wild turkey foraging along the riverbanks, and great horned owls perching quietly on the neighboring cliffs.

For those who don't wish to wander, many species congregate around the feeders that line the stone patio. Numerous hummingbird feeders bring dozens of black-chinned hummingbirds to the property daily.

In the evening you can relax to the sounds of the Chuck-will's-widow and watch swallows flying their erratic patterns as they catch insects.

DIRECTIONS
From Court House Square in Glen Rose, go south on Elm Street/ SR 144 for 0.7 mile to Hwy 56 South. Turn left on Hwy 56 and go 0.6 mile to CR 413. Turn left (northeast) on CR 413 and follow 2.0 miles to a dead end at the gate. Continue 0.3 mile to the bed and breakfast.

CONTACT INFORMATION
Fees here run from $100.00 to around $150.00. For more information Call: 254-898-1000 / Website: www.cedarsonthebrazos.com

PRAIRIES AND PINEYWOODS WEST

PRAIRIES AND PINEYWOODS - WEST
Somervell County Park

#36

GLEN ROSE, TEXAS

KEY BIRDS
Downy woodpecker, lark sparrow, scissor-tailed flycatcher, red-bellied woodpecker

BEST SEASON
All seasons

AREA DESCRIPTION
Large trees, some low brush, with open grass and pasture around lakeside habitat

Somervell County Park is centered on an open soccer playing field which can hold surprises for the wildlife watcher. The lark sparrow can be found feeding in the short grass and scissor-tailed flycatchers often perch on the goal posts.

Common green darners and black saddlebags patrol overhead while eastern bluebirds often perch in the trees around the edge. The pond near the entrance hosts the red-winged blackbird and great-tailed grackle.

Downy woodpeckers fly about from tree to tree uttering their high-pitched calls, while red-bellied woodpeckers are more likely to stay hidden in the oaks. A careful ear is required when listening to birds in this area, because the park's northern mockingbirds are accomplished mimics with an impressive repertoire.

DIRECTIONS
From the intersection of FM 56 and US 67 in Glen Rose, go north on US 67 for 1.3 miles to Bo Gibbs Blvd. Turn left (west), go 0.1 mile and turn right onto Texas Drive. Travel east 0.1 mile on Texas Drive and turn left into the park.

CONTACT INFORMATION
Site open for day use only. Phone: 254-897-4509.

Scissor-tailed Flycatcher

PRAIRIES AND PINEYWOODS WEST

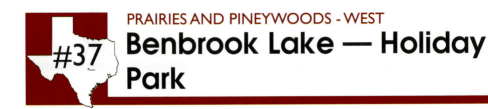

PRAIRIES AND PINEYWOODS - WEST

Benbrook Lake — Holiday Park

#37

SOUTHWEST AREA OF FORT WORTH, TEXAS

KEY BIRDS
Northern bobwhite, western kingbird, great crested and scissor-tailed flycatchers

BEST SEASON
All seasons

AREA DESCRIPTION
Open parkland with shrubs on the western margin and a few towering trees dotting the shoreline

HOLIDAY PARK DAY-USE AREA

Holiday Park's day-use area grants visitors access to the western shore of Benbrook Lake via a 7.3-mile hiking trail. This area is primarily open parkland with shrubs on the western margin and a few towering trees dotting the shoreline. Look carefully among the tree branches for eastern and western kingbirds and great crested and scissor-tailed flycatchers. The winter months attract birds such as cedar waxwing, while the brushy areas provide perches for painted bunting and cover for northern bobwhite. Quail are visible along the roadsides early in the morning or late in the afternoon. Benbrook Lake itself is worth a look any time of year, with double-crested cormorant, white pelican, Franklin's or ring-billed gulls, and perhaps a more unusual vagrant.

DIRECTIONS
To get to Holiday Park day use area from I-20 exit 429A, go 2.4 miles southwest on US Highway 377 to Stephens Drive, then east 0.25 mile and left into the park on Lakeview Drive, across from the Benbrook VFW hall.

CONTACT INFORMATION
Call: 817-292-2400 / Website: www1.swf-wc.usace.army.mil/benbrook

HOLIDAY PARK CAMPGROUND

Just south of Holiday Park Day-Use Area is the Holiday Camp Campground. This area of lakefront includes grasslands, interspersed shrub land, and a number of majestic oak trees. The oaks bring welcome shade, and in spring and fall are filled with migrants. Birds to look for include white-eyed vireo, summer tanager, and yellow-billed cuckoo.

Watch along the shoreline for roosting black and turkey vultures or the occasional migrant, such as yellow warbler. The small inlet of Benbrook Lake near the campground is

PRAIRIES AND PINEYWOODS WEST

a good place to look for great blue, little blue, and green herons, as well as great egret and wood duck. This area provides a clear view of the lake, with numerous cliff swallows and chimney swifts skirting its surface for a drink. To get a great picture of these and others, follow the park's quarter-mile level-grade hiking trail to the photography blind located along the north river bank of the Trinity River's Clear Fork's mouth. The photography blind has no fee and no reservations. It's on a first-come first-served basis.

DIRECTIONS

From the intersection of US 377 and FM 1187, go northeast 0.6 mile on US 377, crossing the bridge over the Clear Fork of the Trinity River, to Pearl Ranch Drive. Turn right (east) on Pearl Ranch Drive, go 1.7 miles to the park entrance.

Northern Bobwhite

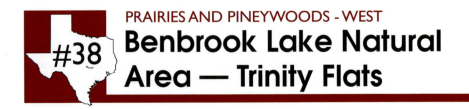

PRAIRIES AND PINEYWOODS - WEST
Benbrook Lake Natural Area — Trinity Flats

#38

SOUTHWEST AREA OF FORT WORTH, TEXAS

KEY BIRDS
Indigo bunting, eastern kingbird, red-bellied and downy woodpeckers, Rio Grande turkey

BEST SEASON
Spring, winter, summer

AREA DESCRIPTION
Forested bottomland and open prairie

The area consists of 1,069 total park acres (including natural areas) and four developed parks comprising approximately 120 acres.

The first thing a visitor to Trinity Flats will notice during spring or summer is the considerable nesting colony of cliff swallows under the US 377 bridge. Careful inspection will reveal dozens of these architectural wonders of mud. From here, go east along the edge of the Trinity River's Clear Fork. A dirt road parallels the forest and at times runs between open prairie and bottomland. Because of the diversity, this road is ideal for seeing species of both habitats, and numerous side trails allow a more in-depth study of either. Look along the bottoms for barred owl, red-bellied and downy woodpeckers, Carolina wren, and summer tanager. On the prairie side of the road, keep a look out for indigo bunting and eastern kingbird. Watch the road proper for red-shouldered hawks in search of their next meal.

Early risers often have a chance to see Rio Grande turkeys. Please note that public access may be limited from September 1st till the end of January annually, when the area is open to (restricted) hunting.

DIRECTIONS
From intersection of US 377 and FM 1187 East in southwest Ft. Worth, go 0.1 mile northeast on US 377 and turn right (east) to go below the US 377 bridge over the Clear Fork of the Trinity River. This will take you to a parking area and access point.

CONTACT INFORMATION
Camping is available and a fee is charged. There is no fee for day use at this time.
Please call: 817-292-2400
Website: www1.swf-wc.usace.army.mil/Benbrook

PRAIRIES AND PINEYWOODS - WEST
Wheaton: Pyramid Road

#39

BENBROOK, TEXAS

KEY BIRDS
Scissor-tailed flycatcher, grasshopper warbler, dickcissel, quail

BEST SEASON
All seasons

AREA DESCRIPTION
Rolling prairie and shrub land

Before Fort Worth exploded to its current size, much of the area must have looked something like Pyramid Road. These few acres of rolling prairie and shrub land offer great wildlife watching opportunities. Listening to the birds on an early summer morning will make you wonder if the bobwhite and dickcissel are in a singing competition, since both songs can be heard from every direction. Add to that the eastern meadowlark and you have a beautiful cacophony of sound that needs to be heard to be believed. Listen carefully and you may be able to pick out the insect-like calling of the grasshopper warbler among the rest of the songsters. The scissor-tailed flycatcher and western kingbird can be seen performing their always-impressive aerial display, and the painted buntings can be seen perching on top of their respective bushes.

DIRECTIONS
From the intersection of Hwy 377 and I-20 in Benbrook, drive south on Hwy 377 for 6.7 miles. At the highway crossover, turn left onto Pyramid Road and follow this gravel road 1.5 miles into the subdivision.

CONTACT INFORMATION
This location is only open during daylight hours.
Phone: 817-237-1111 and ask for Fort Worth Audubon contact information.
Website: www.fwas.org

PRAIRIES AND
PINEYWOODS WEST

PRAIRIES AND PINEYWOODS - WEST
Winscott Plover Road

#40

FORT WORTH, TEXAS

KEY BIRDS
Northern harrier, red-tailed hawk, golden eagle, and prairie falcon

BEST SEASON
Winter

AREA DESCRIPTION
Roadway with over four miles of open prairie

Winscott Plover Road spans over four miles of open prairie complete with fence rows and telephone lines, making it a haven for wintering raptors. In fact, almost every raptor recorded in north-central Texas has been found along this road. This includes not only the northern harrier and red-tailed hawk, but the golden eagle and prairie falcon as well. In summer, look and listen for dickcissel, eastern meadowlark, loggerhead shrike, and the occasional grasshopper sparrow. The area is also frequented by roosting common nighthawks, which are often found perched on fence poles.

Harris's Hawk

DIRECTIONS
From the intersection of US 377 and FM 1187 East in southwest Ft. Worth, go 3.9 miles east on FM 1187. Turn right onto Winscott-Plover Road and proceed 1.6 miles to railroad tracks. After the railroad tracks, turn right and follow 2.6 miles to the stop sign.

CONTACT INFORMATION
This is a day-use-only location.
For more information, call 817-237-1111 and ask for Fort Worth Audubon contact information.
Website: www.fwas.org

PRAIRIES AND PINEYWOODS - WEST

#41 Benbrook Lake — Mustang Park and Mustang Point Campground

SOUTHWEST AREA OF FORT WORTH

KEY BIRDS
Foster's tern, Franklin's gull, laughing gull

BEST SEASON
Winter, spring, fall

AREA DESCRIPTION
A thin peninsula and the best vantage to view the southern end of Lake Benbrook

Mustang Point is perhaps the best vantage to view the southern end of Lake Benbrook, a wildlife haven on the outskirts of metropolitan Fort Worth. This thin peninsula, complete with access road and parking at its tip, permits visitors to venture out into the lake.

Area regulars such as Forster's tern and Franklin's gull, as well as migrant shorebirds such as spotted sandpiper and white-rumped sandpiper, come to perch out on the point. In contrast to 15-20 years ago when turkey were extinct in Tarrant County, visitors today can catch a glimpse of a Rio Grande turkey in the mornings. The lake has produced several unusual species for the area, including laughing gull and whimbrel. Waterfowl frequent the lake in winter and the common loon may be seen at times. Great blue herons and great egrets can be observed along the shoreline, while great crested flycatchers can be heard calling from the surrounding, taller trees. Look for white-tailed deer grazing on the roadside or the occasional roadrunner darting after a lizard.

DIRECTIONS
From the intersection of US 377 and FM 1187 East in southwest Ft. Worth, go 3.9 miles east on FM 1187, then left (north) on CR 1042/ Winscott Plover Road for 1.2 miles to the park entrance.

CONTACT INFORMATION
This site is open daily with some developed camping available for an overnight fee. For more information call: 817-292-2400 / Website: www1.swf-wc.usace.army.mil/benbrook

Laughing Gull

PRAIRIES AND
PINEYWOODS WEST

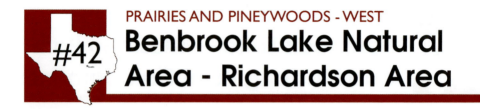

PRAIRIES AND PINEYWOODS - WEST

#42 Benbrook Lake Natural Area - Richardson Area

SOUTHWEST AREA OF FORT WORTH

KEY BIRDS
American kestrel, eastern meadowlark, wood duck, little blue heron

BEST SEASON
All seasons

AREA DESCRIPTION
Mostly lakeshore habitat, open fields, and low brush

In spring, the Richardson Area of the Benbrook Lake Natural Area is a riot of color with thousands of wildflowers. The open fields of wildflowers are also frequented by dickcissel and eastern meadowlark. Raptors, such as American kestrel, can also be seen. For the adventurous, a hike along the eastern shore of Benbrook Lake can produce sightings of wood duck, little blue heron, and many other species including the Rio Grande turkey, which at one point was extinct from the area.

Birdwatching is a favorite pastime of many visitors to Benbrook Lake. All kinds of songbirds, hawks, and even an occasional bald eagle visit the area. Great blue heron, ducks, and geese in the winter, and various other shore birds frequent the area and give the birdwatching public something to see year-round.

Visitors to the Richardson area will get a glimpse into what pristine Texas looked like. Over the last 60 years this land has been well managed, having been neither cultivated nor over-grazed.

***Please note, however, that public access to the area may be limited from September 1st to January 31st annually for (restricted) hunting. Birders should call ahead for closures.

DIRECTIONS
From I-20 in southwest Fort Worth, take Exit 434A for Granbury Road. Go southwest 2.7 miles to Alta Mesa Boulevard. Continue straight ahead on Granbury Road south for 1.0 mile to a T-junction at Colombus Road. Turn right onto Colombus Road and go 0.5 mile to Old Granbury Road/ CR 1902. Turn left and go 0.8 mile to the parking area and access point on the right.

CONTACT INFORMATION:
Site open for day use only. Phone: 817-292-2400 / Website: www1.swf-wc.usace.army.mil/benbrook

PRAIRIES AND PINEYWOODS - WEST
Fort Worth Oakmont Park

#43

7000 BELLAIRE DRIVE S.
FORT WORTH, TEXAS 76132

KEY BIRDS
Great-tailed grackle, purple martin, chimney swift, and Bewick's wren

BEST SEASON
Birding is best during the warmer months of spring through fall

AREA DESCRIPTION
Open playgrounds and hardwood bottomland located along the northern branch of the Clear Fork of the Trinity River

Oakmont Park offers miles of cement trails rolling across a gently changing habitat. This city park is fully accessible and does offer birders some of the best urban wildlife watching in the Fort Worth area.

The playground areas and a playground are combined with hardwood bottomland of a northern branch of the Clear Fork of the Trinity River.

Birders should watch for western kingbirds, which are present along with numerous great-tailed grackle, purple martin, and chimney swift. While hiking through the riparian woodland, watch for tufted titmouse and Carolina chickadee flocks as well as for less common species such as blue-gray gnatcatcher, downy woodpecker, or perhaps a migrant warbler or two. Listen for noisy chattering from the Carolina wren or perhaps a Bewick's wren. Watch carefully to see several great blue herons wading in this tiny stream. Herons actually nest just a mile or so down the trail and several pairs are usually in evidence at the rookery.

DIRECTIONS
From I-20 in southwest Fort Worth, take Exit 431 for Bryant Irvin Boulevard. Go southwest 1.4 miles to Oakmont Boulevard. Turn right onto Oakmont Boulevard and go 0.7 mile to Bellaire Drive South. Turn right and go 0.1 mile to the park on the left.

CONTACT INFORMATION
Birders are welcome to use the park during daylight hours. For additional information and information about park sightings call: 817-871-6763.

PRAIRIES AND PINEYWOODS - WEST
Fort Worth Forest Park
#44

NEAR THE FORT WORTH ZOO IN FORT WORTH, TEXAS

KEY BIRDS
Barn swallow, cliff swallow, purple martin, great-tailed grackle, and eastern bluebird

BEST SEASON
Birding is best during the warmer months of spring through fall

AREA DESCRIPTION
City park with open grassy areas as well as wooded areas along the river

This city park completely encircles the Fort Worth Zoo. For visitors, Forest Park affords a little bit of wilderness along the Trinity River in downtown Fort Worth. The river attracts numerous barn swallows, cliff swallows, and purple martins which come to drink, therefore making the channel of the Trinity River a prominent spot to start searching for wildlife.

Watch carefully throughout the open grassy areas of the park for the ever present great-tailed grackle as well as eastern bluebird. And through the thick wooded areas crisscrossing the park, typical woodland species can be found including red-bellied and downy woodpeckers, Carolina wren, blue jay, and some interesting migrants in spring and fall. The wooded areas will also host the resident red-shouldered hawk, both in the trees and hunting from above.

DIRECTIONS
In Fort Worth, from I-30, take Exit 12/ University Drive. Go south on University for 0.8 mile to Colonial Parkway and turn left. Follow Colonial Parkway 0.3 mile into the park.

CONTACT INFORMATION
Site open for day use only. Phone: 817-871-PARK / 817-871-7698.

PRAIRIES AND PINEYWOODS - WEST
Fort Worth Botanic Gardens

#45

3220 BOTANIC GARDEN BLVD.
FORT WORTH, TEXAS 73107

KEY BIRDS
Western kingbird, red-tailed hawk, and wild turkey

BEST SEASON
All seasons, with late spring the best choice

AREA DESCRIPTION
Best described as a showplace for plants, the exhaustive landscape attracts many species of birds

The Fort Worth Botanic Gardens have over a hundred acres of woods and gardens filled with more than 2,500 species of native and exotic plants.

Many bird species native to eastern North America can be seen here, including neotropical migrants in the spring and fall. What really makes the Botanic Gardens stand out are the numerous streams and ponds scattered throughout. These water sources provide year-round habitats for the skulking green heron and basking red-eared slider. After seeing the rose gardens and Japanese gardens, be sure to visit the plantings at the far northern entrance on Conservatory Drive. These gardens feature native plant species requiring limited water and maintenance. Watch for western kingbird, red-tailed hawk, and wild turkey.

DIRECTIONS
From I-30 heading west in Fort Worth, take Exit 12/ University Drive. Go north on University Drive to the two entrances on your left; the Garden Center is located at the second entrance after 0.4 mile.

CONTACT INFORMATION
Open daily. Call for more information: 817-871-7686 / Website: www.fwbg.org

PRAIRIES AND
PINEYWOODS WEST

PRAIRIES AND PINEYWOODS - WEST
Tanglewood

#46

FORT WORTH, TEXAS

KEY BIRDS
Yellow-billed cuckoo, northern cardinal, blue jay, and wood duck

BEST SEASON
Spring and fall migrations

AREA DESCRIPTION
Streamside habitat and water make up this park

This urban park, although small, and its associated stream is bursting with wildlife and offers a perfect short break spot to stretch your legs and enjoy the wildlife or perhaps turn up some exciting warblers during migration. It is another good stopping place for the traveling birder as well as locals alike. The stream here is a birder's best friend.

The creek itself holds green heron and the beautiful wood duck roosting quietly on fallen logs along the stream or using the numerous nest boxes found throughout the park.

Northern Cardinal

The skulking yellow-billed cuckoo, whose insect-like call can regularly be heard in the park, joins familiar parkland birds such as northern cardinal and blue jay in summer. Another summer resident is the great crested flycatcher, which is often to be found perched among the highest branches surveying the park and its visitors far below.

DIRECTIONS
From I-30 in southwest Fort Worth, take Exit 10 and go south on Hulen Road for 1.7 miles. Turn left on Hartwood, and proceed 0.3 mile to Pebblebrook Court. Turn right and note the park on the right as you follow Pebblebrook.

CONTACT INFORMATION
Open during the daylight hours. Please call for additional information: 817-735-9560

PRAIRIES AND PINEYWOODS - WEST
Foster Park

FORT WORTH, TEXAS

KEY BIRDS
Red-bellied and downy woodpeckers, yellow-billed cuckoo, white-eyed vireo, summer tanager, and indigo bunting

BEST SEASON
All seasons

AREA DESCRIPTION
Open park area with streamside habitats

Foster Park is another of Fort Worth's green oases in the city. This park runs along a cattail-filled creek, which is crisscrossed by a paved walking trail. Numerous other trails branch off from the pavement making a large area of the park accessible to visitors. Search the park in spring and fall for neotropical migrants. Resident birds include downy and red-bellied woodpeckers and the Carolina wren. During the summer the yellow-billed cuckoo and white-eyed vireo join these species. While walking the trails remember to keep an eye out for chimney swift or perhaps a white-winged dove. Careful inspection of the creek can produce green heron and other wading birds.

DIRECTIONS
From I-820 in southwest Fort Worth, take Exit 434A/ Granbury Road. Follow the access road 0.5 mile to South Drive. Turn right (east) on South Drive and follow 1.0 mile to Foster Park.

CONTACT INFORMATION
For basic park information only call: 817-237-1111
Website: www.naturecenterfriends.org

PRAIRIES AND PINEYWOODS - WEST
#48 Fort Worth Nature Center & Refuge

ON THE SHORE OF LAKE WORTH – FORT WORTH, TEXAS

KEY BIRDS
Red-bellied and downy woodpeckers, yellow-billed cuckoo, white-eyed vireo, summer tanager, and indigo bunting

BEST SEASON
All seasons weather permitting

AREA DESCRIPTION
Lake Worth shoreline, leading from prime Trinity River bottomland, through Cross Timbers oak savannah, to prairie grassland

The Fort Worth Nature Center encompasses several thousand acres of the best habitats north-central Texas has to offer. The area molds around the northern shores of Lake Worth leading from prime Trinity River bottomland, through Cross Timbers oak savannah, to prairie grassland. This park also has a herd of American bison. The entire property makes for great wildlife viewing. Of particular interest is the short boardwalk that leads the visitor out onto a lily-pad-covered arm of Lake Worth. In summer this area hosts prothonotary warbler and blue grosbeak calling from the shoreline. Watch for Mississippi kite above the lake. This area also supports a variety of herons and egrets, and waterfowl are plentiful in the winter months.

The woodland canopy hosts numerous red-eyed vireos and yellow-billed cuckoos and the fortunate observer may find a pileated woodpecker.

Throughout the prairie areas, birders should watch for the scissor-tailed flycatcher and painted bunting. Walking along the trails, birders will find a variety of species such as red-bellied and downy woodpeckers, yellow-billed cuckoo, white-eyed vireo, summer tanager, and indigo bunting.

If all these viewing opportunities are not enough, the Fort Worth Nature Center also offers an interpretive center that regularly holds educational events, as well as an impressive set of exhibits covering the local flora and fauna. They even have a gift shop where you can stock up on gifts or the latest field guides.

DIRECTIONS
From I-820 in Fort Worth, take Exit 10A and follow Hwy 199 west 3.7 miles. Exit at Confederate Road and turn right into the refuge at the stop sign. Follow the signs 1.6 miles to the Visitor Center.

CONTACT INFORMATION
This is a day-use area only, call for information: 817-237-1111
Website: www.naturecenterfriends.org

PRAIRIES AND PINEYWOODS - WEST
#49 Camp Joy and Wildwood Park

ON LAKE WORTH'S SOUTHWEST SHORE – FORT WORTH, TEXAS

KEY BIRDS
Gulls, terns, common loon, eared grebe, and bald eagle

BEST SEASON
Fall, winter, spring

AREA DESCRIPTION
Open expanses with a mixture of large trees along the lake's shoreline and undisturbed tract of bottomland forest

Camp Joy and Wildwood Park are located near one another along Lake Worth's southwest shore. Camp Joy, the smaller of the two, is a mostly open expanse with a mix of large trees scattered along the shoreline.

This area provides an excellent vantage point to search the lake, which in the winter months support a variety of waterfowl as well as the common loon and eared grebe.

Spring and fall migration brings the chance to see white pelicans and a variety of gulls and terns, some of which are notably rare in the area.

Wildwood Park is located west of Camp Joy and combines shoreline access with a largely undisturbed tract of bottomland forest. This area is best known for occasionally hosting bald eagles, which have been known to nest here. Other species to look for include red-bellied and downy woodpeckers, yellow-billed cuckoo, white-eyed vireo, summer tanager and indigo bunting.

DIRECTIONS
From I-820 in Fort Worth, take Exit 10A. Go west onto SR 199/ Lake Worth Blvd. for 3.7 miles. Turn off onto the ramp (FM 1886/ Confederate Park Rd.) and go left (west) on FM 1886/ Confederate Park Road for 0.8 mile to Lakeridge Road. Turn left (south) and follow 0.6 mile to Watercress Drive and Lake Worth. At the end of the road, Camp Joy is to the left and Wildwood Park is to the right.

CONTACT INFORMATION
A day-use area. Call: 817-871-PARK - 817-871-9650.

PRAIRIES AND
PINEYWOODS WEST

Laughing Gull

PRAIRIES AND PINEYWOODS - WEST
#50 Old State Fish Hatchery, Lake Worth

PRAIRIES AND PINEYWOODS WEST

NEAR THE LAKE WORTH DAM – FORT WORTH, TEXAS

KEY BIRDS
Little blue heron, snowy egret, white-faced ibis, and waterfowl

BEST SEASON
Weather permitting, all seasons

AREA DESCRIPTION
Open areas, several old fish ponds, and river bottom habitat

The Old State Fish Hatchery is located just below the Lake Worth dam and hugs the Trinity River. The area's original use as a hatchery has left numerous ponds and levees for the enjoyment of wildlife and wildlife watchers.

This area is a great place to see waterfowl in the winter months as well as herons and egrets during the summer. Birders should inquire at the headquarters about water levels in the various ponds.

Ponds with little water and lots of moist mud can attract birds such as little blue heron, snowy egret, white-faced ibis, and a variety of migrant shore birds. Ponds with floating vegetation are better suited for waterfowl.

Follow the entrance road to its end to experience the Trinity River bottomland, with red-eyed vireo and Carolina wren filling the woods with their songs.

DIRECTIONS
From the Northwest Loop of I-820 in Fort Worth, take Exit 10A to Jacksboro Highway/Hwy 199. Proceed southeast on Jacksboro Hwy toward downtown Fort Worth for 2.5 miles to River Oaks Blvd. Turn right onto River Oaks Blvd. and proceed 1.2 miles to Roberts Cutoff Road. Turn right onto Roberts Cutoff Road. Proceed on Roberts Cutoff for about 100 yards and take the first left onto Meandering Road. Stay on Meandering Road. It will cross the Trinity River and after 1.3 miles take a right turn onto Sand Springs Road. The road turns left at the entrance to Camp Carter. Keep going until you see the Lake Worth dam on your left. Parallel the dam until you see the entrance to the fish hatchery on the right after 0.6 mile. Park inside the entrance on the fish hatchery grounds.

CONTACT INFORMATION
Entrance to this location is restricted and no fees are charged. Birders are asked to please call ahead: 817-732-0761.

PRAIRIES AND PINEYWOODS - WEST
#51 Tarrant County Junior College

NW Campus And Marine Creek Lake

NORTHWEST FORT WORTH, TEXAS

KEY BIRDS
Waterfowl, red-winged blackbird, rails, brown thrasher, and eastern and western kingbirds

BEST SEASON
All seasons

AREA DESCRIPTION
Lakeshore habitats and grassy areas

Similar to the other lakes in Fort Worth, Marine Creek Lake is best known for attracting waterfowl during the winter months.

The lake also supports a variety of wading birds year round, including great blue, little blue, and green herons, and both great and snowy egrets. Red-winged blackbirds and rails can be seen in the lake's shallow inlets.

The lakeshore is mostly open with areas of interspersed brush, where brown thrasher and eastern and western kingbirds can be observed.

DIRECTIONS
From the Northwest Loop of I-820 in Fort Worth, take the Marine Creek Parkway Exit 0.1 mile to the college. Turn left onto campus and proceed 0.2 mile to the first stop sign. Turn left and go 0.1 mile to the parking area.

CONTACT INFORMATION
This is a day-use-only area. Birders may call for any new campus regulations or information. Call: 817-515-7100.

Long-billed Thrasher

PRAIRIES AND PINEYWOODS WEST

PRAIRIES AND PINEYWOODS - WEST
Cement Creek Lake

#52

NEAR THE MEACHAM AIRPORT – FORT WORTH, TEXAS

KEY BIRDS
Red-winged blackbird, great-tailed grackle, king rail, and least bittern

BEST SEASON
All seasons

AREA DESCRIPTION
A shallow, reed-filled lake

Cement Creek Lake is a shallow reed-filled lake very close to the busy I-820 Loop in Fort Worth, just across from the Meacham Airport. Even in the heart of this urban area, Cement Creek Lake hosts a great variety of wildlife.

The lake's extensive reed beds provide habitat for roosting red-winged blackbird and great-tailed grackle. King rail and least bittern have also been seen here. Where the reeds give way to open water, look for blue-winged teal and pied-billed grebe. The muddy banks attract killdeer and spotted sandpiper, as well as snowy egret, little blue heron, and occasionally a white-faced ibis.

At the northern end of the lake a culvert supports a healthy population of nesting cliff swallows, who perform endless aerial acrobatics as they skim the surface of the lake.

DIRECTIONS
From the Northwest Loop of I-820 in Fort Worth, take the Hwy 287 Business Exit and go south toward downtown about 0.5 mile. Turn right onto a gravel road which parallels the Meacham Airfield fence line until you reach the parking area.

CONTACT INFORMATION
A day-use-only area, for information call: 817-237-1111. Birders may also ask for Fort Worth Audubon information. Their website is: www.fwas.org

Red-winged Blackbird

PRAIRIES AND PINEYWOODS - WEST
#53 Walnut Grove Park/Lake Grapevine

N. WHITE CHAPEL BLVD.
SOUTHLAKE, TEXAS

KEY BIRDS
Common yellowthroat, black-and-white warbler, yellow-breasted chat, Kentucky warbler, red-eyed vireo, warbling vireo, and indigo bunting

BEST SEASON
Spring, fall, and winter

AREA DESCRIPTION
Riparian and lakeside habitat

Lake Grapevine is managed by the U.S. Army Corps of Engineers. There are several parks around the lake, including Marshall Creek, Meadowmere, Oak Grove, Silver Lake, Rockledge, Rocky Point, Knob Hills, and Northshore. In addition to these parks, several nature trails are available for hikers, mountain bikers, and horseback riders, including the Northshore Trail, Knob Hills Trail, Bluestem Nature Trail, Walnut Grove Trail, Cross Timbers Trail, and the Rocky Point Trail.

The trail from the parking area leads visitors into open areas where vines blanket low shrubs. Dead trees provide perches for red-bellied woodpecker, indigo bunting, and other birds. Listen for the songs of the northern cardinal, Carolina wren, tufted titmouse, and other resident birds within the riparian habitat. Patient birders might hear the common yellowthroat, black-and-white warbler, yellow-breasted chat, Kentucky warbler, red-eyed vireo, warbling vireo, and blue-gray gnatcatcher. Snowy egrets are sometimes seen flying up the stream channel.

DIRECTIONS
From SH 114 and N. White Chapel Blvd. in Southlake, head north on N. White Chapel Blvd. for 1.7 miles to the entry, which is on the right (east) side. Enter the parking area and the trailhead is marked with a sign.

CONTACT INFORMATION
The area is for flood and water storage. Please call for information: 817-481-4541 / Website: www.swf-wc.usace.army.mil/grapevine/

PRAIRIES AND PINEYWOODS - WEST
Bob Jones Park

#54

NEAR SOUTHLAKE, TEXAS

KEY BIRDS
Scissor-tailed flycatcher, Acadian flycatcher, downy woodpecker, yellow-throated warbler

BEST SEASON
All seasons

AREA DESCRIPTION
Post and blackjack oak, eastern red cedar, American and cedar elm, and honey mesquite vegetation

Bob Jones Park near Lake Grapevine includes post and blackjack oak, eastern red cedar, American and cedar elm, and honey mesquite vegetation. The park offers a number of trails – both paved and unpaved – for birders.

The open woodlands provide habitat for resident birds such as northern cardinal, Carolina chickadee, tufted titmouse, red-bellied woodpecker, American robin, western and eastern kingbirds, scissor-tailed flycatcher, Acadian flycatcher, downy woodpecker, yellow-throated warbler, indigo and painted buntings, and many others.

DIRECTIONS
From SH 114 and N. White Chapel Blvd. in Southlake, head north on N. White Chapel Blvd. for 1.8 miles to the pipe-rail fence entry for Bob Jones Park, which is on the right (east) side. Enter the parking area and take the loop road east until it ends in the small parking area. Walnut Grove and Cross Timbers habitat lies all in and around Kirkwood Branch to the south/southwest and north/northeast.

CONTACT INFORMATION
Open during daylight hours. For information call 817-481-2374.

Downy Woodpecker

PRAIRIES AND PINEYWOODS - WEST
Colleyville Nature Center

#55

INTERSECTION OF MILL CREEK AND MILLWOOD DRIVE
COLLEYVILLE, TEXAS 76034

KEY BIRDS
Mallard, geese, barn swallow, purple martin, woodpeckers, flycatchers, hummingbirds, herons

BEST SEASON
Most seasons, depending on the weather

AREA DESCRIPTION
Large creek, forested wetlands, and nine lakes with post oak, cottonwood, pecan, and American elm trees

Part of a plan to preserve Colleyville's remaining natural areas, this 46-acre riparian forest is protected by the city of Colleyville. This riparian natural area, with a large creek, forested wetlands, and nine lakes, offers a unique opportunity to enjoy riparian habitats within an urban area.

The natural area acts as a buffer between Little Bear Creek and the surrounding residential areas. Visitors are first drawn to the ponds near the parking area. A short wooden pier allows for viewing mallard, geese, barn swallow, purple martin, and green heron on the ponds.

An easily-accessible paved trail leads into a densely wooded area near Little Bear Creek. From here unpaved nature trails loop around the area. Birds such as the Carolina chickadee, flycatchers, and titmice are often seen. There are many benches and picnic tables placed along the trails.

The trails lead to five more interconnected lakes teeming with kingfishers, woodpeckers, flycatchers, hummingbirds, herons, egrets, ducks, and owls. Northern rough-winged swallows swoop over the ponds picking insects off the surface.

DIRECTIONS
From the Northeast Loop of I-820 in North Richland Hills, take the Hwy 26/ Grapevine Hwy Exit and follow Hwy 26/ Grapevine Hwy northeast for 4.8 miles. Turn left onto Glade Road and proceed 0.6 mile to Mill Creek Drive. Turn left and follow Mill Creek Drive through a subdivision for 0.3 mile to the park entrance.

CONTACT INFORMATION
A day-use-area only. Call 817-656-7275.

PRAIRIES AND PINEYWOODS WEST

PRAIRIES AND PINEYWOODS - WEST
Village Creek Drying Beds

#56

JUST OFF GREEN OAKS BLVD. IN ARLINGTON, TEXAS

KEY BIRDS
Red-winged blackbird, great egret, great blue heron, killdeer, pied-billed grebe, green-winged teal, greater and lesser yellowlegs, white-rumped sandpiper, and Sprague's pipit

BEST SEASON
All seasons

AREA DESCRIPTION
Open water and wetlands surrounded by willows and oaks

As is the case with many similar facilities, visitors to this water treatment facility will be pleasantly surprised by the abundance and diversity of wildlife using this man-made habitat. The lagoons are a patchwork of cattails and open water. A large levee borders the entire facility and divides the site in the middle. You can walk or drive these levees.

Habitats include open water and wetlands surrounded by willows and oaks. The lagoons host red-winged blackbird, great egret, great blue heron, killdeer, pied-billed grebe, green-winged teal, greater and lesser yellowlegs, white-rumped sandpiper, and Sprague's pipit.

Other species during the spring and summer include western and eastern kingbirds, scissor-tailed flycatcher, little blue heron, wood duck, snowy egret, red-tailed hawk, mourning dove, spotted sandpiper, chimney swift, and cliff and barn swallows. The fortunate visitor may see black-necked stilt, white-faced ibis, black-bellied whistling- and ruddy ducks, glossy ibis, green heron, and American kestrel. A fall or winter visit could reveal a gadwall. In addition to the lagoon and wooded areas, upland grasslands host painted and indigo buntings, as well as white-crowned and savannah sparrows.

DIRECTIONS
From I-30 in Arlington, take the Fielder Street Exit. Go north on Fielder for 1.3 miles until it dead ends at an intersection with Green Oaks Blvd. Turn right (east) and go 0.3 mile to the Village Creek entrance on the left side of the street.

CONTACT INFORMATION
This is a controlled and restricted site for daytime use only.
For access and information call: 817-392-4900
Website: www.fwas.org

River Legacy Parks

#57

703 NW GREEN OAKS BLVD.
ARLINGTON, TEXAS 76006

KEY BIRDS

Belted kingfisher, great egret, little blue heron, tricolored heron, wood duck, cliff swallow, common yellowthroat, and orange-crowned warbler

BEST SEASON

All seasons

AREA DESCRIPTION

Riparian forest along the Trinity River

River Legacy Parks is a stunning example of how community involvement and vision can preserve important wildlife habitat – in this case, riparian forest along the Trinity River. This 1,300-acre park forms a corridor extending along the river. The property was acquired piece by piece through purchase, grants, and donations. It protects valuable riparian wetlands and hardwood forests. The paved trails offer easy access to a variety of habitats representative of the Trinity River riparian system.

Birders should watch for yellow-billed cuckoo, downy woodpecker, Carolina chickadee, tufted titmouse, northern cardinal, ruby-throated hummingbird, northern flicker, and brown thrasher.

Because of its location on the Trinity River, watch for belted kingfisher, great egret, little blue heron, tricolored heron, wood duck, and cliff swallow. Birders have also recorded nesting Cooper's hawks and broad-winged hawks. During the spring, Bell's vireo, common yellowthroat, and scarlet tanager along with merlin or white-tailed kite frequent the area.

As the weather cools during the winter months, bird species may include pine warbler, passing snow geese, hooded merganser, common yellowthroat, orange-crowned warbler, rusty blackbird, purple finch, and on a rare occasion, Harris's hawk. Blue-winged, golden-winged, black-throated blue, blackpoll, hooded, Kentucky, worm-eating, and Swainson's warblers are rare but have been seen here.

The park is currently being expanded to include additional land north of the Trinity River. A visitor center and footbridge connecting the two areas are planned.

DIRECTIONS

From I-30 in Arlington, take the Cooper Street Exit. Drive north on Cooper Street about 1.5 miles to where it ends at Green Oaks Boulevard with the science center at the intersection across from Cooper. Turn left on Green Oaks and go west 0.1 mile to park entrance on the right.

CONTACT INFORMATION
Call for access information: 817-860-6752
Website: www.riverlegacy.org

PRAIRIES AND
PINEYWOODS WEST

Tricolored Heron

PRAIRIES AND PINEYWOODS - WEST
#58 The Dallas Arboretum and Botanical Garden

8525 GARLAND ROAD
DALLAS, TEXAS

KEY BIRDS
Tufted titmouse, American robin, and common nighthawk

BEST SEASON
All seasons

AREA DESCRIPTION
Display gardens that showcase incredible seasonal flowers, ornamental shrubs, trees, and plant collections in a serene setting on White Rock Lake

The gardens offer a great opportunity to learn about native Texas plants and associated wildlife. Watch for birds such as tufted titmouse, American robin, and common nighthawk. White Rock Lake, located nearby, provides an opportunity to see a variety of ducks, egrets, and herons.

Native Texas trees at the arboretum include Texas madrone, rough-leaf dogwood, Texas ash, cherry laurel, escarpment live oak, and Texas mountain laurel.

The arboretum and gardens have five major water features, including ponds and waterfalls, which do attract many species of birds. Visit this site to learn more about gardening with native plants to attract a diversity of wildlife.

DIRECTIONS
From I-30 East in Dallas, take the Barry/ East Grand Exit. Stay straight on the service road crossing Barry and turn left on East Grand Ave./ Hwy 78. Stay on East Grand Ave. for approximately 3.0 miles as it becomes Garland Road. The Dallas Arboretum & Botanical Garden is on the left.

CONTACT INFORMATION
The site is available for day use only with fees ranging from $12.00 for adults to $8.00 for children.
For additional information call: 214-515-6500
Website: www.dallasarboretum.org

Black-crested Titmouse

PRAIRIES AND PINEYWOODS WEST

PRAIRIES AND PINEYWOODS - WEST

#59 Leonhardt Lagoon / Dallas Museum of Natural History

3535 GRAND AVENUE AND 1318 S. 2ND AVENUE IN FAIR PARK, TEXAS

KEY BIRDS
Least bittern, wood duck, mallard, killdeer, common nighthawk, red-winged blackbird, American kestrel, chimney swift, downy woodpecker, and western kingbird

BEST SEASON
Fall, summer, and spring

AREA DESCRIPTION
Open areas with ponds and large trees growing at the edge of the lagoon

Fascinating sculptures on both ends of the lagoon draw visitors out to the pond for a closer look. Birders can sit on one of the benches and watch for western kingbirds as they dive and hover over the pond, picking insects off the lily pads. Barn swallows can also be seen swooping around the pond, while the occasional green heron or one or more species of egret stalks its prey along the shore.

Large trees growing at the edge of the lagoon attract an amazing diversity of birds. Nesting species have included least bittern, wood duck, mallard, killdeer, common nighthawk, red-winged blackbird, American kestrel, chimney swift, downy woodpecker, and western kingbird. Other species that frequent the pond include eastern phoebe, common yellowthroat, ruby-throated hummingbird, Cooper's hawk, double-crested cormorant, Baltimore oriole, American goldfinch, American coot, yellow warbler, and black-and-white warbler.

The Dallas Museum of Natural History, located at the west end of the lagoon, documents the natural history of Texas through 50 dioramas of Texas wildlife, as well as Texas dinosaurs and other prehistoric creatures. With a wonderful collection of permanent and traveling exhibits, the Dallas Museum of Natural History is sure to please both the casual visitor and the serious student of nature.

DIRECTIONS
From I-30 heading east in Dallas, take Exit 47A (2nd Avenue/ Fair Park). Bear right as you exit and continue to Grand Avenue. Turn left on Grand Avenue to enter the park. Turn right just inside the gate and park. The DMNH is directly across the street from the parking lot. The lagoon is on the other side of the museum.

CONTACT INFORMATION
This is a day-use site only. Membership and day use fees are charged. For information call: 214-421-3466 / Website: www.dallasdino.org

PRAIRIES AND PINEYWOODS - WEST
Cedar Ridge Preserve
#60

7171 MOUNTAIN RIDGE PARKWAY
DALLAS, TEXAS

KEY BIRDS
Carolina wren, tufted titmouse, eastern bluebird, eastern kingbird, western kingbird, ruby-throated hummingbird, black-chinned hummingbird, and yellow-rumped warbler

BEST SEASON
Spring and fall migrations

AREA DESCRIPTION
Open oak woodlands with streams, ponds, and the geology of the escarpment

Make a quick stop at the visitor's center for a trail guide and then head to the trails. Ten miles of trails through open oak woodlands offer beautiful views of streams, ponds, and the geology of the escarpment. Look for fossils in the rock formations. Wildflowers add color to the forest greenery.

Future plans for this 633-acre preserve – a favorite among many local Audubon Society members – include habitat restoration for the black-capped vireo. Watch closely for white-eyed vireo, Carolina chickadee, scissor-tailed flycatcher, Carolina wren, tufted titmouse, eastern bluebird, eastern and western kingbirds, ruby-throated hummingbird and black-chinned hummingbirds, and yellow-rumped warbler. Listen for the characteristic calls of downy, ladder-backed, and red-bellied woodpeckers.

DIRECTIONS
From I-20 in southwest Dallas, take Exit 458 for Mountain Creek Parkway. Turn left (south) onto Mountain Creek Parkway and follow it 2.5 miles to Cedar Ridge Preserve.

CONTACT INFORMATION
This site is open for day-use only except Mondays, call for more information: 972-293-5150 / Website: www.audubondallas.org

For additional area birding information contact the Trinity River Audubon Center at 214-398-8722 or visit their website at: http://www.trinityriveraudubon.org/

PRAIRIES AND
PINEYWOODS WEST

PRAIRIES AND PINEYWOODS - WEST
Cedar Hill State Park

#61

1570 FM 1382
CEDAR HILL, TEXAS

KEY BIRDS
American wigeon, ruddy duck, solitary sandpiper, Wilson's phalarope, and greater yellowlegs

BEST SEASON
All seasons

AREA DESCRIPTION
Tallgrass prairie with rolling black clay soil and changing to rugged limestone escarpment

This unique 1,800-acre state park is located where two climax ecosystems converge. The tallgrass prairie and its rolling black clay soil meet the rugged limestone escarpment.

Joe Pool Lake is a beautiful reservoir with wetland edges where birders can see great blue heron, great egret, little blue heron, double-crested cormorant, green-backed heron, American wigeon, ruddy duck, solitary sandpiper, Wilson's phalarope, and greater yellowleg in the springtime. Fall and winter birders may see Bonaparte's and ring-billed gulls, least sandpiper, belted kingfisher, and Forster's tern.

The trails in the park offer secluded locations for wildlife viewing and enjoyment. The DORBA Trail leads visitors through a native tallgrass prairie where dickcissel, northern bobwhite, indigo and painted buntings, field sparrow, and eastern meadowlark are common. Savannah, song, and Lincoln's sparrows and Lapland longspur are often seen during the winter.

A hike along the Talala Trail provides good birding opportunities as it winds through open oak woodlands. During spring and summer look for white-eyed vireo, scissor-tailed flycatcher, Carolina chickadee, summer tanager, Carolina wren, downy woodpecker, blue-gray gnatcatcher, eastern bluebird, Swainson's thrush, tufted titmouse, black-throated green warbler, and loggerhead shrike. Fall and winter species include ruby-crowned kinglet, brown creeper, eastern wood-pewee, and orange-crowned warbler.

DIRECTIONS
From I-20 West in Dallas, take Exit 457 (FM 1382/ Grand Prairie/ Cedar Hill). Turn left (south) on FM 1382/ S. Belt Line Road and follow it south 3.8 miles to Cedar Hill State Park.

Cedar Hill
State Park

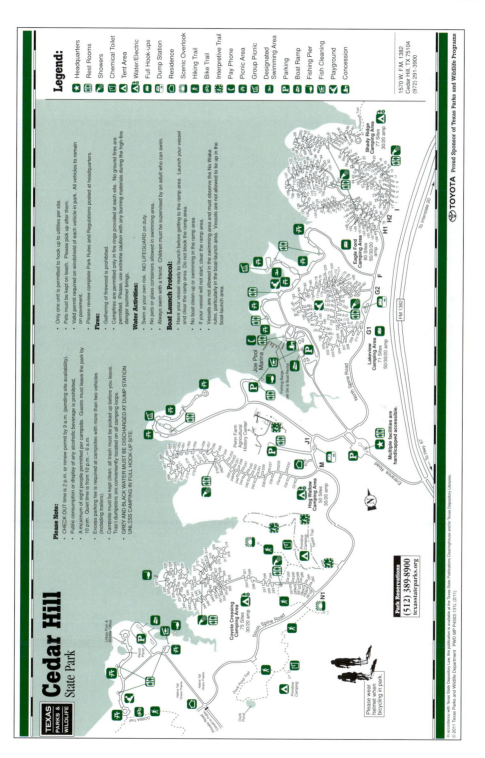

Legend:

- Headquarters
- Rest Rooms
- Showers
- Chemical Toilet
- Tent Area
- Water/Electric
- Full Hook-ups
- Dump Station
- Residence
- Scenic Overlook
- Hiking Trail
- Bike Trail
- Interpretive Trail
- Pay Phone
- Picnic Area
- Group Picnic
- Designated Swimming Area
- Parking
- Boat Ramp
- Fishing Pier
- Fish Cleaning
- Playground
- Concession

1570 W. F.M. 1382
Cedar Hill, TX 75104
(972) 291-3900

Please Note:

- CHECK OUT time is 2 p.m. or renew permit by 9 a.m. (pending site availability).
- Public consumption or display of any alcoholic beverage is prohibited.
- A maximum of eight people permitted per campsite. Guests must leave the park by 10 p.m. Quiet time is from 10 p.m. – 6 a.m.
- Excess parking fee is required at campsites with more than two vehicles (including trailers).
- Campsite must be kept clean; all trash must be picked up before you leave. Trash dumpsters are conveniently located on all camping loops.
- GREY AND BLACK WATER MUST BE DISCHARGED AT DUMP STATION UNLESS CAMPING IN FULL HOOK-UP SITE.
- Only one unit is permitted to hook up to utilities per site.
- Pets must be kept on leash. Please pick up after them.
- Valid permit required on windshield of each vehicle in park. All vehicles to remain on pavement.
- Please review complete Park Rules and Regulations posted at headquarters.

Fires:

- Gathering of firewood is prohibited.
- Campfires are permitted only in fire rings provided at each site. No ground fires are permitted. Please, use extreme caution with any burning materials during the high-fire danger summer brings.

Water Activities:

- Swim at your own risk. NO LIFEGUARD on duty.
- No pets or glass containers allowed in swimming area.
- Always swim with a friend. Children must be supervised by an adult who can swim.

Boat Launch Protocol:

- Have your vessel ready to launch before getting to the ramp area. Launch your vessel and clear the ramp area. Do not block the ramp area.
- No boat clean-up or swimming in the ramp area.
- If your vessel will not start, clear the ramp area.
- Vessels are not allowed in the swimming area and must observe the No Wake rules, particularly in the boat-launch area. Vessels are not allowed to be up in the boat-launch area.

Park Reservations
(512) 389-8900
texasstateparks.org

Please wear helmet when bicycling in park.

Multiple facilities are handicapped accessible.

Shady Ridge Camping Area
30/20 amp

Eagle Ford Camping Area
80 Sites
50/30/20 amp

Lakeview Camping Area
71 Sites
50/30/20 amp

Hog Wallow Camping Area
50 Sites
30/20 amp

Coyote Crossing Camping Area
75 Sites
30/20 amp

Penn Farm Agricultural History Center

Joe Pool Marina

North Spine Road

South Spine Road

Entrance Road

To Interstate 20

To Hwy 67

In accordance with Texas State Depository Law, this publication is available at the Texas State Publications Clearinghouse and/or Texas Depository Libraries.
© 2011 Texas Parks and Wildlife Department   PWD MP P4500-131L (2/11)

TOYOTA   Proud Sponsor of Texas Parks and Wildlife Programs

PRAIRIES AND PINEYWOODS WEST

PRAIRIES AND PINEYWOODS EAST

CONTACT INFORMATION

The standard Texas park day-use and camping fees apply. Information and prices are subject to change. Please call the park (972-291-3900) or park information (1-800-792-111) for the latest updates.

Ruddy Duck

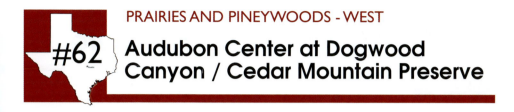

PRAIRIES AND PINEYWOODS - WEST

#62 Audubon Center at Dogwood Canyon / Cedar Mountain Preserve

ADJACENT TO AND PART OF CEDAR HILL STATE PARK

KEY BIRDS
Bewick's wren, red-bellied, and ladder-backed woodpeckers, scissor-tailed flycatcher, eastern and western kingbirds, painted and indigo buntings

BEST SEASON
All seasons

AREA DESCRIPTION
Grasslands and rocky areas

This site is under development as a major education facility operated by the Audubon Society and partners. Once completed, the trails and other educational programming that will be available at the center and preserve will provide an excellent opportunity to learn about Texas birds.

Permanent residents of the escarpment and adjacent grasslands include eastern phoebe, eastern bluebird, northern cardinal, Carolina chickadee, tufted titmouse, Carolina and Bewick's wrens, red-bellied and downy woodpeckers, with an occasional ladder-backed woodpecker. Summer birders may spot Chuck-will's widow, black-chinned hummingbird, ruby-throated hummingbird, scissor-tailed flycatcher, eastern and western kingbirds, painted and indigo buntings, white-eyed and red-eyed vireos, summer tanager, and blue-gray gnatcatcher. During the winter watch for hermit thrush, cedar waxwing, American robin, brown creeper, yellow-rumped and orange-crowned warblers, and ruby-crowned and golden-crowned kinglets.

Once the Audubon Society and its partners have acquired the remaining parcels of land for the Audubon Center at Dogwood Canyon, birders may be able to see the endangered golden-cheeked warbler.

DIRECTIONS
From I-20 West in Dallas, take Exit 457 (FM 1382/ Grand Prairie/ Cedar Hill). Turn left (south) onto FM 1382/ S. Belt Line Road and follow it south approximately 5.2 miles. Dogwood Canyon is located on FM 1382 between I-20 and SH 67, about 0.5 mile southeast of the entrance to Cedar Hill State Park.

CONTACT INFORMATION
At the time of this writing, the location is only open during daylight hours. Expect some construction and workers. For addition information and construction status call: 972-293-5150 or 972-291-5130 / Website: www.audubondallas.org

PRAIRIES AND PINEYWOODS WEST

PRAIRIES AND PINEYWOODS - WEST

Woodland Basin Nature Area

#63

2332 E. MILLER ROAD
GARLAND, TEXAS

KEY BIRDS
Common yellowthroat, red-winged blackbird, Carolina chickadee, Carolina wren, tufted titmouse, blue jay, and northern cardinal

BEST SEASON
All seasons

AREA DESCRIPTION
Creek and lakeside habitats with a large area of woodlands

Located at the confluence of Rowlett Creek and Lake Ray Hubbard, this moist woodland – subject to periodic flooding – provides habitat for a diversity of wildlife.

A walk along the creek will reveal large willow, pecan, sycamore, and oak trees. Understory plants include green ash, eastern redbud, and soapberry. Vegetation growing along the creek provides habitat for birds such as common yellowthroat, red-winged blackbird, Carolina chickadee, Carolina wren, tufted titmouse, blue jay, and northern cardinal.

DIRECTIONS
From I-635 in Dallas take the Centerville Road Exit. Go north on Centerville Road for 3.75 miles to Miller Road. Turn right and go 0.5 mile to the entrance drive on the right.

CONTACT INFORMATION
This location is only available during the daylight hours.
Call: 972-205-2750.

PRAIRIES AND PINEYWOODS - WEST
Rowlett Creek Greenbelt

#64

PRAIRIES AND PINEYWOODS WEST

2525 CASTLE DRIVE
GARLAND, TEXAS

KEY BIRDS
Cliff swallow, scissor-tailed flycatcher, and western kingbird

BEST SEASON
All seasons, depending on the weather

AREA DESCRIPTION
Open prairie and dense, moist riparian woodlands

This 350-acre site consists of open prairie and dense, moist riparian woodland. A very large American elm tree shades a picnic area near the beginning of the trail, where you can watch open grassland birds such as cliff swallow, scissor-tailed flycatcher, and western kingbird. Watch and listen for indigo and painted buntings as you approach the wooded area.

The dominant trees in wooded areas include pecan, oak, American elm, and cottonwood.

Please check the bulletin board for trail information. The trails move through many low-lying areas, so be careful of flooding during heavy rains. This site is maintained by the Dallas Off-Road Bicycle Association and is a favorite for off-road bicycling, so birders should watch for low flying bikes and riders.

Tree Swallow

DIRECTIONS
From I-635 in Dallas take the Centerville Road Exit. Go north on Centerville Road 5.5 miles to Castle Drive. Turn right at Castle Drive into the parking lot.

CONTACT INFORMATION
Site open for day use only.
Phone: 972-205-2750
Website for Dallas Off-Road Bicycle Association:
www.dorba.org

PRAIRIES AND PINEYWOODS - WEST
Lake Lavon Trinity Trail

#65

WYLIE, TEXAS

KEY BIRDS
American white pelican, double-crested cormorant, tricolored heron, great egret, black-crowned night-heron, white-faced ibis, wood duck, marsh wren, and Cooper's hawk

BEST SEASON
All seasons

AREA DESCRIPTION
Open prairie and dense, moist riparian woodlands

Operated by the U.S. Army Corps of Engineers, the Trinity Trail is a nine-mile trail that follows the southwest edge of Lake Lavon from the trailhead near the intersection of CR 384 and CR 389 to Brockdale Park. The trail traverses a variety of habitats that support over 550 species of plants and animals.

A wildlife checklist is available from the Corps of Engineers office. Birds to look for include common loon, American white pelican, double-crested cormorant, tricolored heron, great egret, black-crowned night-heron, white-faced ibis, wood duck, marsh wren, Cooper's hawk, ferruginous hawk, black-necked stilt, Forster's tern, black-billed cuckoo, whip-poor-will, belted and green kingfishers, golden-fronted, ladder-backed, and pileated woodpeckers, willow flycatcher, loggerhead shrike, horned lark, red-breasted nuthatch, brown creeper, northern waterthrush, and common yellowthroat.

Birders should watch carefully near prairie dog mounds for burrowing owls.

DIRECTIONS
Lake Lavon Trinity Trail is located on the southwest portion of Lavon Lake, approximately one mile east of Wylie, Texas. To get to the south end of the lake from Wylie, go northeast on SR 78/ Lavon Pkwy for 0.5 mile. Turn left (north) onto Eubanks and follow 0.5 mile to CR 384 and the entrance to East Fork Park. Turn left (west) on CR 384. Immediately to the right is the entrance to the trailhead marked with a white pipe-rail fence.

CONTACT INFORMATION
Site open for day use only.
Phone: 972-442-3141
Website: www.swf-wc.usace.army.mil/lavon/

Double-crested Cormorant

PRAIRIES AND PINEYWOODS - WEST

#66 Spring Creek Park Preserve & Spring Creek Forest Preserve

HOLFORD ROAD
NORTHEAST OF DALLAS METROPOLITAN AREA

KEY BIRDS
Carolina wren, tufted titmouse, great crested flycatcher, Swainson's hawk, white-eyed vireo, olive-sided flycatcher, catbird, clay-colored sparrow, and blue-headed vireo

BEST SEASON
All seasons

AREA DESCRIPTION
Pristine bottomland forest in the floodplain of Spring Creek

On the east side of Holford Road, the preserve has a paved trail through woodlands to Spring Creek. In summer look for common bird species such as Carolina wren, tufted titmouse, great crested flycatcher, Swainson's hawk, and white-eyed vireo. Pay careful attention and birders may see an olive-sided flycatcher, catbird, clay-colored sparrow, and blue-headed vireo during their annual migrations.

Some of the more unusual sightings include: American woodcock, blue-winged warbler, cerulean warbler, golden-cheeked warbler, Swainson's warbler, hooded warbler, Bell's vireo, grasshopper sparrow, Le Conte's sparrow, veery, American tree sparrow, sedge wren, and Henslow's sparrow.

The west side of Holford Road has a denser understory with unpaved, more primitive trails. This area offers solitude and excellent bird watching opportunities. The sound of the running stream relaxes visitors as they sit on benches beneath the dense tree canopy.

The Preservation Society for Spring Creek Forest maintains the preserve. Future plans include educational activities and guided tours. With their help, this preserve will continue to protect valuable wildlife habitat and provide excellent wildlife viewing opportunities.

DIRECTIONS
From Hwy 75 North/ Central Expressway in Dallas, take the SH 190/ President George Bush Hwy Exit. Turn right and go east approximately 4.5 miles to Holford Road. Turn right (southwest) and go south 0.5 mile to the driveway on the left. Continue another 0.1 mile to the driveway on the right.

CONTACT INFORMATION
Site open for day use only. For information please call: 972-205-2750
Website: www.springcreekforest.org

PRAIRIES AND PINEYWOODS WEST

PRAIRIES AND PINEYWOODS - WEST
Arbor Hills Nature Preserve

#67

6701 W PARKER ROAD
PLANO, TEXAS

KEY BIRDS
Blue jay, scissor-tailed flycatcher, Carolina wren, blue-gray gnatcatcher, tufted titmouse, and Carolina chickadee

BEST SEASON
All seasons

AREA DESCRIPTION
Open woodlands and prairie habitats

When you enter the preserve, listen for common birds such as blue jay, scissor-tailed flycatcher, Carolina wren, blue-gray gnatcatcher, tufted titmouse, and Carolina chickadee.

The paved and unpaved hiking and biking trails lead into the open woodlands and prairies characteristic of this 200-acre park on the western border of Plano.

The stream provides habitat for a variety of birds, and gulf fritillary, giant swallowtail, and monarch-mimicking viceroy butterflies are common. A variety of damselflies and dragonflies also patrol the stream. This nature preserve offers many opportunities for outdoor activities and an escape from the bustle of the city.

DIRECTIONS
From I-35 East in Dallas, take Exit 448A and go northeast on SR 121 approximately 4 miles to FM 544/Parker Road. Follow Parker Road east approximately 3 miles to Arbor Hills Nature Preserve.

CONTACT INFORMATION
Park hours are 5am - 11pm.
For additional information call: 972-941-7250 or 972-941-7255
Website: www.planoparks.org

PRAIRIES AND
PINEYWOODS WEST

PRAIRIES AND PINEYWOODS - WEST
Connemara Conservancy

#68

ALLEN, TEXAS

KEY BIRDS
Cliff swallow, scissor-tailed flycatcher, and American kestrel

BEST SEASON
All seasons, weather permitting

AREA DESCRIPTION
Open meadows

This 72-acre property is an oasis of open meadow in a suburban, residential area. Rowlett Creek borders the property and provides habitat for fish, amphibians, and insects. A bird and plant checklist is available from the Connemara office.

Walk through the pecan grove, along the stream, and follow the trail around the meadow. Watch the fence rows for cliff swallow, scissor-tailed flycatcher, and American kestrel; more than 100 bird species have been observed here. Begun in 1981, The Connemara Conservancy is a land trust dedicated to the preservation of open space areas in north-central Texas. Because the foundation does its best to protect the biodiversity of the meadow preserve, dogs and other pets are not allowed in the meadow.

DIRECTIONS
From Hwy 75 North/ Central Expressway in Allen, take Exit 34 to McDermott Drive. Turn west on McDermott Drive and go 1.0 mile to Alma Drive. Turn left (south) on Alma Drive and go 0.8 mile to Tatum Drive, an unpaved road on the left. Park on Tatum Drive and then walk along it until you reach the bridge. Walk across the bridge to enter the Connemara Meadow. A pecan grove will appear on your left as you do so.

CONTACT INFORMATION
This site is access-restricted so please call ahead. Phone: 214-351-0990 / Website: www.connemaraconservancy.org

American Kestrel

PRAIRIES AND PINEYWOODS - WEST

#69 Heard Natural Science Museum and Wildlife Sanctuary

1 NATURE PLACE
McKINNEY, TEXAS

KEY BIRDS
Prothonotary and parula warblers, hooded merganser, wood duck, and anhinga

BEST SEASON
All seasons

AREA DESCRIPTION
Somewhat hilly with a large lake and trails lined with large trees and underbrush

This 289-acre wildlife sanctuary has over three miles of interpreter-led or self-guided nature trails. Approximately two-thirds of the sanctuary lies within the floodplain of Wilson Creek. Habitats include permanent and ephemeral wetlands, bottomland hardwood forests, and upland prairie that attract many birders each year, including most of the member of the local Audubon Society chapters. There is also a photo/observation blind located near the main building. No reservations are required for the blind.

This is not a location in which to spend only a few hours. My visit lasted the better part of two days and there was still much to see, birds to watch, and photographs to take.

The sanctuary is a haven for more than 240 species of birds, mammals, reptiles, and amphibians and almost 150 species of wildflowers. Upland portions of the sanctuary are being managed to provide habitat for the Texas horned lizard.

A walk through the native plant garden helps visitors identify and learn about native wildflowers, plants, and trees. The science museum features excellent exhibits and educational opportunities. Don't miss the snake exhibit, with live snakes representing all eco-regions of Texas.

After a tour through the museum, obtain a self-guided trail brochure and take a hike. The Hoot-Owl Trail meanders through bottomland hardwood forest. Birders should be aware of and stay clear of the numerous poison-ivy plants.

This sanctuary offers unique opportunities to view a wide diversity of bird species year-round. Nesting species include prothonotary and parula warblers, hooded merganser, wood duck, and anhinga.

There is also a well-established heron rookery, and it is always a birder's attraction during the breeding season. As a point of interest, the oldest bird banding station in the state is located here, offering unique interpretive opportunities during the spring and fall banding of neotropical migratory songbirds.

PRAIRIES AND PINEYWOODS WEST

DIRECTIONS

On Hwy 75 North/ Central Expressway in Dallas, go north approximately 20 miles to Exit 38A. Go east on Hwy 121 for 0.75 mile to Hwy 5. Go right (south) on Hwy 5 for 0.75 mile to FM 1378. Turn left on FM 1378 and drive 1.0 mile to the museum entrance.

CONTACT INFORMATION

Phone: 972-562-5566
Website: www.heardmuseum.org

Anhinga

PRAIRIES AND
PINEYWOODS WEST

PRAIRIES AND PINEYWOODS - WEST
Eisenhower State Park

#70

50 PARK ROAD 20
DENISON, TEXAS

KEY BIRDS
Eastern phoebe, eastern kingbird, scissor-tailed flycatcher, white pelican, and pied-bill grebe

BEST SEASON
All seasons

AREA DESCRIPTION
Grassy uplands, including rare remnants of the tall-grass prairie, terminating in rocky, shoreline bluffs and woodlands

The 423-acre Eisenhower State Park is located northwest of Denison on the shores of Lake Texoma, that is part of the Red River which forms the border between Texas and Oklahoma. Activities include camping, picnicking, hiking, biking, nature study, and birding.

A four-mile nature trail is available for hiking and mountain biking. Grassy uplands, including tallgrass prairie remnants, terminate in rocky, shoreline bluffs and woodlands. Visitors can enjoy a large variety of colorful wildflowers blooming throughout the growing season.

Birders should expect to see during the correct seasons: bald eagle, white pelican, pied-bill grebe, and a variety of gulls and waterfowl during winter months. Birders should be especially observant in the wooded areas between the campgrounds for Carolina wren, northern cardinal, and blue jay. Watch the open grassy fields, which provide habitat for eastern phoebe, eastern kingbird, and scissor-tailed flycatcher.

DIRECTIONS
From US 75 in Denison, take Exit 72 for Hwy 91. Go north on Hwy 91 for 1.7 miles to Denison Dam. Turn left (west) on FR 1310 and follow 1.8 miles to the park entrance.

CONTACT INFORMATION
Daily fees are $5 per day, per person 13 years and older. The standard Texas park day-use and camping fees apply. Information and prices are subject to change. Please call the park (1- 903-465-1956) or park information (1-800-792-1112) for the latest updates.

PRAIRIES AND
PINEYWOODS WEST

PRAIRIES AND PINEYWOODS WEST

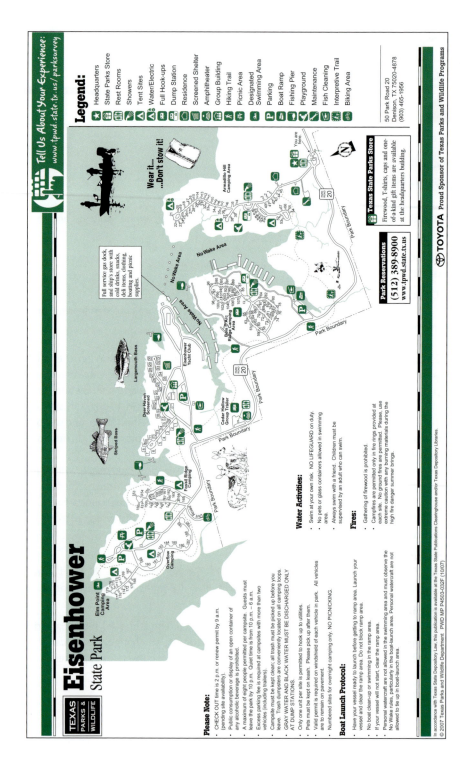

Eisenhower
State Park

TEXAS PARKS & WILDLIFE

Legend:

- Headquarters
- State Parks Store
- Rest Rooms
- Showers
- Tent Sites
- Water/Electric
- Full Hook-ups
- Dump Station
- Residence
- Screened Shelter
- Amphitheater
- Group Building
- Hiking Trail
- Picnic Area
- Designated Swimming Area
- Parking
- Boat Ramp
- Fishing Pier
- Playground
- Maintenance
- Fish Cleaning
- Interpretive Trail
- Biking Area

Please Note:

- CHECK OUT time is 2 p.m. or renew permit by 9 a.m. (pending site availability).
- Public consumption or display of an open container of any alcoholic beverage is prohibited.
- A maximum of eight people permitted per campsite. Guests must leave the park by 10 p.m. Quiet time is from 10 p.m. – 6 a.m.
- Excess parking fee is required at campsites with more than two vehicles (including trailers).
- Campsite must be kept clean; all trash must be picked up before you leave. Trash dumpsters are conveniently located on all camping loops.
- GRAY WATER AND BLACK WATER MUST BE DISCHARGED ONLY AT DUMP STATIONS.
- Only one unit per site is permitted to hook up to utilities.
- Pets must be kept on leash. Please pick up after them.
- Valid permit is required on windshield of each vehicle in park. All vehicles are to remain on pavement.
- Numbered sites for overnight camping only. NO PICNICKING.

Boat Launch Protocol:

- Have your vessel ready to launch before getting to ramp area. Launch your vessel and clear the ramp area. Do not block ramp area.
- No boat clean-up or swimming in the ramp area.
- If your vessel will not start, clear the ramp area.
- Personal watercraft are not allowed in the swimming area and must observe the No Wake rules, particularly in the boat-launch area. Personal watercraft are not allowed to tie up in boat-launch area.

Water Activities:

- Swim at your own risk. NO LIFEGUARD on duty.
- No pets or glass containers allowed in swimming area.
- Always swim with a friend. Children must be supervised by an adult who can swim.

Fires:

- Gathering of firewood is prohibited.
- Campfires are permitted only in fire rings provided at each site. No ground fires are permitted. Please, use extreme caution with any burning materials during the high fire danger summer brings.

Tell Us About Your Experience:
www.tpwd.state.tx.us/parksurvey

Wear it... ...Don't stow it!

Full service gas dock, and ship's store with cold drinks, snacks, deli items, clothing, boating and picnic supplies.

Elm Point Camping Area

Largemouth Bass

Striped Bass

Eisenhower Yacht Club

Deer Haven Screened

Cedar Hollow Group Trailer

Fossil Ridge Camping

Overflow Camping

Bois D'Arc Ridge Camping Area

Armadillo Hill Camping Area

No Wake Area

Park Boundary

You are here.

Texas State Parks Store

Firewood, T-shirts, caps and one-of-a-kind gift items are available at the headquarters building.

50 Park Road 20
Denison, TX 75020-4878
(903) 465-1956

Park Reservations

(512) 389-8900
www.tpwd.state.tx.us

TOYOTA Proud Sponsor of Texas Parks and Wildlife Programs

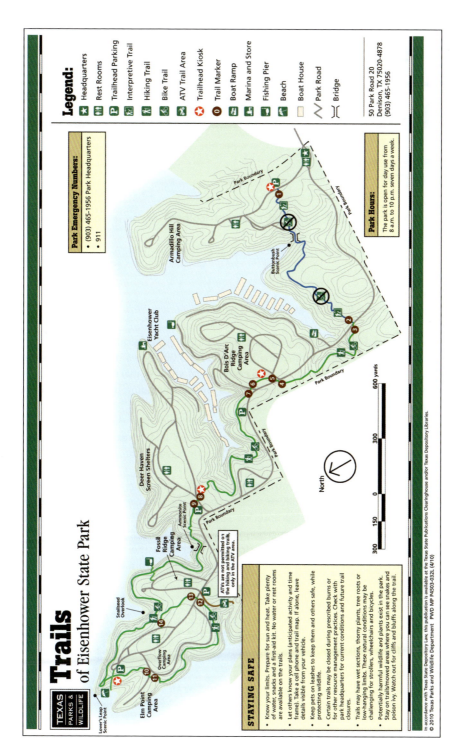

Trails
of Eisenhower State Park

TEXAS PARKS & WILDLIFE

Legend:

- Headquarters
- Rest Rooms
- Trailhead Parking
- Interpretive Trail
- Hiking Trail
- Bike Trail
- ATV Trail Area
- Trailhead Kiosk
- Trail Marker
- Boat Ramp
- Marina and Store
- Fishing Pier
- Beach
- Boat House
- Park Road
- Bridge

50 Park Road 20
Denison, TX 75020-4878
(903) 465-1956

Park Emergency Numbers:
- (903) 465-1956 Park Headquarters
- 911

Park Hours:
The park is open for day use from 8 a.m. to 10 p.m. seven days a week.

North

300 150 0   300   600 yards

ATVs are not permitted on the hiking and biking trails, only in the ATV area.

Armadillo Hill Camping Area

Buttonbush Scenic Point

Eisenhower Yacht Club

Bois D'Arc Ridge Camping Area

Park Boundary

Deer Haven Screen Shelters

Ammonite Scenic Point

Fossil Ridge Camping Area

Snailseed Overlook

Overflow Camping Area

Elm Point Camping Area

Lover's Leap Scenic Point

STAYING SAFE

- Know your limits. Prepare for sun and heat. Take plenty of water, snacks and a first-aid kit. No water or rest rooms are available on the trails.

- Let others know your plans (anticipated activity and time frame). Take a cell phone and trail map. If alone, leave details visible from your vehicle.

- Keep pets on leashes to keep them and others safe, while protecting wildlife.

- Certain trails may be closed during prescribed burns or for other resource management practices. Check with park headquarters for current conditions and future trail closures.

- Trails may have wet sections, thorny plants, tree roots or low-hanging limbs. These natural conditions may be challenging for strollers, wheelchairs and bicycles.

- Potentially harmful wildlife and plants exist in the park. Stay on trails/mowed areas where you can see snakes and poison ivy. Watch out for cliffs and bluffs along the trail.

PRAIRIES AND PINEYWOODS - WEST
Hagerman National Wildlife Refuge

#71

6465 REFUGE ROAD
SHERMAN, TX

KEY BIRDS
Waterfowl during fall and spring migrations, tricolored heron, roseate spoonbill, and wood stork

BEST SEASON
All seasons

AREA DESCRIPTION
Marsh and water and 8,000 acres of upland habitat

Hagerman National Wildlife Refuge spans over 11,000 acres along the Big Mineral Arm on the southern shores of Lake Texoma, and includes 3,000 acres of marsh and water and 8,000 acres of upland and farmland. This complex of shallow marshlands, deep bays, and riparian woodland hosts an impressive array of wildlife, including thousands of geese and other waterfowl during the winter.

In spring and early summer, the grasslands are filled with the songs of dickcissels, indigo buntings, and blue grosbeaks, as well as herons and egrets, including great blue, little blue, green herons and great, snowy, and cattle egrets that are common along the shoreline.

During the late summer months and early fall, watch for wading species such as tricolored heron, roseate spoonbill, or wood stork. Late summer is also the time to look for wandering terns, especially the interior subspecies of least tern, which occasionally move to the lake from their nesting grounds on the Red River.

A driving loop brings visitors into close contact with the wildlife and provides an opportunity to observe the numerous bird species. Take this drive slowly and watch carefully.

DIRECTIONS
From US 75 between Denison and Sherman, take Exit 65 for FM 691. Go west on FM 691 for 3.5 miles to the county airport and FM 1417. Turn right (north) on FM 1417 and follow 1.4 miles to Refuge Road, heading west 6.2 miles to the refuge headquarters.

CONTACT INFORMATION
The refuge is only open during daylight hours and, at this time, no fees are charged. For more information phone: 903-786-2826 / Website: southwest.fws.gov/refuges/texas/hagerman/

PRAIRIES AND PINEYWOODS - WEST
Cross Timbers Hiking Trail

#72

NEAR SHERMAN, TEXAS

KEY BIRDS
Yellow-billed cuckoo, painted bunting, great blue heron

BEST SEASON
All seasons

AREA DESCRIPTION
Lakeside and woodland habitats

The Cross Timbers Hiking Trail meanders 14 miles along the southern shore of Lake Texoma, providing an intimate look at the undeveloped shoreline and adjacent woodland. Along the way, hikers will be accompanied in summer by the tireless song of the painted bunting, the insect-like croaking of the yellow-billed cuckoo, and the wheeze of the blue-gray gnatcatcher. With a quiet search along the shoreline, birders might discover a great blue heron stalking small fish and frogs along the shore.

The winter months are great for a variety of waterfowl. Pay attention to the open water for wintering loons and grebes among the rafts of diving ducks.

DIRECTIONS
From the intersection of US 82 and US 377 in Whitesboro, travel north 13.7 miles to Juniper Point West Recreation Area on the left, just before crossing Lake Texoma. The trail starts from a parking area on the west end of the park.

CONTACT INFORMATION
The trail is open during daylight hours. Permit required for camping. Call: 903-523-4022 for additional information.

PRAIRIES AND
PINEYWOODS WEST

PRAIRIES AND PINEYWOODS - WEST
Miss Kitty's Bird & Bath

#73

NORTH OF GAINESVILLE, TEXAS ON FM373

KEY BIRDS
Northern bobwhite, green heron, wood duck, eastern meadowlark

BEST SEASON
Winter, fall, and spring

AREA DESCRIPTION
Streambeds and ponds, hardwood forest, and open grasslands

Miss Kitty's Bird & Bath offers an excellent escape from the bustle of city life. The newly refurbished house was the homestead of the Felty family for almost 100 years. The caring hands of the Walter family have restored the house to its original glory.

Visitors can relax in a quiet country setting and listen to the wind blowing through the grass, the constant turning of the windmill, and the characteristic whistle of the northern bobwhite. Habitats on the ranch include streambeds and ponds, hardwood forest, and open grasslands. Check along the stream for green heron and the occasional wood duck, or watch overhead for the aerial hunting of the Mississippi kite.

In the uplands, look for eastern meadowlark and lark sparrow or hike over 300 acres to catch sight of deer and wild turkey.

DIRECTIONS
From I-35 North in Gainesville, take Exit 498B for US 82. Turn left (west) on US 82 and follow 12.4 miles to FM 373 in Muenster. Turn left (south) onto FM 373 and follow 7.7 miles. The farm is on the left (east) side of FM 373 and 0.2 mile in from the road.

CONTACT INFORMATION
This location is listed as restricted so please call ahead. Phone: 940-759-2712 or 940-736-1147.

American Goldfinch

PRAIRIES AND PINEYWOODS WEST

PRAIRIES AND PINEYWOODS - WEST
#74 LBJ National Grasslands

NEAR DECATUR, TEXAS

KEY BIRDS
Northern bobwhite, wild turkey, neotropical migratory birds

BEST SEASON
All seasons

AREA DESCRIPTION
Grasslands with wooded areas

The Caddo and Lyndon B. Johnson (LBJ) National Grasslands are located in two areas: northeast and northwest of the Dallas-Fort Worth metroplex.

The most popular activities are hiking, bird watching, wildlife viewing, and photography. You will have plenty of room to do all these things — the grasslands cover 38,098 acres. The recreation areas on the Caddo-LBJ National Grasslands offer a variety of facilities for camping, picnicking, and other outdoor activities.

Waterfowl, northern bobwhite, wild turkey, and songbirds thrive in the diverse habitats provided by the grasslands. In spring, almost anywhere on the grasslands, visitors enjoy viewing neotropical migratory birds, and the spring show of wildflowers is sure to please photographers.

The Black Creek Lake Recreation Area is one developed access point which provides a good starting point for exploration. Species to be on the lookout for include the summer's Mississippi kite and turkey vulture overhead and a variety of large hawks during the winter months.

Black Creek Lake and the other roadside water sources could turn up cattle egret and little blue heron, while the woods ring with the sounds of painted bunting and blue-gray gnatcatcher.

For those interested in a more adventurous hike, the Cottonwood Black Creek Trail starts at the far end of the recreation area and can be followed for several miles through the riparian forest along Black Creek.

Cottonwood Creek Lake Recreation Area provides another point of reference for the sea of habitat that is LBJ National Grasslands. The small camping and picnic area along the lakeshore is a great place to view wildlife.

Watch in the numerous trees near the boat landing for red-bellied woodpecker and scan the far shore for little blue or great blue herons or wood duck. Winter months support a large variety of waterfowl, and the roadside shrubs and woodlands support a large diversity of wintering sparrows and raptors.

Directions

From the intersection of US 380 and US 287 in Decatur, travel north on US 287 for 9.7 miles to FM 1655 in Alvord. Turn right and go 0.7 mile through downtown Alvord and across the raildroad tracks to E. Pine Road. Turn right on E. Pine Road and go 4.9 miles to CR 2372. Turn left onto CR 2372 and proceed 1.4 miles to CR 2461.

For the Cottonwood Creek Lake Recreation Area

Turn left onto CR 2461 and go 3.2 miles to CR 2560. Turn left again onto CR 2560 and continue 2.2 miles to Cottonwood Lake on the left. Turn left and proceed 0.4 mile to the recreation area.

For the Black Creek Lake Recreation Area

Turn left onto CR 2461 and go 0.4 mile to FS 902. Turn left again onto FS 902 and continue 0.4 mile to the recreation area.

Contact Information

These locations are open year round and daily. A fee is charged for developed camping areas.
For information call: 940-627-5475
Website: www.fs.fed.us/r8/texas/recreation/

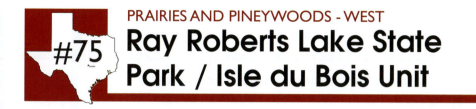

PRAIRIES AND PINEYWOODS - WEST

Ray Roberts Lake State Park / Isle du Bois Unit

#75

NEAR SANGER, TEXAS

KEY BIRDS
Mississippi kite, bald eagle, and greater roadrunner

BEST SEASON
Fall and winter

AREA DESCRIPTION
Wooded terrain bordering the blackland prairies

The Isle du Bois Unit of Ray Robert Lake State Park provides excellent access to the southern shores of Lake Ray Roberts. Although the park offers great wildlife viewing opportunities year round, it is especially appealing during fall and winter months when the waterfowl arrive and the summer crowds thin. Wintering bald eagles are occasionally seen.

A summer attraction are the two pair of Mississippi kites that frequent the park. These aerial acrobats are wonderful to watch as they pursue dragonflies and proceed to eat them on the wing. Other birds well worth some extended watching are the greater roadrunners, which are entertaining to watch at any time. Watch closely for brilliantly colored painted buntings in the trees and great egrets stalking frogs in the shallows.

The park is located in the Eastern Cross Timbers, a narrow strip of wooded terrain bordering the blackland prairies of north central Texas.

DIRECTIONS
From I-35 in Sanger, take Exit 478 for FM 455. Go east on FM 455 for 10.2 miles to the park entrance on the left. Turn left and continue 0.4 mile to the entry gate.

CONTACT INFORMATION
Site open daily. The standard Texas park day use and camping fees apply. Information and prices are subject to change. Please call the park (940-686-2148) or park information (1-800-792-1112) for the latest updates.

PRAIRIES AND
PINEYWOODS WEST

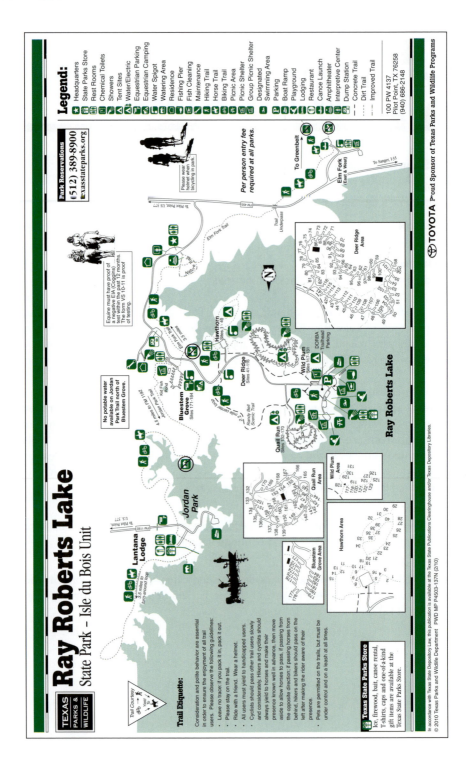

Ray Roberts Lake
State Park – Isle du Bois Unit

Trail Etiquette:

Consideration and polite behavior are essential in order to ensure the enjoyment of all trail users. Please observe the following guidelines:

- Leave no trace: if you pack it in, pack it out.
- Please stay on the trail.
- Ride with a friend. Wear a helmet.
- All users must yield to handicapped users.
- Cyclists should pass other trail users slowly and considerately. Hikers and cyclists should always yield to horses and make their presence known well in advance, then move aside to allow horses to pass. If passing from behind, hikers and bikers should pass on the left after making the rider aware of their presence.
- Pets are permitted on the trails, but must be under control and on a leash at all times.

Texas State Parks Store

Ice, firewood, bait, canoe rental, T-shirts, caps and one-of-a-kind gift items are available at the Texas State Parks Store.

Legend:

Headquarters
State Parks Store
Rest Rooms
Chemical Toilets
Showers
Tent Sites
Water/Electric
Equestrian Parking
Equestrian Camping
Water Spigot
Watering Area
Residence
Fishing Pier
Fish Cleaning
Maintenance
Hiking Trail
Horse Trail
Biking Trail
Picnic Area
Picnic Shelter
Group Picnic Shelter
Designated Swimming Area
Parking
Boat Ramp
Playground
Lodging
Restaurant
Canoe Launch
Amphitheater
Interpretive Center
Dump Station
-- - Concrete Trail
----- Dirt Trail
--- Improved Trail

Park Reservations
(512) 389-8900
texasstateparks.org

Equine must have proof of a negative EIA (Coggins) test within the past 12 months. The form VS 10-11 is proof of testing.

Per person entry fee required at all parks.

Please wear helmet when bicycling in park.

No potable water available on Jordan Park Trail north of Bluestem Grove.

100 PW 4137
Pilot Point, TX 76258
(940) 686-2148

TOYOTA Proud Sponsor of Texas Parks and Wildlife Programs

PRAIRIES AND PINEYWOODS - WEST
#76 Greenbelt Corridor At Ray Roberts Lake State Park

NORTHEAST OF DENTON, TEXAS

KEY BIRDS
Herons, egrets, red-bellied and downy woodpeckers, American redstart, blue-gray gnatcatcher, and white-eyed vireo

BEST SEASON
All seasons

AREA DESCRIPTION
Forests, well-maintained trail, riparian forest, then open farmlands with a thin buffer of trees

Ray Roberts Lake State Park's Greenbelt Corridor follows the Elm Fork of the Trinity River from where it leaves Lake Ray Roberts to where it enters Lake Lewisville 11 miles downstream.

This well-maintained trail offers easy access to the the Elm Fork of the Trinity River, making it an excellent area for wildlife viewing in the midst of a major metropolitan area.

Upon entering the Greenbelt from its northern entrance, check the drainage canals just below the dam for herons and egrets and listen for indigo buntings calling from the forest edge.

Upon entering the woods, listen for the calls of red-bellied and downy woodpeckers. Watch for the small flocks of Carolina chickadee and tufted titmouse and migrating songbirds, such as northern parula, Nashville warbler, American redstart, blue-gray gnatcatcher, and white-eyed vireo.

Only 4.5 miles downstream from the dam at Ray Roberts Lake, the riparian forest along the Elm Fork of the Trinity River gives way to open farmlands with a thin buffer of trees.

These open areas host the eastern meadowlark and scissor-tailed flycatcher, and in winter attract a variety of sparrows to the brushy edges.

At the southern entry to the Greenbelt, the riparian forest associated with the Elm Fork of the Trinity is at its most impressive. Here numerous cottonwoods, sycamores, and pecans tower over the trail providing excellent wildlife watching opportunities and some welcome shade from the sun.

The stately woodland here supports healthy numbers of eastern woodland species such as Carolina wren and northern cardinal. The yellow-billed cuckoo can be spotted creeping through the canopy in search of its favorite meal of caterpillars, while blue grosbeaks venture in from their normal haunts along the forest edge. Also look for both red-eyed and white-eyed vireos.

PRAIRIES AND
PINEYWOODS WEST

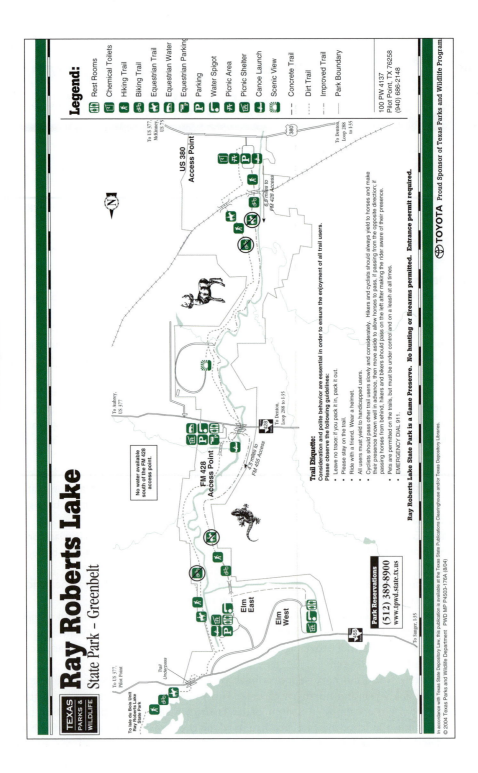

Ray Roberts Lake
State Park – Greenbelt

Legend:

- Rest Rooms
- Chemical Toilets
- Hiking Trail
- Biking Trail
- Equestrian Trail
- Equestrian Water
- Equestrian Parking
- Parking
- Water Spigot
- Picnic Area
- Picnic Shelter
- Canoe Launch
- Scenic View
- — Concrete Trail
- ···· Dirt Trail
- —·· Improved Trail
- —— Park Boundary

100 PW 4137
Pilot Point, TX 76258
(940) 686-2148

No water available
south of the FM 428
access point.

Park Reservations
(512) 389-8900
www.tpwd.state.tx.us

US 380
Access Point

FM 428
Access Point

Elm
East

Elm
West

Trail Etiquette:
Consideration and polite behavior are essential in order to ensure the enjoyment of all trail users.
Please observe the following guidelines:
- Leave no trace: if you pack it in, pack it out.
- Please stay on the trail.
- Ride with a friend. Wear a helmet.
- All users must yield to handicapped users.
- Cyclists should pass other trail users slowly and considerately. Hikers and cyclists should always yield to horses and make their presence known well in advance, then move aside to allow horses to pass, if passing from the opposite direction; if passing horses from behind, hikers and bikers should pass on the left after making the rider aware of their presence.
- Pets are permitted on the trails, but must be under control and on a leash at all times.
- EMERGENCY DIAL 911.

Ray Roberts Lake State Park is a Game Preserve. No hunting or firearms permitted. Entrance permit required.

TOYOTA Proud Sponsor of Texas Parks and Wildlife Program

DIRECTIONS

Elm Fork of the Trinity River at FM 455

From I-35 in Sanger, take Exit 478 for FM 455. Go east on FM 455 for 9.3 miles to the entrance to Elm Fork Park. Turn right and go 0.9 mile to the first parking area on the left below Ray Roberts Dam.

Elm Fork of the Trinity River at FM 428

From I-35 North in Denton take Exit 470 for TX 288 Loop. Go east on North SR 288 Loop for 3.6 miles to FM 428. Turn left (north) onto FM 428 and follow it 5.5 miles to the middle access point just after crossing the river on the left.

Elm Fork of the Trinity River at Hwy 380

From I-35 in Denton, take Exit 469 for US 380/ W. University Drive. Bear right (east) onto US 380/ US 377 for 7.6 miles to the third access point on the left just after crossing the river.

CONTACT INFORMATION

Site open for day use only. Phone: 940-686-2148.

PRAIRIES AND PINEYWOODS WEST

Great Blue Heron

PRAIRIES AND PINEYWOODS - WEST
Lost Creek Reservoir State Trailway

#77

LOCATED AT FORT RICHARDSON AND JACKSBORO, TEXAS

KEY BIRDS
Lark sparrow, painted bunting, northern bobwhite, red-bellied woodpecker, great egret, and great blue heron

BEST SEASON
All seasons

AREA DESCRIPTION
Many shaded areas of pecan and oak trees and runs by the creek or lakes much of the route

Located at Fort Richardson and Jacksboro, this approximately 10-mile hike, bike, and equestrian trail runs adjacent to Fort Richardson and along Lost Creek. The trail follows scenic Lost Creek and travels the east side of Lake Jacksboro and Lost Creek Reservoir. The trail crosses the dam at Lost Creek Reservoir and winds along the west side until you enter the trailhead.

There is a trailhead at Fort Richardson State Park and a trailhead on Lost Creek Reservoir. The trail passes shaded areas of pecan and oak trees and runs by the creek or lakes much of the route, providing many opportunities to fish and swim.

Watch the area around the lake and water for grassland birds such as lark sparrow, painted bunting, and northern bobwhite. Look in areas of dense brush for white-eyed vireo and yellow-billed cuckoo. Check the shoreline for a variety of shore birds during spring and fall migrations. Look for the red-bellied woodpecker, great egret, and great blue heron downstream from the FM 59 bridge, and check the bridge for nesting cliff swallows.

DIRECTIONS
From the intersection of US 380 and US 281 and FM 59 in Jacksboro, go north 2.3 miles on FM 59 to the parking area on the right.

CONTACT INFORMATION
The standard Texas park day-use and camping fees apply. Information and prices are subject to change. Please call the park or park information 1-800-792-1112 or 940-567-3506 for the latest updates.

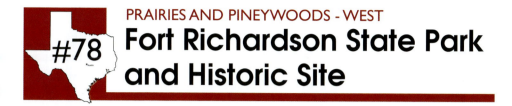

PRAIRIES AND PINEYWOODS - WEST
#78 Fort Richardson State Park and Historic Site

NEAR JACKSBORO, TEXAS

KEY BIRDS
Painted bunting, white-eyed vireo, herons, and migratory waterfowl

BEST SEASON
Summer and fall

AREA DESCRIPTION
Prairie grasslands and the low brush and hardwoods following Lost Creek

Established in 1867, Fort Richardson was the northernmost of a line of federal forts established after the Civil War. The 454-acre fort was abandoned in May, 1878. Historical structures include seven of the original buildings which have been restored: the post hospital, the officers' quarters, a powder magazine, a morgue, a commissary, a guardhouse, and a bakery. There are also two replicas of the officers' and enlisted men's barracks. The officers' barracks houses the Interpretive Center.

Birders should be on the lookout for painted buntings in open areas near the historical buildings and white-eyed vireos in the dense groves of oaks. Watch the pond behind park headquarters for herons and migratory waterfowl. Taking a slow walk along Lost Creek is where the best birding will be.

DIRECTIONS
From the intersection of US 380 and US 281 in Jacksboro, go south 0.8 mile on US 281 to Fort Richardson State Historical Site.

CONTACT INFORMATION
The standard Texas park day-use and camping fees apply. Information and prices are subject to change. Please call the park or park information (1-800-792-1112) or 940-567-3506 for the latest updates. Web Site: http://www.tpwd.state.tx.us/spdest/findadest/parks/fort_richardson/

Canada Geese

PRAIRIES AND PINEYWOODS WEST

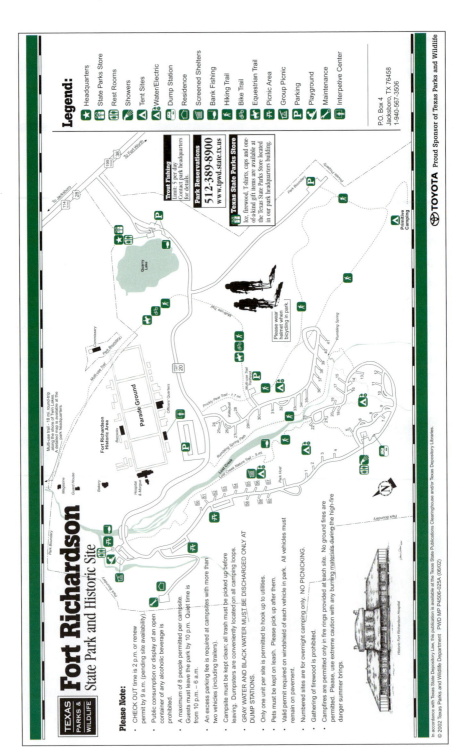

PRAIRIES AND PINEYWOODS - WEST
Clark Gardens

#79

MINERAL WELLS, TEXAS

KEY BIRDS
Swallows, painted bunting, and some waterfowl in addition to some domestic species

BEST SEASON
All seasons

AREA DESCRIPTION
Native plants such as mesquite with ponds, and many species of flowers and trees

This 83-acre botanical garden was created to serve as a working model for achieving aesthetically pleasing, sustainable landscapes. By demonstrating the techniques of using adapted plants, minimizing lawns, using compost and mulch, and conserving and collecting water, they hope to inspire and educate visitors.

The numerous ponds and fountains in the gardens are excellent spots for birders to spend some time observing the species of birds that are attracted here.

Check the large pond next to the parking area for swallows and the nearby mesquite trees for painted bunting. The gardens are a demonstration of how to use native plants and water features to enhance habitat for wildlife.

DIRECTIONS
From the intersection of US 281 and US 180 in Mineral Wells, go east on US 180 for 4.6 miles to Maddux Rd. Go left (north) on Maddux Rd. for 0.9 mile to Clark Gardens.

CONTACT INFORMATION
This location is open daily, all year. General Admission Fees: $7.00 per adults, $5.00 per seniors (65 and over) and $5.00 per child 5 to 12 years old. Call 940-682-4856 for more information or go to their web site: www.clarkgardens.com

PRAIRIES AND PINEYWOODS - WEST
#80 Lake Mineral Wells State Park and Trailway

EAST OF MINERAL WELLS, TEXAS

KEY BIRDS
Waterfowl, shore birds, woodpeckers

BEST SEASON
All seasons

AREA DESCRIPTION
River habitats as well as pasture and upland areas

Lake Mineral Wells State Park is located along Rock Creek, a large tributary of the Brazos River. The 3,282.5-acre park includes Lake Mineral Wells in its boundary.

This area was an early home to several Native American tribes including the Comanche. White settlers began arriving in the early 1850s, and intermittent warfare occurred until the late 1870s. Rugged terrain and lush native grasses attracted many early-day ranchers to this area, including Charles Goodnight, Oliver Loving, and C. C. Slaughter, who ran large herds of longhorn cattle.

Limestone cliffs line the southern edge of the reservoir, providing habitat for canyon wrens and several species of common and rare songbirds. Watch for several species of woodpecker in the trees and dead standing timber. Waterfowl and shorebirds are common during spring and fall migration. The Texas Parks & Wildlife website listed below contains a field bird checklist for the park.

DIRECTIONS
From the intersection of US 281 and US 180 in Mineral Wells, go east on US 180 for 3.9 miles to PR 71. Turn left (north) on PR 71 and follow it 0.3 mile into the park.

CONTACT INFORMATION
This site open for day use only. The standard Texas park day-use and camping fees apply. Information and prices are subject to change. Please call the park or park information (1-800-792-1112) for the latest updates. Phone: 940-328-1171 / Website: http://www.tpwd.state.tx.us/spdest/findadest/parks/lake_mineral_wells/

Lake Mineral Wells

State Park and Trailway

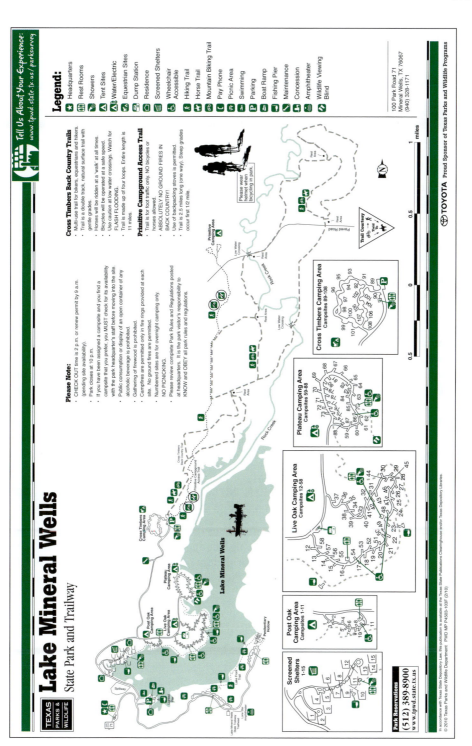

Tell Us About Your Experience:
www.tpwd.state.tx.us/parksurvey

Legend:

- Headquarters
- Rest Rooms
- Showers
- Tent Sites
- Water/Electric
- Equestrian Sites
- Dump Station
- Residence
- Screened Shelters
- Wheelchair Accessible
- Hiking Trail
- Horse Trail
- Mountain Biking Trail
- Pay Phone
- Picnic Area
- Swimming
- Parking
- Boat Ramp
- Fishing Pier
- Maintenance
- Concession
- Amphitheater
- Wildlife Viewing Blind

Cross Timbers Back Country Trails

- Multi-use trail for bikers, equestrians and hikers.
- Trail is a double track, natural surface trail with gentle grades.
- Horses will be ridden at a 'walk' at all times.
- Bicycles will be operated at a safe speed.
- Use caution at low water crossings. Watch for FLASH FLOODING.
- Trail is made up of four loops. Entire length is 11 miles.

Primitive Campground Access Trail

- Trail is for foot traffic only. NO bicycles or horses allowed.
- ABSOLUTELY NO GROUND FIRES IN BACK COUNTRY!
- Use of backpacking stoves is permitted.
- Trail is 2.5 miles long (one way). Steep grades occur first 1/2 mile.

Please Note:

- CHECK OUT time is 2 p.m. or renew permit by 9 a.m. (pending site availability).
- Park closes at 10 p.m.
- If you have been assigned a campsite and you find a campsite that you prefer, you MUST check for its availability with the park headquarter's staff before moving into the site.
- Public consumption or display of an open container of any alcoholic beverage is prohibited.
- Gathering of firewood is prohibited.
- Campfires are permitted only in fire rings provided at each site. No ground fires are permitted.
- Numbered sites are for overnight camping only. NO PICNICKING.
- Please review complete Park Rules and Regulations posted at headquarters. It is the park visitor's responsibility to KNOW and OBEY all park rules and regulations.

100 Park Road 71
Mineral Wells, TX 76067
(940) 328-1171

TOYOTA Proud Sponsor of Texas Parks and Wildlife Programs

Please wear helmet when bicycling in park.

Cross Timbers Camping Area
Campsites 89-108

Plateau Camping Area
Campsites 59-88

Live Oak Camping Area
Campsites 12-58

Post Oak Camping Area
Campsites 1-11

Screened Shelters 1-15

TEXAS PARKS & WILDLIFE

Park Reservations
(512) 389-8900
www.tpwd.state.tx.us

© 2010 Texas Parks and Wildlife Department   PWD MP P4503-103F (2010)

In accordance with Texas State Depository Law, this publication is available at the Texas State Publications Clearinghouse and/or Texas Depository Libraries.

PRAIRIES AND PINEYWOODS WEST

PRAIRIES AND PINEYWOODS - WEST
#81 Possum Kingdom State Park

WEST OF MINERAL WELLS, TEXAS AND SOUTH OF GRAHAM, TEXAS

KEY BIRDS
Chipping sparrow, painted bunting, canyon and Bewick's wrens, plus herons, egrets, and shore birds

BEST SEASON
Winter, summer, and spring

AREA DESCRIPTION
Rugged canyon country of the Palo Pinto Mountains and Brazos River Valley

This 1,528-acre state park adjacent to Possum Kingdom Lake, is located in the rugged canyon country of the Palo Pinto Mountains and Brazos River Valley and offers camping, bird watching, hiking, nature and study along with many other activities.

In early summer, birders will hear the calls of singing chipping sparrows and painted buntings. Access to several shallow coves provides an opportunity to watch for herons, egrets, and shorebirds.

The lake will also attract and hold waterfowl and bald eagles during the winter along with canyon and Bewick's wrens in the brushy uplands, as well as the black-chinned hummingbird and lark sparrow.

DIRECTIONS
From the intersection of US 180 and US 281 in Mineral Wells go west on US 180 for 34.9 miles to PR 33. Turn right (north) on PR 33 for 16.1 miles to the park entrance.

CONTACT INFORMATION
The standard Texas park day-use and camping fees apply. Information and prices are subject to change. Please call the park or park information 1-800-792-1112 or call: 940-549-1803 for the latest updates. Website: http://www.tpwd.state.tx.us/spdest/findadest/parks/possum_kingdom/

PRAIRIES AND PINEYWOODS - WEST
Wildcatter Ranch and Resort

#82

SOUTHEAST OF GRAHAM, TEXAS

KEY BIRDS
Hawks, white-eyed vireo, yellow-billed cuckoo, belted kingfisher, painted bunting, egrets, and herons

BEST SEASON
All seasons

AREA DESCRIPTION
Hilly and rocky landscape and Hill Country habitats sloping down to riverside with trees and brush

Located amid the rolling Palo Pinto Hills and the Brazos River, the 1500-acre Wildcatter Ranch and Resort offers visitors a chance to enjoy a landscape steeped in history and overflowing with natural beauty. An afternoon spent with the general manager sent me off to enthusiastically explore the outdoors and the bird life that is always present.

The main ridge running north to south through the ranch will eventually hold a series of comfortable cabins and be the starting point for numerous trails to be explored on horseback or on foot. Look for white-eyed vireo, yellow-billed cuckoo, and painted bunting in the open woodland and rolling shrub land. At the southern end of the ranch is a wetland that provides habitat for egrets, herons, and belted kingfishers. The winter months attract a diversity of ducks and geese.

Take a slow drive down to the Brazos River and watch for flycatchers and the black-crested titmouse. Careful observance will let you see several species of hawks and owls near evening.

DIRECTIONS
From the intersection of US 380/ SR 16 and Hwy 67/ 7th St. in Graham, go south on SR 16/ Elm Street for 9.2 miles to Wildcatter Ranch. The ranch is located 8.9 miles south of the Courthouse Square in Graham on Hwy 16. The main entrance is on the west side of the highway.

CONTACT INFORMATION
This is a restricted-access site and commercial. Please call ahead.
Phone: 940-549-3500; 888-462-9277
Website: www.wildcatterranch.com

PRAIRIES AND PINEYWOODS - WEST
Hockaday Ranch B & B

#83

NEAR GRAHAM, TEXAS

KEY BIRDS
Ash-throated flycatcher, black-crested titmouse, roadrunners, and lark sparrow

BEST SEASON
All seasons

AREA DESCRIPTION
Juniper-oak woodland and open brush and grassland

Located on the Brazos River this B & B and RV park offers the quiet and seclusion for some careful birdwatching.

One hundred and fifty years ago the ranch was part of the Brazos Indian Reservation. The ranch supports a variety of habitats. Birders should watch the roadsides for greater roadrunners.

The fence rows provide perches for the ash-throated flycatcher and curious black-crested titmouse. Where the trees give way to grassland, look for lark sparrow and listen for northern bobwhite whistling from deep cover or scurrying down the road as you approach.

DIRECTIONS
From the intersection of US 380/ SR 16 and Hwy 67/ 7th Street in Graham, go south on SR 16 for 4.8 miles to Old Hwy 16. Turn right and go 0.3 mile to Pettus Lane, turn right and go 0.9 mile to the Hockaday Ranch B & B.

CONTACT INFORMATION
Call ahead for lodging and RV fees. Call: 940-549-0087 or 940-550-8041
Website: www.hockadayranch.com

PRAIRIES AND PINEYWOODS - WEST
#84 Backside

RACE TRACK ROAD
GRAHAM, TEXAS

KEY BIRDS
Great blue heron, great egret, belted kingfisher, red-tailed hawk

BEST SEASON
All seasons, depending on the weather

AREA DESCRIPTION
Brazos River frontage, with cottonwoods lining the banks and neighboring mesquite scrubland habitat

The Backside offers one of those unique combinations that only Texas can offer: abundant wildlife in an easily accessible area combined with a great steak restaurant.

The Backside offers tent and RV camping along the banks of the Brazos River. The river displays an impressive diversity of species, with great blue heron and great egret along its banks and the occasional belted kingfisher. The numerous cottonwoods lining the banks and neighboring mesquite scrubland hold numerous painted and indigo buntings, calling from all directions.

Red-shouldered Hawk

In winter the river attracts an impressive variety of raptors with numerous red-tailed hawk and the occasional bald eagle cruising down stream. A mountain lion has been seen in this area.

DIRECTIONS
From the intersection of US 380/ SR 16 and Hwy 67/ 7th Street in Graham go south on Hwy 67/ 7th Street for 6.0 miles to Rosser Ranch Road. Turn left (east) onto Rosser Ranch Road and go 2.8 miles to Race Track Road. Turn right and go 0.8 mile to the entrance.

CONTACT INFORMATION
This is a commercial site and is open daily. Developed camping and RV spaces are available for a fee. For more information call: 940-549-8422.

PRAIRIES AND
PINEYWOODS WEST

PRAIRIES AND PINEYWOODS - WEST
Lucy Park

#85

WICHITA FALLS, TEXAS

KEY BIRDS
Snowy egret, killdeer, Mississippi kite, and mourning and Inca doves

BEST SEASON
All seasons

AREA DESCRIPTION
Several large areas bordered by the Wichita River and its associated woodland

A well-maintained trail accompanies the river for its length through the park, providing excellent bird watching opportunities. In summer, the park hosts several pairs of Mississippi kite.

The woodlands provide habitat for Carolina wren and Carolina chickadee, while the more open edges provide foraging grounds for mourning and Inca doves. Along the Wichita River, look for snowy egret, killdeer, and migrating songbirds during spring and fall.

DIRECTIONS
From US 82 in south Wichita Falls take the Kemp Street Exit north 1.7 miles to Seymour Street. Turn right (east) on Seymour Street and go 0.3 mile to Sunset Drive. Turn left (north) on Sunset Drive and follow it 0.1 mile into the park.

CONTACT INFORMATION
This city park is open for day use only. Phone: 940-761-7490 / Website: www.wichitafallstx. gov/?NID=69

PRAIRIES AND PINEYWOODS - WEST
#86 Lake Arrowhead State Park

229 PARK ROAD 63, WICHITA FALLS, TX 76310

KEY BIRDS
Quail, wild turkey, neotropic cormorant, scissor-tailed flycatcher, waterfowl, and wading birds

BEST SEASON
All seasons

AREA DESCRIPTION
Lake habitat surrounded by semi-arid, gently rolling prairie, much of which has been covered by mesquite

Lake Arrowhead acts as an oasis of water surrounded by semiarid, gently rolling prairie, much of which has been covered by mesquite in recent decades.

Waterfowl and wading birds are commonly seen in the park. The mesquite brush provides habitat for scissor-tailed flycatcher and western kingbird. Northern bobwhite and wild turkey can often be seen in the campgrounds and picnic areas.

The lake itself attracts a diversity of birds and other wildlife. In late summer, look for Forster's and least terns as well as the neotropic cormorant.

In winter, large numbers of waterfowl and American white pelican visit the lake. The black-tailed prairie dog town at the park can provide lots of entertaining viewing. Be sure to watch for burrowing owls near and inside the prairie dog town.

DIRECTIONS
From the intersection of US 281 and US 82 in Wichita Falls, go south on US 281 for 6.8 miles to RR 1954. Turn left (east) on RR 1954 and follow it 7.2 miles to Lake Arrowhead State Park.

CONTACT INFORMATION
The standard Texas park day-use and camping fees apply. Information and prices are subject to change. Please call the park or park information 1-800-792-1112 for the latest updates or call 940-528-2211 / Website: http://www.tpwd.state.tx.us/spdest/findadest/parks/lake_arrowhead/

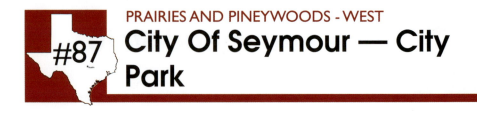

PRAIRIES AND PINEYWOODS - WEST
City Of Seymour — City Park

#87

SEYMOUR, TEXAS

KEY BIRDS
Wild turkey, killdeer, black-bellied whistling-duck, and herons

BEST SEASON
All seasons

AREA DESCRIPTION
Creekside habitat and grassy areas with low brush

The story goes that early settlers noticed that Seymour Creek was one of the best places for wild turkey anywhere along the Brazos River. Because of this, they settled there and the town of Seymour was founded. If the story is true, the residents of Seymour have done right by their turkeys and respectfully set aside 83 acres along Seymour Creek as parkland.

More regular residents include nesting blue jay, northern mockingbird, common grackle, and mourning dove.

In the heat of the summer the muddy banks of the creek provide excellent habitat for killdeer and herons. In summer, be sure to climb the slight rise on the east side of the park and look back over the city for Mississippi kites. Also, look for the recently arrived black-bellied whistling-ducks, which nest in large trees around town.

DIRECTIONS
From the intersection of US 183 and US 82 in Seymour go south 0.4 mile to E. McLain Street. Turn left on E. McLain and go 0.4 mile to the park on the left.

CONTACT INFORMATION
This is a day-use-only site, please call: 940-889-3148
Website: www.cityofseymour.org

PRAIRIES AND PINEYWOODS - WEST
#88 Ranger Creek Ranch

COUNTY ROAD 3150
VERA, TEXAS
(17 MILES WEST OF SEYMOUR, TEXAS)

KEY BIRDS
Lark sparrow, Mississippi kite, roadrunners, and geese and ducks

BEST SEASON
Spring, summer, fall

AREA DESCRIPTION
West Texas rolling plains with plenty of mesquite trees, fertile wheat fields, and striking mesas and canyons

The Walker Family has lived, farmed, and hunted thousands of acres of west Baylor County for over a hundred years. During this time they have developed an appreciation for the land and a love for its wildlife.

Fifteen years ago they started Ranger Creek Ranch to share this love with others. They have made many improvements and have carefully managed the land for a wide diversity of wildlife. Their extensive system of blinds offers excellent opportunities to observe and photograph wildlife up close.

The canyons host lark sparrows and roadrunners in abundance and are one of the few remaining places where seeing Texas horned lizards is a daily occurrence. The ponds are also frequented by Mississippi kites, which cruise overhead in search of their dragonfly prey. During the winter months, the managed wetlands are seasonally flooded to attract geese and ducks in great numbers.

The history of the ranch can be seen in several old rock buildings that are nearly a century old. Ranger Creek Ranch offers a unique glimpse at one of Texas' most striking landscapes and an opportunity to enjoy its great wildlife and hospitality.

DIRECTIONS
From the intersection of US 183 and US 82/ W. California Street in Seymour, go west on US 82/ W. California Street for 17.6 miles to the town of Vera and CR 3150. From Vera, go west 1.0 mile on CR 3150 to the ranch on the right.

CONTACT INFORMATION
Ranger Creek Ranch, 2591 CR 3185, Seymour, TX, 76380. This ranch is a commercial operation and entrance is restricted please call ahead. Phone: 940-888-2478 / Website: www.rangercreekranch.com

PRAIRIES AND
PINEYWOODS WEST

American Wigeon

Wildlife Management Areas Of Texas

The rural landscape of Texas offers a natural beauty and character unsurpassed. Texas boasts some of the most beautiful and abundant populations of plants and wildlife to be found anywhere.

Past generations of Texas families lived in or near rural, natural areas of the state, and understood the value and necessity of healthy natural systems. But today most Texans live near cities and towns, and many of us have lost our connection with the land.

The Wildlife Management Areas (WMAs) of Texas offer a unique opportunity for the public to learn and experience the natural part of Texas and the systems that support life. WMAs are operated by the Wildlife Division of Texas Parks and Wildlife. Today, we have 51 Wildlife Management Areas, encompassing some 756,464 acres of land. WMAs are established to represent habitats and wildlife populations typical of each ecological region of Texas. Today, nearly every ecological region in the state is represented, with the exception of the Cross Timbers and Prairies in north-central Texas.

WMAs were established as sites to perform research on wildlife populations and habitat, conduct education on sound resource management, and to provide public hunting, hiking, camping, bird watching, and a host of other outdoor recreational opportunities - all of which are compatible with the conservation of this valuable resource.

WMAs offer a chance to experience Texas's natural beauty - from the high, wide skies of the Panhandle in the north to the southern tropical thorn forests of the Lower Rio Grande Valley; and from the spectacular western vistas of the Trans-Pecos to the lush green mystery of the Pineywoods in East Texas.

You must have a permit to visit a WMA. The only exceptions are driving tours and special educational events.

Limited Public Use (LPU) Permit - $12

- A $12 Limited Public Use (LPU) Permit is also available which allows an adult to enter these lands, but does not authorize them to hunt.
- The LPU Permit provides entry to Texas Parks & Wildlife Department Wildlife Management Areas at times when they are open for general visitation.
- Only permit holders receive a map booklet listing available areas, facilities, rules, and schedules.

LPU Permits are available at TPWD offices and all license vendors (a place which sells hunting and fishing licenses), or by calling 1-800-TX-LIC-4U (menu choice 1 for license sales) and paying by Visa, Discover, or MasterCard). If the permit is purchased at a TPWD office, the map booklet and supplement will be provided immediately at the time of purchase; otherwise, the publications will be mailed to the purchaser within two weeks of purchase.

Here are five tips to help enjoy Wildlife Management Areas to the fullest:
1. Bring your own drinking water.
2. Insect repellant is recommended for mosquitoes.
3. High heat and humidity in the summer should be taken into consideration when planning a visit.
4. Keep in mind there are no restroom facilities.
5. The WMA is not wheel chair accessible.

Users must have a $48.00 Texas Public Lands Permit available from TPW vendors. This one permit will allow entry to most Texas wildlife management areas.

Texas State Parks

Fee information for specific parks is available on that particular park's website by clicking on the "Fees" link. You can also inquire about specific fees by calling the Park Information line (Monday-Friday from 8am – 5pm) at 1-800-792-1112 (option 3 - option 3). The Central Reservation Center will also give you rates when you make reservations at 512-389-8900. The Reserve America Internet Reservations website (www.reserveamerica.com) also contains fee information for specific parks.

TEXAS STATE PARKS PASS

The Texas State Parks Pass is an annual pass that offers many special benefits. As a pass holder, you and your guests can enjoy unlimited visits to more than 90 State Parks, without paying the daily entrance fee (card holder and physical pass must be present). You can also receive exciting discounts on camping (restrictions apply), park store merchandise, and recreational equipment rentals, and you are eligible for other specials.

BIRDING TRAILS: TEXAS

Chambers of Commerce and Convention & Visitors Bureaus

TEXAS PANHANDLE

Abilene CVB / 800-727-7704 / www.abilenevisitors.com
Abilene COC / 915-677-7241 / www.abilene.com/chamber
Albany COC / 915-762-2525 / www.albanytexas.com
Amarillo CVB / 806-374-1497 / 800-692-1338 / www.Amarillo-cvb.org
Big Spring CVB / 915-264-2315 / www.bigspringtx.com
Bronte COC / 915-473-6451 / www.brontetxs.com
Borger COC / 806-274-2211 / 800-687-5694 / www.borger.com
Breckenridge COC / 254-559-2301 / www.breckenridgetexas.com
Crosbyton COC / 806-675-2261 / www.crosbytoncoc.com
Canadian COC / 806-323-6234 / www.canadiantx.com
Clarendon COC / 806-874-2421, 800-579-4023 / www.clarendonedc.org
Dumas COC / 806-935-2123 / www.dumaschamber.com
Dalhart Area COC / 806-244-5646 / www.dalhart.org
Eastland COC / 254-629-2332 / www.eastland.net/eastland/
Floydada COC / 806-983-3434 / www.floydadachamber.com
Lubbock COC / 806-761-7000, 800-321-5822 / www.lubbockchamber.com
Lubbock CVB / 806-747-5232, 800-692-4035 / www.lubbocklegends.org
Llano Estacado Tourism Society / 806-698-6530 / www.llanoestacado.com
Miami COC / 806-868-3291 / www.miamitexas.org
Muleshoe Chamber of Commerce / 806-272-4248 / www.muleshoechamber.org
Plainview COC / 800-658-2685 / www.plainviewtex.com
Perryton COC / 806-435-6575 / www.perryton.org
Post COC / 806-495-3461 / www.postcitytexas.com
Quitaque COC / 806-455-1456 / www.quitaque.org
Quanah COC / 940-663-2222 / www.quanah.org
Robert Lee EDC / www.robertleetx.com
Ralls COC / 806-253-2342
San Angelo COC / 915-655-4136, 800-375-1206 / www.sanangelo-tx.com
Spur COC / 806-271-3363 / www.spurchamber.com
Spearman COC / 806-659-5555 / www.spearman.org
Texas Prairie Rivers Region Inc. / 806-323-5397 / www.texasprairierivers.com
Texas Forts Trail / 915-676-1762 / www.texasfortstrail.com

Texas Panhandle Tourism Marketing Council / www.texasptmc.org
Wheeler COC / 806-826-3408 / www.wheelertexas.com
Wellington COC / 806-447-5848

TEXAS PRAIRIES & PINEYWOODS

Arlington CVB /817-265-7721 / www.arlington.org
Athens / 888-294-AVIP(2847) / athenstx.org
Athens COC / 800-755-7878 / www.athenscc.org
Allen COC / 927-727-5585 / www.allenchamber.com
Benbrook Area COC / 817-249-4451 / www.benbrookchamber.org
Bosque County / 254-435-2382 / users.htcomp.net/bosque
Brenham/Washington County / 888-BRENHAM (273-6426) / www.brenhamtexas.com
Burleson County COC / 979-596-2383 / www.rtis.com/reg/somerville
Bryan-College Station CVB / 800-777-8292 / www.bryan-collegestation.org
Centerville COC / 903-536-7261 / www.rtis.com/reg/centerville
Corsicana COC / 877-376-7477 / www.corsicana.org
Calvert COC / 979-364-2559 / www.rtis.com/reg/calvert
Crockett Area COC / 936-544-2359 / www.crockettareachamber.org
Clifton COC / 800-344-3720 / www.cliftontexas.org
City of Tyler / 800-235-5712 / www.cityoftyler.org
City of Nacogdoches / www.ci.nacogdoches.tx.us
City of Rusk / 903-683-2213 / www.rusktx.com
City of Gilmer / 903-797-8888 / www.gilmer-tx.com
City of Gladewater / 903-845-2196 / cityofgladewater.com
City of Longview / 903-237-4000 / www.longviewtx.com
City of Mineola / 800-MINEOLA (646-3652) / www.mineola.com
City of Mount Vernon / 903-573-4495 / www.mtvernon-texas.com
City of Sulphur Springs 903-885-7541 / sulphurspringstx.org
City of Uncertain / 903-789-3443 / www.cityofuncertain.com
City of Seymour / 940-889-3148 / www.cityofseymour.org
City of Garland / 972-205-2000 / www.ci.garland.tx.us
City of North Richland Hills / 817-427-6000 / www.ci.north-richland-hills.tx.us
City of Paris / 903-784-2501 / www.paristexas.com
City of Ennis / 972-878-1234 / www.ennis-texas.com
Dallas CVB / 800-232-5527 / www.dallascvb.com
Duncanville COC / 972-780-4990 / www.duncanvillechamber.org
Decatur / 940-627-3107 / www.decaturtx.org
Denison Area COC / 903-465-1551 / www.denisontexas.com
Denton CVB / 888-381-1818 / www.discoverdenton.com
Franklin County COC / 903-537-4365 / www.mt-vernon.com/~chamber
Fort Worth CVB / 800-433-5747 / www.fortworth.com
Graham / 800-256-4844 / www.visitgraham.com
Grand Saline / 903-962-7147 / www.grandsaline.com

Greenville COC / 903-455-1510 / www.greenville-chamber.org
Glen Rose CVB / 888-346-6282 / www.glenrosetexas.net
Granbury CVB / 800-950-2212 / www.granburytx.com
Gainesville / 940-668-4500 / www.gainesville.tx.us/default.asp
Grapevine CVB / 800-457-6338 / www.grapevinetexasusa.com
Hillsboro Area COC / 800-HILLSBORO (445-5726) / www.hillsborochamber.org
Hamilton / 254-386-3216 / hamiltontexas.com
Hico / 800-361-HICO (4426) / www.hico-tx.com
Huntsville CVB / 800-289-0389 / www.huntsvilletexas.com
Jefferson/Marion County COC / 888-GO-RELAX (467-3529) / www.jefferson-texas.com
Jacksonville COC / 800-376-2217 / www.jacksonvilletexas.com
Jacksboro COC / 940-567-2602 / www.jacksborochamber.com
Livingston-Polk County COC / 936-327-4929 / www.livingston-polkcountychamber.com
Lufkin/Angelina County COC / 936-634-6644 / www.lufkintexas.org
La Grange Area COC / 800-524-7264 / www.lagrangetx.org
McKinney CVB / 888-649-8499 / www.mckinneycvb.org
Meridian COC / 254-435-2381 / users.htcomp.net/meridian
Mexia Area COC / 888-535-5476 / mexiachamber.com
Mineola COC / 903-569-2087 / www.chamber.mineola.com
Marshall COC / 903-935-7868 / www.marshall-chamber.com
Mineral Wells Area COC / 800-252-6989 / www.mineralwellstx.com
Nacogdoches CVB / 888-OLDEST-TOWN (653-3786) / www.visitnacogdoches.org
Palestine CVB / 800-659-3484 / www.visitpalestine.com
Palestine COC / 903-729-6066 / www.palestinechamber.org
Plano CVB / 800-81-PLANO (7-5266) / www.planocvb.com
Riverside/ Lake Livingston Area COC / 936-594-1414 / www.lakelivingstonarea.org
Red River County COC / 903-427-2645 / www.red-river.net
Richardson CVB / 888-690-7287 / www.richardsontexas.org
Rosebud COC / 254-583-7979 / www.rtis.com/reg/rosebud
Sanger / 940-458-7702 / www.sangertexas.com
Sherman / 888-893-1188 / www.shermantexas.com
Sabine County COC 409-787-3732 / www.sabinecountytexas.org
San Augustine COC / 936-275-3610 / www.sanaugustinetx.com
Sabine County COC (409) 787-3732, www.sabinecountytexas.com
Shelby County COC / 936-598-3682 / www.shelbycountychamber.com
Southlake / 817-481-5581 / www.ci.southlake.tx.us
Trinity Peninsula COC / 936-594-3856 / www.trinitychamber.org
Tawakoni Area COC / 903-447-3020 /www.tawakoni.org
Texarkana COC / 903-792-7191 / www.texarkana.org
Wichita Falls / 940-716-5500 / www.wichitafalls.org
Wills Point / 903-873-3111 / www.willspointchamber.com
Winnsboro Area COC / 903-342-3666 / www.winnsboro.com
Wylie COC / 972-442-2804 / www.wyliechamber.org

Texas Audubon Society Chapters

Audubon Dallas

PO Box 12713
Dallas, TX 75225
www.audubondallas.org

Bastrop County Audubon Society

Bastrop, TX
www.bastropcountyaudubon.org

Bexar Audubon Society

PO Box 6084
San Antonio, TX 78209
www.bexaraudubon.org

Big Country Audubon Society

PO Box 569
Abilene, TX 79604
325-691-8981
www.bigcountryaudubon.org

Central Texas Audubon Society

1308 Circlewood
Waco, TX 76712
www.centexaudubon.org

Coastal Bend Audubon Society

PO Box 3604
Corpus Christi, TX 78463
361-885-6203
www.coastalbendaudubon.org

El Paso Trans Pecos Audubon Society

PO Box 972441
El Paso, TX 79997
www.trans-pecos-audubon.org

Fort Worth Audubon Society

PO Box 16528
Fort Worth, TX 74162
www.fwas.org

Golden Triangle Audubon Society

PO Box 1292
Nederland, TX 77627
www.goldentriangleaudubon.org

Houston Audubon Society

440 Wilchester Blvd.
Houston, TX 77079
713-932-1639
www.houstonaudubon.org

Huntsville Audubon Society

PO Box 6818
Huntsville, TX 77342
www.huntsvilleaudubon.org

Llano Estacado Audubon Society

PO Box 6066
Lubbock, TX 79493
www.leas.bizland.com

Monte Mucho Audubon Society

PO Box 200
Realitos, TX 78376
956-764-5701
www.audubon.org/chapters/monte-mucho-audubon-society

Prairie and Timbers Audubon Society

c/o Heard Natural Science Museum
One Nature Place
McKinney, TX 75069
972-562-5566
www.prairieandtimbers.org

Rio Brazos Audubon Society

PO Box 9055
College Station, TX 77842
www.riobrazosaudubon.org

Rio Grande Delta Audubon Society

8801 Boca Chica
Brownsville, TX 878521
956-831-4653 or 1-866-279-1775
www.riograndedeltaaudubon.org

Texas Panhandle Audubon Society

PO Box 30939
Amarillo, TX 79120
806-656-0036
www.TXPAS.org

Travis Audubon Society

3710 Cedar St.
Box 5
Austin, TX 78705
512-300-2473
www.travisaudubon.org

Twin Lakes Audubon Society

PO Box 883
Belton, TX 76513
www.twinlakesaudubon.org

Tyler Audubon Society

PO Box 132926
Tyler, TX 75713
www.tyleraudubon.org

Texas Bird List

The following is a list of bird species accepted for Texas by the Texas Bird Records Committee (TBRC) of the Texas Ornithological Society.

I = Introduced
E = Extinct
u = uncertain origin of introduced/native origin
* = birds expected to be accepted by the TBRC

LOONS

ORDER GAVIIFORMES, FAMILY GAVIIDAE
Red-throated Loon
Pacific Loon
Common Loon
Yellow-billed Loon

GREBES

ORDER PODICIPEDIFORMES, FAMILY DIOMEDEIIDAE
Least Grebe
Pied-billed Grebe
Horned Grebe
Red-necked Grebe
Eared Grebe
Western Grebe
Clark's Grebe

SHEARWATERS, PETRELS AND ALBATROSSES

ORDER PROCELLARIIFORMES, FAMILY PROCELLARIIDAE
Yellow-nosed Albatross
White-chinned Petrel
Black-capped Petrel *
Cory's Shearwater
Greater Shearwater
Sooty Shearwater
Manx Shearwater
Audubon's Shearwater

FAMILY SULIDAE
Masked Booby
Blue-footed Booby
Brown Booby
Red-footed Booby
Northern Gannet

PELICANS FRIGATEBIRDS

ORDER PELECANIFORMES, FAMILY FREGATIDAE
Magnificent Frigatebird

ORDER PELECANIFORMES, FAMILY PELICANIDAE
American White Pelican
Brown Pelican

CORMORANTS

(ORDER PELECANIFORMES, FAMILY PHALACROCORACIDAE)
Double-crested Cormorant
Neotropic Cormorant

DARTERS

ORDER PELECANIFORMES, FAMILY ANHINGIDAE
Anhinga

BITTERNS AND HERONS

ORDER CICONIIFORMES, FAMILY ARDEIDAE
American Bittern
Least Bittern

Great Blue Heron
Great Egret
Snowy Egret
Little Blue Heron
Tricolored Heron
Reddish Egret
Cattle Egret
Green Heron
Black-crowned Night-Heron
Yellow-crowned Night-Heron

STORM-PETRELS

ORDER PROCELLARIIFORMES, FAMILY HYDROBATIDAE
Wilson's Storm-Petrel
Leach's Storm-Petrel
Band-rumped Storm-Petrel

TROPICBIRDS

ORDER PELECANIFORMES, FAMILY PHAETHONTIDAE
Red-billed Tropicbird

IBISES AND SPOONBILLS

ORDER CICONIIFORMES, FAMILY THRESKIORNITHIDAE
White Ibis
Glossy Ibis
White-faced Ibis
Roseate Spoonbill

STORKS

ORDER CICONIIFORMES, FAMILY CICONIIDAE
Jabiru
Wood Stork

AMERICAN VULTURES

ORDER CICONIIFORMES
Black Vulture
Turkey Vulture

FLAMINGOES

ORDER PHOENICOPTERIFORMES, FAMILY PHOENICOPTERIDAE
Greater Flamingo

SWANS, GEESE AND DUCKS

ORDER ANSERIFORMES, FAMILY ANATIDAE
Black-bellied Whistling-Duck
Fulvous Whistling-Duck
Greater White-fronted Goose
Snow Goose
Ross's Goose
Canada Goose
Brant
Trumpeter Swan
Tundra Swan
Muscovy Duck
Wood Duck
Gadwall
Eurasian Wigeon
American Wigeon
American Black Duck
Mallard
Mottled Duck
Blue-winged Teal
Cinnamon Teal
Northern Shoveler
White-cheeked Pintail
Northern Pintail
Garganey
Green-winged Teal
Canvasback
Redhead
Ring-necked Duck
Greater Scaup
Lesser Scaup
Harlequin Duck
Surf Scoter
White-winged Scoter
Black Scoter
Oldsquaw
Bufflehead
Common Goldeneye
Barrow's Goldeneye
Hooded Merganser
Red-breasted Merganser
Common Merganser
Masked Duck
Ruddy Duck

KITES, HAWKS, EAGLES AND ALLIES

ORDER FALCONIFORMES, FAMILY ACCIPITRIDAE

Osprey
Hook-billed Kite
Swallow-tailed Kite
White-tailed Kite
Snail Kite
Mississippi Kite
Bald Eagle
Northern Harrier
Sharp-shinned Hawk
Cooper's Hawk
Northern Goshawk
Crane Hawk
Gray Hawk
Common Black-Hawk
Harris's Hawk
Roadside Hawk
Red-shouldered Hawk
Broad-winged Hawk
Short-tailed Hawk
Swainson's Hawk
White-tailed Hawk
Zone-tailed Hawk
Red-tailed Hawk
Ferruginous Hawk
Rough-legged Hawk
Golden Eagle

CARACARAS AND FALCONS

ORDER FALCONIFORMES, FAMILY FALCONIDAE

Crested Caracara
Collared Forest-Falcon
American Kestrel
Merlin
Aplomado Falcon
Prairie Falcon
Peregrine Falcon

GUANS

ORDER GALLIFORMES, FAMILY CRACIDAE

Plain Chachalaca

PHEASANTS, GROUSE AND TURKEYS

ORDER GALLIFORMES, FAMILY PHASIANIIDAE

Ring-necked Pheasant (I)
Greater Prairie-Chicken
Lesser Prairie-Chicken
Wild Turkey

NEW WORLD QUAIL

ORDER GALLIFORMES, FAMILY ODONTOPHORIDAE

Montezuma Quail
Northern Bobwhite
Scaled Quail
Gambel's Quail

RAILS, GALLINULES AND COOTS

ORDER GRUIFORMES, FAMILY RALLIDAE

Yellow Rail
Black Rail
Clapper Rail
King Rail
Virginia Rail
Sora
Paint-billed Crake
Spotted Rail
Purple Gallinule
Common Moorhen
American Coot

CRANES

ORDER GRUIFORMES, FAMILY GRUIDAE

Sandhill Crane
Whooping Crane

THICK-KNEES

ORDER CHARADRIIFORMES, FAMILY BURHINIDAE

Double-striped Thick-knee

PLOVERS

ORDER CHARADRIIFORMES, FAMILY CHARADRIIDAE

Black-bellied Plover
American Golden-Plover

Collared Plover
Snowy Plover
Wilson's Plover
Semipalmated Plover
Piping Plover
Killdeer
Mountain Plover

OYSTERCATCHERS
ORDER CHARADRIIFORMES, FAMILY HAEMATOPODIDAE
American Oystercatcher

STILTS AND AVOCETS
ORDER CHARADRIIFORMES, FAMILY RECURVIROSTRIDAE
Black-necked Stilt
American Avocet

JACANAS
ORDER CHARADRIIFORMES, FAMILY JACANIDAE
Northern Jacana

SANDPIPERS AND ALLIES
ORDER CHARADRIIFORMES, FAMILY SCOLOPACIDAE
Greater Yellowlegs
Lesser Yellowlegs
Solitary Sandpiper
Willet
Wandering Tattler
Spotted Sandpiper
Upland Sandpiper
Eskimo Curlew
Whimbrel
Long-billed Curlew
Hudsonian Godwit
Marbled Godwit
Ruddy Turnstone
Surfbird
Red Knot
Sanderling
Semipalmated Sandpiper
Western Sandpiper

Red-necked Stint
Least Sandpiper
White-rumped Sandpiper
Baird's Sandpiper
Pectoral Sandpiper
Sharp-tailed Sandpiper
Purple Sandpiper
Dunlin
Curlew Sandpiper
Stilt Sandpiper
Buff-breasted Sandpiper
Ruff
Short-billed Dowitcher
Long-billed Dowitcher
Common Snipe
American Woodcock
Wilson's Phalarope
Red-necked Phalarope
Red Phalarope

GULLS, TERNS AND SKIMMERS
ORDER CHARADRIIFORMES, FAMILY LARIDAE
Pomarine Jaeger
Parasitic Jaeger
Long-tailed Jaeger
Laughing Gull
Franklin's Gull
Little Gull
Black-headed Gull
Bonaparte's Gull
Heermann's Gull
Mew Gull
Ring-billed Gull
California Gull
Herring Gull
Thayer's Gull
Iceland Gull
Lesser Black-backed Gull
Slaty-backed Gull
Western Gull
Glaucous Gull
Great Black-backed Gull
Kelp Gull

Black-legged Kittiwake
Sabine's Gull
Gull-billed Tern
Caspian Tern
Royal Tern
Elegant Tern
Sandwich Tern
Roseate Tern *
Common Tern
Arctic Tern *
Forster's Tern
Least Tern
Bridled Tern
Sooty Tern
Black Tern
Brown Noddy
Black Noddy
Black Skimmer

PIGEONS AND DOVES

ORDER COLUMBIFORMES, FAMILY COLUMBIDAE
Rock Dove (I)
Red-billed Pigeon
Band-tailed Pigeon
Eurasian Collared-Dove (I)*
White-winged Dove
Mourning Dove
Passenger Pigeon (E)
Inca Dove
Common Ground-Dove
Ruddy Ground-Dove
Ruddy Quail-Dove
White-tipped Dove

PARAKEETS AND PARROTS

ORDER PSITTACIFORMES, FAMILY PSITTACIDAE
Monk Parakeet (I)
Carolina Parakeet (E)
Green Parakeet (u)
Red-crowned Parrot (u)

CUCKOOS, ROADRUNNERS AND ANIS

ORDER CUCULIFORMES, FAMILY CUCULIDAE
Black-billed Cuckoo
Yellow-billed Cuckoo
Mangrove Cuckoo
Greater Roadrunner
Groove-billed Ani

BARN OWLS

ORDER STRIGIFORMES, FAMILY TYTONIDAE
Barn Owl

TYPICAL OWLS

ORDER STRIGIFORMES, FAMILY STRIGIDAE
Flammulated Owl
Eastern Screech-Owl
Western Screech-Owl
Great Horned Owl
Snowy Owl
Northern Pygmy-Owl
Ferruginous Pygmy-Owl
Elf Owl
Burrowing Owl
Mottled Owl
Spotted Owl
Barred Owl
Long-eared Owl
Stygian Owl *
Short-eared Owl
Northern Saw-whet Owl

NIGHTJARS

ORDER CAPRIMULGIFORMES, FAMILY CAPRIMULGIDAE
Lesser Nighthawk
Common Nighthawk
Pauraque
Common Poorwill
Chuck-will's-widow
Whip-poor-will

SWIFTS

ORDER APODIFORMES, FAMILY APODIDAE
White-collared Swift
Chimney Swift
White-throated Swift

HUMMINGBIRDS

ORDER APODIFORMES, FAMILY TROCHILIDAE
Green Violet-ear
Green-breasted Mango
Broad-billed Hummingbird
White-eared Hummingbird
Berylline Hummingbird *
Buff-bellied Hummingbird
Violet-crowned Hummingbird
Blue-throated Hummingbird
Magnificent Hummingbird
Lucifer Hummingbird
Ruby-throated Hummingbird
Black-chinned Hummingbird
Anna's Hummingbird
Costa's Hummingbird
Calliope Hummingbird
Broad-tailed Hummingbird
Rufous Hummingbird
Allen's Hummingbird

TROGONS

(ORDER TROGONIFORMES, FAMILY TROGONIDAE
Elegant Trogon

KINGFISHERS

ORDER CORACIIFORMES, FAMILY ALCEDINIDAE
Ringed Kingfisher
Belted Kingfisher
Green Kingfisher

WOODPECKERS AND ALLIES

(ORDER PICIFORMES, FAMILY PICIDAE)
Lewis's Woodpecker
Red-headed Woodpecker
Acorn Woodpecker
Golden-fronted Woodpecker

Red-bellied Woodpecker
Yellow-bellied Sapsucker
Red-naped Sapsucker
Red-breasted Sapsucker *
Williamson's Sapsucker
Ladder-backed Woodpecker
Downy Woodpecker
Hairy Woodpecker
Red-cockaded Woodpecker
Northern Flicker
Pileated Woodpecker
Ivory-billed Woodpecker (E)

TYRANT FLYCATCHERS

ORDER PASSERIFORMES, FAMILY TYRANNIDAE
Northern Beardless-Tyrannulet
Greenish Elaenia
Tufted Flycatcher
Olive-sided Flycatcher
Greater Pewee
Western Wood-Pewee
Eastern Wood-Pewee
Yellow-bellied Flycatcher
Acadian Flycatcher
Alder Flycatcher
Willow Flycatcher
Least Flycatcher
Hammond's Flycatcher
Dusky Flycatcher
Gray Flycatcher
Cordilleran Flycatcher
Black Phoebe
Eastern Phoebe
Say's Phoebe
Vermilion Flycatcher
Dusky-capped Flycatcher
Ash-throated Flycatcher
Great Crested Flycatcher
Brown-crested Flycatcher
Great Kiskadee
Sulphur-bellied Flycatcher
Tropical Kingbird
Couch's Kingbird

Cassin's Kingbird
Thick-billed Kingbird
Western Kingbird
Eastern Kingbird
Gray Kingbird
Scissor-tailed Flycatcher
Fork-tailed Flycatcher
Rose-throated Becard
Masked Tityra

SHRIKES

ORDER PASSERIFORMES, FAMILY LANIIDAE
Northern Shrike
Loggerhead Shrike

VIREOS

ORDER PASSERIFORMES, FAMILY VIREONIDAE
White-eyed Vireo
Bell's Vireo
Black-capped Vireo
Gray Vireo
Blue-headed (Solitary) Vireo
Cassin's (Solitary) Vireo
Plumbeous (Solitary) Vireo
Yellow-throated Vireo
Hutton's Vireo
Warbling Vireo
Philadelphia Vireo
Red-eyed Vireo
Yellow-green Vireo
Black-whiskered Vireo
Yucatan Vireo

JAYS, MAGPIES AND CROWS

ORDER PASSERIFORMES, FAMILY CORVIDAE
Steller's Jay
Blue Jay
Green Jay
Brown Jay
Western Scrub-Jay
Mexican Jay
Pinyon Jay
Clark's Nutcracker

Black-billed Magpie
American Crow
Tamaulipas Crow
Fish Crow
Chihuahuan Raven
Common Raven

LARKS

ORDER PASSERIFORMES, FAMILY ALAUDIDAE
Horned Lark

SWALLOWS

ORDER PASSERIFORMES, FAMILY HIRUNDINIDAE
Purple Martin
Gray-breasted Martin
Tree Swallow
Violet-green Swallow
Bank Swallow
Barn Swallow
Cliff Swallow
Cave Swallow
Northern Rough-winged Swallow

TITMICE AND CHICKADEES

ORDER PASSERIFORMES, FAMILY PARIDAE
Carolina Chickadee
Black-capped Chickadee
Mountain Chickadee
Juniper (Plain) Titmouse
Tufted Titmouse

VERDINS

ORDER PASSERIFORMES, FAMILY REMIZIDAE
Verdin

BUSHTITS

ORDER PASSERIFORMES, FAMILY AEGITHALIDAE
Bushtit

NUTHATCHES

ORDER PASSERIFORMES, FAMILY SITTIDAE
Red-breasted Nuthatch
White-breasted Nuthatch
Pygmy Nuthatch
Brown-headed Nuthatch

CREEPERS

ORDER PASSERIFORMES, FAMILY CERTHIIDAE
Brown Creeper

WRENS

ORDER PASSERIFORMES, FAMILY TROGLODYTIDAE
Cactus Wren
Rock Wren
Canyon Wren
Carolina Wren
Bewick's Wren
House Wren
Winter Wren
Sedge Wren
Marsh Wren

KINGLETS

ORDER PASSERIFORMES, FAMILY REGULIDAE
Golden-crowned Kinglet
Ruby-crowned Kinglet

DIPPERS

ORDER PASSERIFORMES, FAMILY CINCLIDAE
American Dipper

GNATCATCHERS

(ORDER PASSERIFORMES, FAMILY SYLVIIDAE)
Blue-gray Gnatcatcher
Black-tailed Gnatcatcher
(Order Passeriformes, Family Sylviidae)
Blue-gray Gnatcatcher
Black-tailed Gnatcatcher

THRUSHES AND ALLIES

(ORDER PASSERIFORMES, FAMILY TURDIDAE)
Northern Wheatear
Eastern Bluebird
Western Bluebird
Mountain Bluebird
Townsend's Solitaire

Orange-billed Nightingale-Thrush
Veery
Gray-cheeked Thrush
Swainson's Thrush
Hermit Thrush
Wood Thrush
Clay-colored Robin
White-throated Robin
Rufous-backed Robin
American Robin
Varied Thrush
Aztec Thrush

THRASHERS AND ALLIES

ORDER PASSERIFORMES, FAMILY MIMIDAE
Gray Catbird
Black Catbird
Northern Mockingbird
Sage Thrasher
Brown Thrasher
Long-billed Thrasher
Curve-billed Thrasher
Crissal Thrasher

STARLINGS

ORDER PASSERIFORMES, FAMILY STURNIDAE
European Starling (I)

PIPITS

ORDER PASSERIFORMES, FAMILY MOTACILLIDAE
American Pipit
Sprague's Pipit

WAXWINGS

ORDER PASSERIFORMES, FAMILY BOMBYCILLIDAE
Bohemian Waxwing
Cedar Waxwing

SILKY-FLYCATCHERS

ORDER PASSERIFORMES, FAMILY PTILOGONATIDAE
Gray Silky-flycatcher
Phainopepla

OLIVE WARBLER

ORDER PASSERIFORMES, FAMILY PEUCEDRAMIDAE

Olive Warbler

WOOD-WARBLERS

ORDER PASSERIFORMES, FAMILY PARULIDAE

Blue-winged Warbler
Golden-winged Warbler
Tennessee Warbler
Orange-crowned Warbler
Nashville Warbler
Virginia's Warbler
Colima Warbler
Lucy's Warbler
Northern Parula
Tropical Parula
Yellow Warbler
Chestnut-sided Warbler
Magnolia Warbler
Cape May Warbler
Black-throated Blue Warbler
Yellow-rumped Warbler
Black-throated Gray Warbler
Townsend's Warbler
Hermit Warbler
Black-throated Green Warbler
Golden-cheeked Warbler
Blackburnian Warbler
Yellow-throated Warbler
Grace's Warbler
Pine Warbler
Prairie Warbler
Palm Warbler
Bay-breasted Warbler
Blackpoll Warbler
Cerulean Warbler
Black-and-white Warbler
American Redstart
Prothonotary Warbler
Worm-eating Warbler
Swainson's Warbler
Ovenbird
Northern Waterthrush

Louisiana Waterthrush
Kentucky Warbler
Connecticut Warbler
Mourning Warbler
MacGillivray's Warbler
Common Yellowthroat
Gray-crowned Yellowthroat
Hooded Warbler
Wilson's Warbler
Canada Warbler
Red-faced Warbler
Painted Redstart
Slate-throated Redstart *
Golden-crowned Warbler
Rufous-capped Warbler
Yellow-breasted Chat

TANAGERS

ORDER PASSERIFORMES, FAMILY THRAUPIDAE

Hepatic Tanager
Summer Tanager
Scarlet Tanager
Western Tanager
Flame-colored Tanager

SPARROWS, BUNTINGS AND ALLIES

ORDER PASSERIFORMES, FAMILY EMBERIZIDAE

White-collared Seedeater
Yellow-faced Grassquit
Olive Sparrow
Green-tailed Towhee
Eastern Towhee
Spotted Towhee
Canyon Towhee
Bachman's Sparrow
Botteri's Sparrow
Cassin's Sparrow
Rufous-crowned Sparrow
American Tree Sparrow
Chipping Sparrow
Clay-colored Sparrow

Brewer's Sparrow
Field Sparrow
Black-chinned Sparrow
Vesper Sparrow
Lark Sparrow
Black-throated Sparrow
Sage Sparrow
Lark Bunting
Savannah Sparrow
Baird's Sparrow
Grasshopper Sparrow
Henslow's Sparrow
Le Conte's Sparrow
Nelson's Sharp-tailed Sparrow
Seaside Sparrow
Fox Sparrow
Song Sparrow
Lincoln's Sparrow
Swamp Sparrow
White-throated Sparrow
Harris's Sparrow
White-crowned Sparrow
Golden-crowned Sparrow
Dark-eyed Junco
Yellow-eyed Junco
McCown's Longspur
Lapland Longspur
Smith's Longspur
Chestnut-collared Longspur
Snow Bunting

GROSBEAKS AND ALLIES

ORDER PASSERIFORMES, FAMILY CARDINALIDAE
Crimson-collared Grosbeak
Northern Cardinal
Pyrrhuloxia
Rose-breasted Grosbeak
Black-headed Grosbeak
Blue Bunting
Blue Grosbeak
Lazuli Bunting
Indigo Bunting
Varied Bunting
Painted Bunting
Dickcissel

BLACKBIRDS AND ORIOLES

ORDER PASSERIFORMES, FAMILY ICTERIDAE
Bobolink
Red-winged Blackbird
Eastern Meadowlark
Western Meadowlark
Yellow-headed Blackbird
Rusty Blackbird
Brewer's Blackbird
Common Grackle
Boat-tailed Grackle
Great-tailed Grackle
Shiny Cowbird
Bronzed Cowbird
Brown-headed Cowbird
Black-vented Oriole
Orchard Oriole
Hooded Oriole
Altamira Oriole
Audubon's Oriole
Baltimore Oriole
Bullock's Oriole
Scott's Oriole

FINCHES AND ALLIES

ORDER PASSERIFORMES, FAMILY FRINGILLIDAE
Pine Grosbeak
Purple Finch
Cassin's Finch
House Finch
Red Crossbill
White-winged Crossbill
Common Redpoll
Pine Siskin
Lesser Goldfinch
Lawrence's Goldfinch
American Goldfinch
Evening Grosbeak

OLD WORLD SPARROWS

ORDER PASSERIFORMES, FAMILY PASSERIDAE
House Sparrow (I)

Many Thanks To ——

Eric Miller and the Amarillo CVB, Barbara McWilliams at the Hampton Inn, Hotel Shanna Smith Snyder and the Abilene CVB, John English and all the good folks around Abilene, Darla Yarbrough and the Residence Inn hospitality in Abilene, The Geiger Group, Jody Lamb and the people at the U.S. Vanguard Company, Mr. South Texas, Cletus Bianchi, Shelly Plante and the Texas Parks and Wildlife Department, Rebecca Sills with National Audubon Chapter Services, The Texas Audubon Society, Abilene Audubon Members, Bonnie and Joe Thompson, Bill Mead for his bird IDs and coffee, Beth Shumate, and the McKinney CVB, Lee Zigler and the Rio Grande Delta Audubon Chapter, David and Elise Failke for putting me on some fantastic photo ops and photo IDs, Marilyn Reiswig and the Perryton-Ochiltree Chamber of Commerce.

And last but by no means the least, Debbie Foster for putting up with my unusual way of earning a living for a long, long time.

GREAT BLUE HERON

Index